Not Prince Hamlet

Also by Michael Meyer

Novel
The End of the Corridor

Biographies
Ibsen
Strindberg

Plays
The Ortolan
Lunatic and Lover

Translations
Ibsen: Sixteen Plays
Strindberg: Sixteen Plays
Frans G. Bengtsson: The Long Ships

MICHAEL MEYER

Not Prince Hamlet

Literary and Theatrical Memoirs

SECKER & WARBURG
LONDON

First published in England 1989
by Martin Secker & Warburg Ltd

Copyright © 1989 by Michael Meyer

British Library Cataloguing in Publication Data

Meyer, Michael, *1921*–
Not Prince Hamlet. Literary & theatrical memoirs
1.   English literature. Meyer, Michael, *1921*–
I.   Title
828'.91409

ISBN 0 436 27090 0

Typeset in 11/12pt Linotron Bembo by
Hewer Text Composition Services, Edinburgh
Printed by
Mackays of Chatham plc,
Chatham, Kent

For Nora with love

Contents

List of Illustrations

ix

10 reprinted by kind permission of Mrs Rosemary Rollo; 12 of the Oxford University Press Ltd; 13 of Mrs Renée-Jane Etté; 14 of Mrs Claudia Seymer; 16 of Mr Piers Paul Read; 17 of Mrs Clare Penate; 18 of Vernon Richards; 22 of William Heinemann Ltd; 23 of Universal Pictorial Press and Agency Ltd; 24 of Anthony Crickmay; 25 of Miss Dilys Hamlett; 26 of Studio Edmark; 27 of Miss Gillian Herring; 30 of Mr Graham Greene; 34 and 36 of Mr Kevin Cummins; 38 © Bern Schwartz; 40 of Joe Cocks Studio.

Although every effort has been made to trace the copyright holders, we apologize in advance for any unintentional omissions and would be pleased to insert the appropriate acknowledgements in any subsequent edition of this book.

Acknowledgements

I am grateful to the following for permission to quote copyright material: Mr Graham Greene (letters and dedications); 'Canoe' by Keith Douglas © Marie J. Douglas 1978. Reprinted from *The Complete Poems of Keith Douglas*, edited by Desmond Graham (1978), by permission of Oxford University Press. Miss Anne Keyes and Routledge & Kegan Paul Ltd (Sidney Keyes's poems 'Death and the Maiden' and 'William Wordsworth', and Keyes's letters to me); Mr John Heath-Stubbs and David Higham Associates Ltd (Mr Heath-Stubbs's poem 'Simile'); copyright © the Estate of Kenneth Tynan and reproduced by permission of Nick Hern Books and Kathleen Tynan (extracts from Kenneth Tynan's reviews, first printed in *He That Plays The King*, Longman, and Random House Inc, 1953); Faber and Faber Ltd (lines from W. H. Auden); the estate of the late Sonia Brownwell Orwell (letters to me from George Orwell); Macmillan Inc. (Tyrone Guthrie's tribute to Frederick Valk, first printed in Diana Valk's *Shylock for a Summer*); the Peters Fraser & Dunlop Group, Ltd (letter from Rebecca West); A. P. Watt, Ltd, on behalf of the Executors of the Estate of Robert Graves (letter from Robert Graves); Lady Richardson (letter from Sir Ralph Richardson). My memories of George Orwell first appeared in a slightly different form in *The World of George Orwell*, edited by Miriam Gross (Weidenfeld & Nicolson, 1971), my description of the first night of *Brand* at Hammersmith in 1959 in *A Night in the Theatre*, edited by Ronald Harwood (Methuen, 1982), and my reminiscences of the Far East in the Swedish newspaper *Svenska Dagbladet*. My accounts of my visit to Tahiti with Graham Greene, how he became a film actor and how I danced for the headhunters were originally given in an abbreviated form as broadcast talks for the BBC. Some of my anecdotes about Sir Ralph Richardson were used by Garry O'Connor in his biography of Sir Ralph, not always with acknowledgement, and some of the material about Michael Flanders and Michael Elliott first appeared in my obituaries of them for *The Times*. My thanks also to my brother Peter Meyer, Mrs Diana Valk, Mrs Patricia Feltham, and my editors Max Eilenberg and Mark Bryant.

A Jewish Childhood

I was born on 11 June 1921 in Hamilton Terrace in St John's Wood, London, a few hundred yards from Lord's cricket ground which fifty years earlier my great-great-grandfather had owned. My father said it was the only really ugly house he had ever lived in, a big Victorian building of red and yellow brick; he had leased it for three months while our new home was being got ready in Marylebone. That was in Portland Place, a beautiful eighteenth-century house built by the Adam brothers which got bombed during the war. Although my father, a timber importer, was then no more than well-to-do, we had eight servants: a cook, parlourmaid, housemaid, under-housemaid, nurse, nursemaid, kitchenmaid and chauffeur. Their combined salaries totalled £350 a year, from two pounds a week for the cook to ten shillings a week for the nursemaid and kitchenmaid. Although I liked them all, I decided early in life that even if I became a millionaire I would never have servants living in. Our existence was regulated by the need not to inconvenience them. There was no question of raiding the kitchen for snacks or drinks; none of us could sleep late, for the rooms had to be done; nor could we leave clothes or anything on the floor.

We saw more of the servants than of our parents. My two elder brothers and I lived on the second floor, looked after by our nurse and nursemaid; my father and mother occupied the two floors below, the servants the two above. My mother was beautiful, tall, slim and auburn-haired, my father handsome and witty; when they first met at a dance, she told her sisters that he was 'just like Lewis Waller', a famous matinée idol of the time, and Waller's photographs confirm this. But I remember them as gracious people who lived a totally different life downstairs, in which we were sometimes briefly allowed to partake. Had my mother lived longer, my memories would doubtless be different.

When I was seven, my eldest brother, Peter, got flu. My father caught it, then my mother. In her case it turned quickly to bronchitis and pneumonia, and within a few days she was dead. I did not learn of this until a fortnight later. My brothers and I had been sent to our maternal grandparents in Bayswater. We did not know, or care, why; the change was fun, and we were pampered. One afternoon I was sitting upstairs there with my nurse and my mother's old nurse – known as Mother's Ann, whom my grandparents still kept on out of charity – reading a comic by the fire while they chatted. Some remark, I do not recall what, made me look up and ask: 'Is she dead?' They nodded, and showed me the announcement in the 'Deaths' column of *The Times*. I wept a little, but was mainly impressed that any member of our family should be mentioned in the papers.

I have only three memories of my mother: helping her to arrange chocolates in a silver filigree dish for some party she and my father were to give, and sticking one large thin round chocolate, presumably a mint, edge upwards against the side of the dish; her saying to me that we might find ourselves short of food, since something called the General Strike was about to start; and my first visit to a theatre. Mother took me and my brothers to *Peter Pan*, with Dorothy Dickson (still alive as I write, at ninety-one) as Peter and Gerald du Maurier as Captain Hook; we sat in a box and I remember shouting something down at the people in the stalls below during an interval, and their faces looking up and smiling. When Captain Hook descended in a green light to the cave and put poison in Peter's toothglass, I became frightened and Mother told me to turn my face away, which I did. My brother Peter, who was twelve when she died, says she was full of fun, loving and generally enchanting, and everyone who knew her echoes this. I do not know why I remember her so little, and I am sad that this should be.

By contrast, I have many and vivid memories of my nurse, partly no doubt because she stayed with us until I was thirteen, but more because it was she, rather than our parents, who ruled our life. She was Mary Ann Sanford, born in 1865 in the Surrey village of Wonersh; a large woman, stern but benevolent, with apple-pink veins in her cheeks, greying hair fastened at the back in a bun and an unexpectedly cultured voice. Even now, when I look at her photograph, I feel an emotion which the photographs of my parents do not evoke. I imagine the same must be true of many people of my generation and upbringing, and although to later generations this may seem unnatural and even unhealthy, at least it meant that any absence of parental love – not that my mother did not love us, nor my father, eventually, in his way, once we had reached an age when he could converse with us as equals – was less damaging than it is now. Can children today feel the same about *au pairs*, who change so frequently?

Both my parents were Jewish, as were all the ancestors I have been able to trace. My mother was brought up strictly orthodox, my father as an agnostic. They married in 1915 after he had been invalided back from France in bizarre circumstances. He was a corporal motor-cycle dispatch rider and, driving at night with no lights, as regulations demanded near the front, he contrived to get ridden over by a British cavalry officer coming in the opposite direction. My father always swore that the horse was on the wrong side of the road, but if Father on a motor cycle was anything like what he later was with a car, my money would be on the cavalryman. The incident probably saved his life, for he escaped the carnage which was about to begin. On the first morning of their honeymoon he ordered eggs and bacon for himself and fried eggs alone for my mother, who, as an orthodox Jew, had never touched bacon. They all arrived on the same silver dish, so that the bacon fat had seeped across to her eggs. Father, who tended to get angry with waiters, ordered him to bring fresh eggs. Mother, wishing to avoid a scene, and doubtless hungry, asked if he thought it would really matter if she swallowed a little bacon fat. He said: 'You know how I feel', so she ate it, and the next morning ordered eggs and bacon. We children were brought up as agnostics like him, and remained so.

Father and Mother seem to have been completely happy, and although he was only forty-four when she died he never married again, though in due course he took on a sequence of mistresses. Nanny's unguarded comments kept us aware of them; I remember three, all lively, handsome and temperamental. Small children bored my father, and he was not good at concealing this. When he came to take us out for the day from boarding-school, he always returned us an hour before the other boys, on the pretext that there was 'a little mist in the air', although none of our schools lay more than an hour's drive from London. How much that extra hour would have meant to us, and how little it can have meant to him; but he could not bear to be bored, so back to our empty houses we had

3

to go. Once we were old enough to be talked to as adults, he was a marvellous companion.

From my few memories of my mother and what other people have told me about her, I do not recognize anything of her in myself. Peter and my other brother, Dick, both inherited her gentleness and diffidence; though now I think of it, I was pretty diffident and lacking in self-confidence until my father died, when I was thirty-four. Then I think I started to become like him. I inherited his sensuality and, unlike Peter and Dick, his stocky build; and, I like to think, his love of plain speaking and dislike of circumlocution. But, likewise, those traits did not emerge in me until after his death, and they may have been not so much inherited as learned from Raymond Postgate, for whom I had recently begun to work and who was to prove a second – no, not second, for there were others before him – father-figure to me.

A famous actor lived two doors from us in Portland Place. He was always beautifully dressed, and would salute us, and we him, as we passed each other on our way to Regent's Park. This was Allan Aynesworth, who had created the role of Algernon in the original production of *The Importance of Being Earnest* in 1895, and his military bearing was no pretence for he was the son of a general and had actually been born at the Royal Military College in Sandhurst. I wonder what his father thought when his son became a professional actor in the 1880s, remembering the reputation the theatre had then. Other neighbours were Edgar Wallace and the dramatist Sir Arthur Pinero; I probably saw them both on my walks, but I don't remember them. Perhaps Nanny did not recognize them. Portland Place was still gas-lit, each lamp being operated manually by a gaslighter with a long pole as dusk approached. He was a figure to look out for, as was the muffin man with his bell, from whom Nanny would buy fresh crumpets. I remember too the open-topped independent 'pirate' buses in their different colours trying to outpace each other, and how when we crossed the road we had to pick our way through the piles of horse-droppings, since many tradesmen's carts were still horse-drawn.

I suppose I must have had friends, but I do not remember any from those early years. Sometimes we went to tedious parties, with games which I disliked and dreaded. But when I was five I began to have lessons from a governess, and a new world opened for me. Miss Shuttleworth must have been approaching seventy; she came for two hours a day and taught me writing (I could already read), arithmetic, history, geography and, before I was six, the beginnings of French and Latin. She was the most imaginative teacher I was ever to have, apart from one at my preparatory and one at my public schools, but I had them only in English for an hour or two each week, whereas Miss Shuttleworth taught me every day and made everything interesting, even French and Latin grammar. She must, it now occurs to me, have been born in the 1850s and have known in her childhood a number of people who had been born in the eighteenth century; some, perhaps, who remembered the French Revolution.

Even older than Miss Shuttleworth was my maternal great-grand-mother, Charlotte Moses, whom my brothers and I visited occasionally for lunch at her house off Notting Hill Gate, a hideous tall building from the 1870s or 1880s of which I dare say she may have been the original occupant. She had been born in 1844 in Maitland, New South Wales, her father, Samuel Cohen, having emigrated to Australia ten years earlier to set up a trading company with his brothers. At the age of nineteen she married one Alfred Moses, and I have a photograph of her taken that year, 1863, outside her new home in Hobart, only ten years after the abolition of transportation there, when the island's name was changed from Van Diemen's Land to Tasmania. Many of the men she saw daily, perhaps even some of their servants, must have been ex-convicts from the hulks. As a teenager she would have read in the newspapers of the Crimean War and the Indian Mutiny. She gave birth to my grandmother there in 1865, but then they moved to England, I believe as a result of some scandal concerning Alfred Moses and a servant-girl. He died in 1872, aged only thirty-three; handsome, roguish and thoroughly untrustworthy, to judge from a full-length portrait of him which remains in the family.

Great-grandma was a jovial but gruffly alarming old lady, heavily moustached and bearded. Lunch always consisted of veal or lamb cutlets and chocolate puddings shaped like sandcastles, and afterwards she would sing for us in her deep voice the street ballads and music-hall songs of her youth, 'The Ratcatcher's Daughter' or, her favourite, 'Villikins and his Dinah', which ended: 'And a cup of cold poison was found by her side'. At half-past two the maid would announce: 'The carriage is waiting' – the only occasions on which I have ever heard the sentence except in a theatre – and as a special treat we were allowed to accompany Great-grandma on her afternoon ride. Hers must have been one of the last privately owned horse-drawn carriages in London. The coachman was an aged man called Ellis, and the horse, which seemed to us almost equally old, responded with an air of resignation when addressed as Nicholas. We dreaded these rides, for the carriage was both extremely stuffy and dreadfully bumpy. The windows had probably not been opened since the reign of Queen Victoria. But in we would climb, and Nicholas would jolt us along the Bayswater Road and around Hyde Park in an atmosphere of hot leather and stale straw. I don't recall that I was ever actually sick (though I could never travel long journeys in a car until I was almost out of adolescence), but it was always a great relief when the carriage turned right at Alexandra Gate and the homeward half of the journey began. She lived to be eighty-four, surviving my mother, her granddaughter. One of her brothers, Louis Cohen, became the head of Lewis's of Liverpool and the first Jewish Lord Mayor of that city.

In due course I accompanied my father and brothers to Friday evenings at my maternal grandparents in Chepstow Villas. They were a genial old couple. My grandfather, Albert Benjamin, had been born in Hanover in 1863. His father, Joseph, born in 1794, had fought against Napoleon as an ensign under Blücher at Leipzig and Waterloo. When he was sixty-nine his third wife swooned in the street and was rushed into the nearest house, where she gave birth to my grandfather. He came to London as a young man and spent the rest of his life here. Around 1900 or earlier he applied for naturalization, but was rejected on the technical ground that both his referees were New Zealanders instead of, as the law demanded, British subjects. He did not bother to re-apply, since in those pre-1914 days few European countries required passports for entry, and when war was declared he, who had lived in England for thirty years, was interned as an enemy alien, something he never quite forgave. Ironically, the house where he had been born in Hanover happened to be the British consulate, so that he had been born on British soil. Although he knew of my interest in history, he never mentioned that his father had fought at Waterloo, and I only discovered this several decades later.

Albert Benjamin was a jolly, bald old man, who still spoke English with a strong guttural accent. His wife Blanche was tiny and gentle, with white hair fastened at the back in a bun. Because of her Australian upbringing she still pronounced certain words, such as 'grass' and 'dance', with the flat vowels which people nowadays chiefly associate with Americans. Unlike Great-grandma's house, in

6

which everything was dark and sombre, my grandparents' rooms were full of colour, with chairs in bright red and blue velvet and polished silver catching the light everywhere. The food on these Friday evenings – strictly kosher, of course – was very good, especially a green cold fish stew and the best roast veal I have ever tasted, with flat roasted potatoes crinkled brown. We could not understand the Hebrew prayers but enjoyed the meal. Occasionally our aunts' conversation would be interrupted by a warning '*Pas devant les enfants*', and would be continued in ponderous and excruciating French, which we probably understood rather better than they did.

Grandma had a sister, Ray, married to an immensely fat old man named Dave Lewis. They always served curry, which we liked, but it was supposed to be too fierce for us, so that to our disappointment we were given some ordinary dish. Uncle Dave liked his curry very hot, and imagined that everyone else did, so would sprinkle red pepper over not only his own dish but those of everyone else. He began his day by being shaved in bed by his valet, during which operation he would smoke a long Havana cigar and drink a pint of ale. After lunch he would light another cigar and fall asleep; but somehow, while snoring loudly, he contrived to continue smoking his cigar, which would drop regular inches of ash on his succession of stomachs. It seemed to us a great waste of a cigar. Uncle Dave was violent-tempered; once, when the Sunday joint was not to his satisfaction, he threw it back down the kitchen stairs. He gave my great-aunt Ray, who was a talented painter, a rough time.

My grandfather disapproved of our unorthodox upbringing. Once he visited us at teatime to find Nanny frying bacon in a pan. 'You shouldn't cook that for them, nurse.' 'Why not, sir? The pig's a clean animal.' 'How can it be?' he muttered, and a few minutes later stumped out. Once he gave me a penny to play with, but took it back before leaving. He delighted in taking us to the circus each Christmas, and was childishly downcast when one year we asked if we might go to a theatre instead.

I never knew my father's parents, for they both died before I was born. My great-great-great-grandfather on that side was a Pole from Brody in the Ukraine, who came to England in, or shortly before, 1760. He was known as Brody Meyer, and was a fur importer, as were his son and grandson. The latter, my great-grandfather Meyer Meyer, born in the year of Waterloo, had sixteen children, one of whom produced five illegitimate offspring by his cook. The fourth of Meyer Meyer's sons, my grandfather Barry, was described to me by his eldest son, my uncle Montague, as 'a delightful fellow and the biggest bloody fool you ever met'. In those days the stupid son of the family traditionally entered the Army or the Church or, if those careers were barred by religion, was sent to India, where it was regarded as impossible not to make money, but my grandfather created a kind of record by not only not making any but contriving to lose what he had. Walking one day in Bombay, he found himself confronted by an obdurate native who refused to stand aside for him, whereupon my grandfather, with all the family aggressiveness, barged him into the gutter. As a result, the Indian wounded himself on a knife he was carrying in his sleeve, and sued my grandfather for assault. Barry was not worried, for the case would be heard by a British magistrate who would see that justice was done. It was; my grandfather was found guilty and ordered to pay compensation. Deciding that India was no longer a place for a white man, he returned to London, where, after a brief spell as a tobacconist, he became an agent for the Alliance Assurance Company. He married Marian Marsden, whose grandfather, Isaac Montague Marsden, born Moses, had owned Lord's cricket ground from 1860 to 1868, and had fathered twenty-two children by his two marriages.

Isaac had come to own the ground through the incompetence of the Marylebone Cricket Club committee. The previous owner had suggested to them that, since he was now old, they should buy the freehold from him instead of continuing to lease it. They refused, so he sold the ground to Isaac. Six years later, the MCC decided they would, after all, like to own the freehold and, as the committee minutes show, were scandalized when Isaac demanded a handsome profit on his purchase. Remarks were made about Mr Marsden's original name having been Moses. But they had to pay his price. They could have done with him as Treasurer instead of some of the gentlemen who have filled that office since.

My father, the fourth of Barry and Marian's five children, was brought up in straitened circumstances in Adelaide Road near Swiss Cottage. He and his elder brother Montague left University College School at fifteen to earn their keep and, through some family connection, got jobs as clerks and, eventually, salesmen in the timber firm of Bamberger. Both were tough and indeed truculent young men who enjoyed getting into fist fights with brewers' draymen and the like, of which they would boast in later years. Their sister Milly, the eldest of the five, then married a well-to-do tobacco merchant,

Louis Leverson. On their honeymoon he said: 'You've made me so happy. Is there anything you'd like me to do for you?' With good Jewish acumen she replied: 'Monty wants to start his own timber business, and if you could lend him £2,000 I think you'd find it a good investment.' He did, and it was. Two or three years later my father joined him, and they soon became the largest timber importers in the country. It was the best kind of industrial company, in that the board was always open to anyone of talent, and most of its members had worked their way to it from humble positions. For three-quarters of a century it was a proud tradition that no employee ever voluntarily left Montague Meyer. Then in 1982 we merged with a firm half our size, deaths and retirements left them with a majority on the board, and the patriarchal but immensely successful company of old was replaced by a different kind of capitalism, with bigger profits and many redundancies. Father and Uncle Monty never voted anything but socialist all their lives.

Uncle Monty was a fearsome man of great charm but violent temper, famously impossible to work with. My father, though a man of some temper himself, was regarded as a restraining influence on him, insofar as anyone could be. Uncle Monty's rages were legendary, as was the colour of his language. Once I was sitting with my father in his office when through the folding doors I heard Uncle Monty roar: 'Tell the buggers we'll bloody sue them', and so on at length. I said: 'What on earth's that?' 'Oh,' said Father, 'just Monty dictating a letter.'

His turnover of secretaries became such that eventually a little man named Robert Brown, who had been with the firm for forty years and looked exactly like Mr Punch, took over the job, his refusal to be intimidated outweighing such disadvantages as an ignorance of shorthand. Soon after my brother Peter joined the firm he rushed into Father's office and said: 'A dreadful thing has happened. Uncle Monty's given Robert Brown the sack.'

'That's all right,' said Father.

'All right? But he's been with the firm for forty years.'

'It's all right. He won't go.'

'Won't go?'

'He'll look in after lunch and say: "Any letters?", and Monty will say: "I've bloody sacked you", and Robert'll say: "I'm not bloody going after forty years", and Monty'll say: "Well, take this bloody letter, then".'

Which is exactly what happened.

Away from the office, Uncle Monty was generous and hugely amusing. He liked us nephews to invite ourselves to lunch, which he would give us at the Savoy, either in the restaurant or in a private suite which he permanently rented there, for seductions as well as for meals. No menu was ever presented to him; the head waiter would suggest what he thought might be worth Uncle Monty's attention that day. Once a new waiter, sensing a good tip, thrust the menu under Uncle Monty's nose. Uncle Monty looked at it as though, in Damon Runyon's phrase, it was a side dish he hadn't ordered. 'What's this?' he asked, and the waiter was swept away and not seen again. During the war he moved into a flat overlooking Hyde Park. When spring arrived, the trees came into leaf and obstructed his view so he telephoned the appropriate minister and said: 'I don't know everything. I don't pretend to know everything. But one thing I do know when I see it is a rotten tree. One of your trees in Hyde Park is rotten and if you don't do something about it, it'll fall down and kill someone.' 'Which tree?' asked the minister. Uncle Monty identified it. Within a week this perfectly healthy tree was cut down, and Uncle Monty enjoyed an uninterrupted view of the park.

Soon after the Second World War a play called *Edward, My Son* was staged in the West End. The main character, played by Robert Morley, who was also part-author, was a bullying tycoon who so resembled Uncle Monty that his sons persuaded him to see it, without mentioning the similarity. He roared with laughter throughout, and when asked for his opinion said: 'Bloody marvellous. Of course, you never get people like that in real life.'

I got on well with both my brothers, then as later. Dick was lame with polio, which he had contracted at the age of three. His right leg was never thicker than a man's forearm, and he wore, as was the custom then, a hideous iron brace, clearly visible between his shorts and socks. A good musician, he was to become a distinguished psychiatrist at, among other places, Holloway prison, and after his death the governor told me that Dick had been able to get through to the really difficult cases with whom none of the other staff could make contact at all. I wondered why, and she said: 'Because he was lame.' When he limped into their cells, the prisoners recognized him as someone to whom life had dealt a short straw, as it had to them.

When I was seven, I began to attend a day-school called Egerton House in Dorset Square. It was a pleasant enough place, run by the stern but fair Mr Hodgson, who had bright blue eyes that never blinked, and his partner Miss Watson, a red-faced lady who frightened us all. There I made my first two appearances on the stage, as a child in *The Pied Piper* and the Frog Footman in *Alice in Wonderland*, and won a cup for boxing. The teaching was all right, though nothing compared with Miss Shuttleworth. But in 1930, when I was nine and Dick eleven, he and I were sent to boarding-school, and a new and hateful chapter of my life began.

2

Long Corridors

Was Earleywood as grim as I remember it, or was I just a pampered child brought face to face with the realities of life? Looking back, I have no doubt that I was over-protected. But it was not only my first year at Earleywood that I hated. Even at the end of my stay there, when I was in the football eleven, enjoyed my boxing and cricket, had won a scholarship to Wellington and was big enough to bully other boys if I wished (though I don't think I did), I could not wait to leave. Do places like Earleywood still exist? They must, for a few days ago I read in the paper of a prep-school head in Sussex who was sentenced to prison for three months for sadistic flogging. We were not flogged much; it happened only once to me, for eating sweets after lights-out in the dormitory, and I only had three strokes. 'Oo, it did hurt,' I remember announcing to the others when I returned from Dr Pitkin's study. But it was not a very severe punishment. Nor were conditions at the school particularly austere. There was the brass bell that woke us at 6.45 each morning, the runs before breakfast, the cold baths, the lack of privacy and, worst, the fear of Dr Pitkin – so great that the sound of his shoes squeaking on the plum-coloured linoleum of the corridors paralysed our larynxes and he would enter the playroom to absolute silence. 'I will have discipline', was his repeated credo, and disciplined we were; but I wonder what the subsequent effect was on most of us.

Peter had gone to a prep school called Fernden near Haslemere run by a sadist named Brownrigg, and he says that when he came with Father, Dick and me to see Earleywood he immediately recognized Pitkin as the same type and begged Father not to send us there. But Father was deceived by Pitkin's joviality, as he had been by Brownrigg's, and by the impressive rows of polished boards around the walls giving details of scholarships that former pupils had won to public schools. I dare say he was not sorry to get us off his hands, especially since after Mother's death we had moved to a maisonette two doors away in Portland Place, which meant that Nanny and we children lived on the same floor as he did. How well I remember Nanny peering through the curtains as he arrived or left with some ladyfriend. Once, he later told me, she had even opened his bedroom door one night when he was on the job. She would make snide references to them before us. It cannot have been pleasant for him to have her in the house, and when years later I asked why he did not sack her, he said: 'Because she was wonderful with you boys.' He wanted his freedom, so off to Earleywood we went, Dick for two years, myself for four.

The horror of our impending return there blighted the last fortnight of each holiday. At last the dreaded day would arrive. Father would give us lunch at the Hungaria in Lower Regent Street, after which the chauffeur would drive us to Waterloo. The last hundred yards of the journey were along a covered and cobbled approach, and when I drive along it today and hear the change of acoustics as though entering a tunnel, the chill still strikes me after fifty years. A horrid sight on the platform was that of parents conversing with our teachers, evidence of that conspiracy of adults against which we were powerless. What would be the use of reporting to one the cruelty of another? Then the train would start. Staines, Egham, Virginia Water, Sunningdale – the names of those intermediate stations are engraved on my mind, each more hateful than the last because nearer to our destination. At last the grim name of Ascot would appear. We disembarked, walked through a long subway that always smelt of urine, climbed into a dozen grey-padded taxis, and were swept through the pine- and birch-lined lanes until we reached the steep flinty drive and saw the windows of Earleywood glowing coldly out into the night.

Education at Earleywood concentrated on the classics, on which in our two final years we spent twenty hours a week. Pitkin knew his public-school headmasters well enough to be sure that alphas in Greek and Latin would more than counterbalance any number of gammas in other subjects. French, maths, history and the rest were regarded as irrelevancies and perfunctorily taught, with one exception. Dr Pitkin had a partner named Miss Sandwith. In appearance she was not unlike Miss Shuttleworth: tall, thin, very wrinkled and, it seemed to us, infinitely aged, though I suppose she was still in her sixties. She taught English, and her method was simple: she read aloud to us the plays of Shakespeare. But how she read them! Her voice was the voice of a great actress, a mellow contralto of extraordinary range, and she could do anything with it. When she read a male part, she modulated to a sober tenor or even a rough growling baritone. She could imitate any accent, and there was never any need to tell us who was speaking except when a new character appeared. Most of us were unrewarding pupils, for we regarded these hours chiefly as a blessed release from the monotony of the classics, and would punctuate her miraculous readings with the exploding of pistol caps and shrill treble requests to leave the room. But I suppose she knew that not more than half a dozen boys in each class were interested and addressed herself to them.

A year before I left she retired, and Dr Pitkin took a new partner. Mr Aldrich-Blake was smartly dressed and had a large and expensive car, a white blazer with a Cambridge college crest, highly greased hair, an expanse of shining teeth and a playful habit of holding boys under the water in the swimming-bath. He struck us as even nastier than Dr Pitkin, though less dangerous, since being stupid and slightly deaf he was easy to deceive. A year after I left, Dr Pitkin died of cancer and Mr Aldrich-Blake ran the school alone, with markedly less success.

Being at Earleywood had, however, one result for which I have never ceased to be grateful: nothing has seemed quite so awful since. Even Wellington, a spartan place in the 1930s, was liberal by comparison. For over forty years, although I was often in the vicinity of Earleywood, I could not bear even to drive past the school. Then, one summer evening in the seventies, driving home after playing cricket at Bagshot, I saw the signpost off the A3 and on an impulse took the turning. There, unchanged, the building stood with its multitude of windows aglow. Dusk was falling, and I left my car in the road so as not to attract attention and walked up the steep flinty-red drive. My old horror of the place returned. As I walked along its front a window was suddenly flung up and a fierce, bald, very red-faced man demanded to know who I was. I must have seemed a prowler with evil intentions on either the boys or his personal valuables, nor did my explanation that I was an old pupil convince him. He cross-examined me on my knowledge of the place, my naming of Dr Pitkin and Miss Sandwith tilted the scale, and he invited me in for a glass of sherry in the room in which Dr Pitkin had flogged me. We glanced in at the little chapel, where our young blood had been chilled by many a sermon on the danger of an unspecified temptation at the nature of which we could only guess. A brass plaque on the wall informed me that Miss Sandwith had lived to the age of ninety-two. The school, my host explained, now bore a new name. He expounded his views on education and I sensed the shade of Dr Pitkin nodding approval. I believe the place is now the residence of a wealthy Arab.

In the holidays Father took us dutifully to the theatre, mainly to farces and musical comedies. From the welter of trivia which I sat through in the twenties and thirties, a few memories stand out. In 1928 I saw Fred Astaire and his sister Adele in *Funnyface*, with Leslie Henson and Sydney Howard also in the cast. That was an evening, for Henson and Howard were a great pair of comics, Henson tiny and grotesque, Howard large and plump and very precise of speech and movement. The next year I was taken to Noël Coward's *Bitter Sweet* – the American star of which, Peggy Wood, was said to resemble my mother – and another musical, *Silver Wings*, with Lupino Lane, Harry Welchman and, in a minor part, the young Ralph Richardson. When, years later, I became a friend of Ralph, I asked him if he had really sung in this, since he was notoriously unmusical. He replied: 'Sort of.' But mostly we were taken to admire Bobby Howes, a perky little comic of amiable talent, or Marion Lorne, whom I thought much funnier, in a series of plays by her husband Walter Hackett, mostly at the Whitehall Theatre, which he had built for her. These were all written to the same formula, a modern opening scene followed by a flashback to the same setting in some previous century for most of the rest of the play. I laughed dutifully at all these, but much preferred *Richard III*, to which an aunt took me when I was nine, with a fine performance as the King by Baliol Holloway. Why my father, who liked serious theatre, so seldom took us to any I cannot imagine; unless, it now occurs to me, he kept that for his mistresses.

In *The Gay Adventure*, Marion Lorne was partnered by Seymour Hicks, who also presented and staged the play, and I remember how, when the rest of the large cast had taken their curtain calls in their period costumes, there ensued a considerable pause while we all clapped expectantly for Hicks, and how he eventually appeared in white tie and tails, differentiating himself from his company and identifying himself with us in the stalls. Even at that age I sensed something patronizing in the air with which he presented them, in their working clothes, to us, his social equals. I saw Max Reinhardt's production of A. P. Herbert's musical *Helen*, with George Robey as Menelaus, and the same year, 1932, I had my first sight of the young

John Gielgud in J. B. Priestley's adaptation of his novel *The Good Companions*. Next year I saw him in *Richard of Bordeaux*, Gordon Daviot's play about Richard II, and in 1934 his Hamlet. Both these performances would, I am sure, seem impossibly mannered and romanticized today (unlike most actors, the older he has grown the better he has become, so that several of his finest performances have been given since he was seventy), but on both occasions I was profoundly moved, and I have never seen any production of *Hamlet* since which so completely brought across the play as a whole, partly because, directing himself at the age of thirty, he had unselfishly picked the best possible supporting cast. Can there ever have been a more sensual Claudius and Gertrude than Frank Vosper and Laura Cowie, or a better Horatio, Polonius and Osric than Jack Hawkins, George Howe and the twenty-year-old Alec Guinness? Howe was only thirty-four, and when half a century later I asked him why he had been chosen so young to play Polonius, he replied that there was a general lack of middle-aged and oldish actors because of the Great War, so that any young actor who could convincingly act age tended to be cast old, as Howe continued to be.

Amazing as it now seems to me, that *Hamlet*, Baliol Holloway's *Richard III* and a touring *Macbeth* directed by Ben Greet to which we were taken from Earleywood, were the only Shakespeare performances I saw before I went up to Oxford at the age of eighteen. Nor did I see any other classics during that time except, in 1938, Saint-Denis's great production of *The Three Sisters*, *The School for Scandal*, two Shaw plays and, in 1939, *The Importance of Being Earnest* with Edith Evans as Lady Bracknell. I had first seen Edith Evans in a very different role in 1933 giving one of her marvellous peasant performances in *The Late Christopher Bean*. Alas that I missed her *Witch of Edmonton* and her Nurse in *Romeo and Juliet*. In *Theatre Royal*, a play about the Barrymores by Edna Ferber and George S. Kaufman (its original title in the USA was *The Royal Family*, but it was felt that in England this would sound blasphemous), I saw the young Laurence Olivier make a spectacular first entrance vaulting down on to the stage from the top of a high staircase. Years later I reminded him of this, and he said: 'Yes, and do you remember how I slid down the banisters?' He seemed genuinely hurt when I confessed that after half a century I did not. *Theatre Royal* also contained two of the best actresses I was ever to see: Marie Tempest and Madge Titheradge. Marie Tempest, then seventy, was a legendary monster to work with but had marvellous authority and timing. Madge Titheradge seemed to me, the few times I saw her, to have everything, but although she lived well into her seventies illness cut her career short when she was only fifty. Ralph Richardson told me he thought Madge Titheradge the best actress he had ever worked with.

Excited as I was by these visits to the theatre, I don't recall that they made me want to become an actor (that came later). Two things I used to dread after each performance. In the car on the way home, Father and Peter would criticize what we had seen, the way I do today, and for me this spoiled the magic of the evening. Then the car would stop in Manchester Street, where the last and longest-serving of Father's mistresses lived, and he would leave us there to be driven home without him. I remember how savagely I resented this.

My main passion during the first thirteen years of my life was cricket. This must have begun very early, for when my great-uncle Ted Marsden, who had played once or twice for Middlesex around the turn of the century, took me to see England v. the Rest at Lord's in 1930 shortly before my ninth birthday, I remember towards the end of the day longing for either Hobbs or Hammond, who were sharing a glorious partnership of 150, to get out so that my hero Frank Woolley, next on the scorecard, could come in. I was a fervent Surrey supporter, because my nurse came from that county, and would wait eagerly for Father to bring home the evening paper so that I could see how they had fared. The great Jack Hobbs still played for them occasionally (only, I have since read, when the weather promised to be decently warm); I had seen him hit eighty not out in that match at Lord's, and three years later I watched him take the West Indian bowlers apart for a double century in a day when he was in his fifty-first year. Although we lived quite near Lord's, I preferred the long Tube journey to the Oval; and when we went on holiday, in Kent or Sussex, I would persuade my father or some other adult to take me to a match at Canterbury, Folkestone, Dover, Hastings or Hove. At the last-named ground, in that first cricket-watching summer of 1930, I saw Maurice Tate take six Australian wickets before lunch, including Ponsford lbw second ball of the day. They totalled over 300 none the less, Alan Kippax scoring the most graceful century and the last pair, Hurwood and Hornibrook, adding a hundred – to my rage, for they prevented me from seeing Duleepsinhji bat. A child needs heroes, and mine were cricketers. I collected their likenesses on cigarette cards, with which I filled two largish albums, and their autographs in a small

17

red book which I still have, together with those of actors, some of whom were later to become my friends.

I have said cricket was my main childhood passion. Looking back, I think it was the only one. Most people remember their childhood nostalgically. To me it was a period of intense boredom, almost completely lacking in wonder. The countryside was a foreign and virtually unexplored land. Once Nanny took Dick and me to stay with some friends of hers called Jeal who lived in a tiny cottage somewhere, and the evening we arrived Mr Jeal took me outside to pull up some radishes for tea. It was dark, and I can still remember the smell of freshly disturbed earth as something quite new. I wonder when I next smelt it again. I never enjoyed the pleasure of bathing naked. Heaven did not lie about me in my infancy; I longed only to escape into the adult world. For me, growing up signified not so much the loss of innocence as the gaining of knowledge; the winning of freedom, rather than the losing of it.

During my last term at Earleywood, Father appeared unexpectedly one afternoon to tell me that Nanny had died. It was my first experience of grief, the emotion I should have felt when I learned of my mother's death. I felt a similar grief when my father died twenty years later, for by that time he and I had become close. But of my mother I retain only those three trivial memories, and I cannot look at her gravely beautiful face in the family album without a feeling of deprivation and self-reproach.

Father had chosen Wellington for Peter on the recommendation of a friend of Mother; her son had been there, and the pine country which surrounded it was meant to be healthy (Peter had had glandular trouble and had been pronounced delicate). Moreover, Father wanted us to go to a rugger school near London with a decent eating-place nearby, to reduce the, for him, boredom of his twice-termly visits. (He had sent Dick and me to Earleywood rather than to Fernden because Earleywood was near Wellington and so he could take the three of us out together.) It was more difficult to get a good meal in Britain then than now, but at Bray in Berkshire there were two reputable restaurants, the Café de Paris and the Hind's Head, so Dick and I were sent to Earleywood and the three of us to Wellington, all within easy reach of Bray.

To anyone who knew its history, Wellington must have seemed an inappropriate school for us. It had been founded as a memorial to the great Duke shortly after his death, mainly to provide education for the orphaned sons of Army officers, who received special terms, and part of the cost of building had been met by the simple measure of stopping a day's pay from every man in the Army, from the Commander-in-Chief to the newest private. What the non-commissioned ranks must have felt about this is not hard to imagine. F. B. Malim, who was headmaster for my first two years, was in the Victorian mould: a small man of terrifying authority, remote from the boys. I scarcely met him. But he possessed one rare virtue: a willingness to choose for his teachers, in addition to the usual solid types, young mavericks who would probably not remain for long before leaving to become writers, or to pursue some other romantic career. These firebrands caused occasional trouble, but always left before they became really difficult, and Malim doubtless had confidence in his own ability to cope with any seditious ideas they might seek to spread. Outstanding among these mavericks were Cuthbert Worsley and Robin Gordon-Walker. Worsley, later to become a distinguished drama critic and to write a splendid volume of memoirs, *Flannelled Fool*, which revealed details of homosexual goings-on among the masters, taught me English during my first year before leaving to drive an ambulance in the Spanish Civil War, and opened exciting windows. It was he who introduced me to the poetry of Wilfred Owen. Robin Gordon-Walker was to be an even bigger influence on me.

Peter, who went to Wellington in 1930, hated it; by contrast I remember it much more fondly than I remember Oxford. Somehow it had become liberalized between 1930 and 1935. I encountered no bullying nor anti-Semitism, both common at public schools in the 1930s. The absence of anti-Semitism was the more remarkable in that there were very few other Jews at Wellington. It also helped that I liked games where Peter had not (Dick, being lame, was excused them). Admittedly the head boy of each house was allowed to beat, and in my second term we suffered under a horrible boy who averaged a beating a day. But his predecessor and successors were amiable, and the staff, or anyway those I came into contact with, were tolerant; my housemaster was dull but harmless. Above all, Wellington possessed two great advantages over Earleywood: there was no Dr Pitkin with squeaking shoes to paralyse our larynxes, and we had privacy of a sort. Every boy, from his first or, at latest, his second term, had his own room. They were tiny, about nine feet by five, and the partitions separating them stopped several feet from the high ceilings so that there was no privacy from noise, but we became inured to that – as people are said to do who live by a railway line – and each had its own door which we could close behind us.

Many, perhaps most, of the boys were destined for a career in the Army, but the school, thanks largely to Malim, prided itself on its artistic side, especially history and music. An unusual number of my contemporaries achieved success in intellectual and artistic fields. Michael Howard was to be Regius Professor of History at Oxford, Richard Sykes and Christopher Ewart-Biggs became ambassadors and both were to be assassinated by the IRA, John Gardner, Philip Cranmer and Patrick Ireland became professors of music, John Addison and James Bernard successful composers, Constantine Fitzgibbon a distinguished writer, Frank Giles editor of the *Sunday Times*, Robin Dunn and Bob Gatehouse High Court judges, Michael Brock warden of Nuffield College, Oxford, Gordon Campbell Secretary of State for Scotland, Michael Palliser head of the Diplomatic Service and Christopher Lee a film star. (The poet Gavin Ewart had left just before I came.)

During my first two years, we spent only twelve hours a week on the classics compared with twenty a week at Earleywood, but from the age of fifteen, when I passed School Certificate and entered the Classical Lower Sixth, this number increased to thirty-six. For my last three years we studied nothing else except for three hours a week of English. Among other things we had to translate Shakespeare into both Greek iambics and Latin hexameters. The longer I continued with this regimen, the more rapidly my early enthusiasm for the classics decreased. Of the cultural side of ancient Greece and Rome we learned virtually nothing. Translation, whether from these languages into English or the reverse, was our daily stint. Little appeal was made to our imaginations. If anyone had told me then that my career would be principally that of a translator, I would not have believed them; or, if I had, the prospect would have depressed me.

The history teaching at Wellington was far more imaginative. An affected but gifted old aesthete named Talboys had presided over it for years, and shortly before I came he was joined by an even better teacher, Robin Gordon-Walker. Together they achieved a remarkable record of scholarships to Oxbridge, and when Talboys left halfway through my time he was replaced by another fine teacher, Max Reese. I would have learned far more from them than I did in the Classical Sixth, but Malim had been saddened by the fact that Peter and Dick had both abandoned the classics immediately after

1 Aunt Milly, Uncle Dick, Uncle Monty, Father and Grandfather
in the garden at 181 Adelaide Road, c. 1895

2 Father

3 Mother

4 With Mother, Dick and Peter, 1921

taking School Certificate and since I was, mistakenly as it turned out, regarded as a certainty for a classical scholarship to Oxbridge, he extracted from my father a promise that I at least would not transfer to another side. I acceded willingly to this, for the classics were my best subject; I only narrowly scraped School Certificate credits in history and English, and was hopeless at French, maths and the sciences. So I continued with Greek and Latin, becoming progressively disillusioned, and it was not until my final term, when I had twice failed scholarships at Oxford, that I moved to the history side. By that time my dislike of the classics had become so strong that I have never opened a Greek or Latin book since, and I, who once read those languages almost as easily as I did English, now have difficulty in understanding any but the simplest words and phrases. Sometimes, now that I am old, it occurs to me that it might be an amusing exercise to revive my knowledge of, at any rate, Greek by going through Homer or Sophocles with a dictionary and a crib, but I do not suppose that I ever will.

Two years before I left Wellington, Malim retired and was replaced by Robert Longden. Longden was thirty-three and one of the most brilliant classicists of his year at Oxford. He had been a member of that remarkable generation at Eton which included George Orwell, Cyril Connolly, Henry Green, Harold Acton, Steven Runciman, David Cecil and Alec Douglas-Home, and is frequently and always affectionately mentioned in their memoirs, especially those of Orwell and Connolly. Although, or perhaps because, he had had no experience of schoolmastering, having become a don immediately after gaining his degree, he had an instant effect on the school. Malim had been an austere, remote and elderly figure; Longden was younger than most of his staff, possessed great good looks and charm, was a natural administrator, and swept Wellington into the twentieth century. His liberal and humanistic attitude was resented by the older teachers but greatly welcomed by most of the younger ones and by virtually all the boys, whom he addressed by their Christian names as he had his students at Oxford, something which appalled the older masters as I suppose it would have appalled Malim. The common room, like all common rooms, was divided into two factions, and more than his reforms it was his support of the progressives against the diehards that changed the atmosphere of the school. His opponents called him unsound, but he was far from that. It was widely said that he would have succeeded Claude Elliott as the next headmaster of Eton but for his untimely death in 1940 at the age of thirty-seven. A stick of bombs, perhaps intended for the nearby Military College at Sandhurst, dropped across the school grounds, he left a dinner party in his lodge to make sure that no one had been hurt, and a final bomb which had hung up picked him off as he stepped out of his door. Nobody else was touched. He was succeeded by two uninspiring headmasters, and Wellington, to the delight of many of its surviving staff (most of the young ones had by now joined the forces), relapsed into its old conservatism for the next quarter of a century.

About Robin Gordon-Walker I find it difficult to write objectively, for he seems to me to have been the most important person in my life. He possessed what my classics master, for all his solid virtues, lacked: the ability to make fretful adolescents such as myself work and develop our talents. Certain privileged boys, members of the History Sixth and the more intelligent athletes, enjoyed free access to his rooms in their out-of-school hours. This was much disapproved of by the older masters, several of whom had been appointed before the 1914 war, but Robin had strong supporters among the younger masters, was extremely popular with the parents of his pupils and, most importantly, was a favourite of both Malim and Longden. As the result of a poem by me which appeared in the school magazine, I was invited to join this group about a year before I left. One had to get one's housemaster's permission to leave the house after a certain hour in the evening, and looking back I am surprised that my housemaster, one of Robin's adversaries, never refused me permission, though he gained a small revenge by not making me a prefect until my last term and promoting an odious junior named Gilks in my place.

But for my entry into this group, my memories of Wellington would probably be almost as unaffectionate as my memories of Earleywood, for I had no friends in my house and got on ill with both my housemaster and my sixth-form master, though the latter, who became a successful headmaster of two of the biggest grammar schools in the north, seemed a pleasant fellow when I met him afterwards. I am sure I was a recalcitrant pupil, and I don't think he was good with those. Robin, by contrast, specialized in bringing the best out of difficult boys; he sought out their individuality and developed that, while insisting on hard work and intellectual discipline. What windows he opened into my mind! After my nurse and Miss Shuttleworth, he was the first big positive influence on my life, and I can never forget the debt I owe him, any more than I can forget the details of that room off the Long Corridor, with its high windows overlooking the cricket field, its broad divan covered with knobbly little cushions, its rows of bookshelves filled with the gilt-lettered spines of Eliot, Auden, Spender and MacNeice – the excitingly perplexing new poets whom Robin would expound to us – and the red-brick fireplace on which stood a Spanish doll with castanets. There was a short passage leading from the corridor to this room, and great was my disappointment when there was no pinprick of light in the keyhole at the end of it, for that meant that Robin was out and I would have to spend the rest of the evening in my little cubicle, which had seemed such a refuge when I first had it after Earleywood but which now, like the playroom with the plum-coloured lino, seemed something to escape from.

Equally I remember the other nine boys who formed our group and with whom I shared these discoveries. Seven were to be killed in the war; only three of us lived to be twenty-two.

How can I attempt to analyse what qualities in those friends, now dead for nearly half a century, excited me? Any obituary notice of any son killed before his manhood expresses the immense, vague and helpless regret which I still feel for their deaths. They were the friends I should have grown up with, grown old with. A few years later I tried to lay their ghosts in a novel, *The End of the Corridor*. Adolescence was still, then, close enough for me to be able to write about it as I cannot hope to now.

Rowland Hill, everyone said, would have played stand-off half for England and Alan Sykes for Scotland, John Williams would have been a county cricketer, Charles Ruck-Keene and Keith Foottit county hockey players and perhaps internationals. Keith, Andrew Tod and Claud Raymond were talented poets. Only Claud achieved fame, and that after his death in the most unexpected manner. He was a very shy and unathletic boy, and a convinced pacifist, who took part in the war with the greatest reluctance. The official report of his death in Burma bears quoting:

He was in charge of a small party despatched against isolated enemy posts on the road from Letpan to Taungup. Near the village of Talaku they were fired on by a strongly entrenched enemy post on a jungle-covered hill. Raymond charged at the fire. Wounded in the right shoulder he continued up the slope firing from the hip. A Japanese grenade struck him in the face, but he picked himself up and went on. Hit a third time, his wrist shattered, he still carried on, killed two

and wounded a third Japanese. The rest of the enemy fled
into the jungle, leaving their equipment and position in
British hands. Others had been wounded in the attack, and
Raymond refused treatment until last and insisted on walking
back to the landing craft lest delay should endanger the whole
patrol. After walking a mile he collapsed and had to be
carried on an improvised stretcher. He died of wounds soon
after. His self-sacrifice undoubtedly saved the whole patrol by
allowing it to withdraw before the enemy could launch
his counter-attack.

For this he was awarded a posthumous Victoria Cross. Of all the
boys at Wellington in my time, Claud must have seemed the least
likely to achieve that honour. What strange ferocity and self-disregard
suddenly entered into that gentle spirit?

Robin himself left a couple of years after I did, after falling out
with Longden's successor, a cautious and withdrawn bursar from
Oxford. ('We all felt he should have been a don,' said one of the
bursar's ex-prefects at his old high table, to which the Provost
replied: 'We all felt he should have been a schoolmaster.') Robin
married a young and beautiful wife, and three months later died
of a cerebral haemorrhage at the age of thirty-seven. She bore his
daughter, a gifted and attractive girl who was killed in a car accident
soon after her twenty-first birthday.

There was little theatre at Wellington then, but during my last year
I played a comic old woman in a one-act play called *The Bathroom
Door* and Major Petkoff, a comic old man, in Shaw's *Arms and the
Man*. I had something of a success in both roles and decided I would
like to make the stage my profession. Having failed my scholarships,
I asked Longden if I could try for the Royal Academy of Dramatic
Art instead of going to Oxford, but he said that OUDS, the Oxford
University Dramatic Society, which boasted many distinguished
ex-members, offered at least as good an entry to the professional
stage as any drama school, which was probably then true, and urged
me to go up to Oxford, for which I was eventually grateful. I also,
for some reason which I cannot now guess at, decided to take up
a musical instrument. I hankered after the trumpet, but the music
director, Mr Allen, said the orchestra needed a euphonium. I did not
even know what this was. It turned out to be a tuba and to possess
every disadvantage: it was very heavy to carry, and had an enormous
expanse of metal to polish; I sat among the trombones, which was

deafening; and a wrong note was much more noticeable than from any other instrument, especially if, as sometimes happened, I emitted it during what was meant to be a sudden silence.

During that otherwise undistinguished last year at Wellington, I won two minor prizes, one for Latin hexameters and one for the best original English poem. I received these from the hand of our President, the Duke of Connaught, then aged eighty-nine. I had just had my nose broken at cricket, missing a catch in the gully; this had resulted in two black eyes, and when I arrived on the platform, looking very unlike the Shelleyan figure he must have expected, the old Duke turned uneasily to Longden before handing me Aldous Huxley's *Ends and Means*. I shook his already shaking hand, a contact that briefly linked me to the very distant past, for he, Queen Victoria's youngest son, had been the uncle of the last Tsar of Russia and of the German Kaiser, and had been carried to his christening by his godfather, the great Duke of Wellington; and the Duke, born in 1769, must as a child have known people born in the previous century, in which Shakespeare wrote *Hamlet*.

My favourite writers at school were Owen and Sassoon and, later, Auden. Owen has remained my favourite of all English poets. Auden made a tremendous impact on me, as on so many of my generation. 'Taller today, we remember similar evenings', 'Sir, no man's enemy, forgiving all', 'Look, stranger, at this island now' and

> Now the leaves are falling fast,
> Nurse's flowers will not last;
> Nurses to the graves are gone,
> But the prams go rolling on.

I had not thought of these lines for decades but, leafing again through the 1930 *Poems*, which I bought in 1937 when I was sixteen, and *Look, Stranger!*, purchased together with *The Ascent of F6* and *Spain* the following year, I feel again across fifty years the old excitement. Here was someone speaking to us in our own language and on our own level, not from an Olympian height. He made one feel that poetry was something one might partake in oneself as a kind of equal, not just as a reverent auditor. I began to write bad adolescent poems myself about the hopelessness of adolescent love, having developed the, in those days, usual infatuations for other boys, none of them reciprocated.

Novels meant less to me than poetry, though the 1930s were a rich decade for English fiction. Aldous Huxley, Graham Greene, George Orwell, Elizabeth Bowen, Rosamond Lehmann, Evelyn Waugh, Henry Green and Robert Graves were all under forty-five and at or approaching their peak; H. E. Bates, C. S. Forester and L. A. G. Strong, later to write more popular but less good work, were then rightly regarded as being on the same level; and of an older generation, H. G. Wells, Virginia Woolf, Somerset Maugham and P. G. Wodehouse were still active. D. H. Lawrence had died in 1930 and his reputation was in temporary decline. But most of these I did not discover until I went up to Oxford. Huxley and Strong were the novelists I enjoyed most at school; neither is greatly admired today.

In January 1939, between my unsuccessful scholarship attempts, I went for a couple of weeks to ski at Geilo in central Norway, taking with me a large book called Zimmern's *The Greek Commonwealth* of which, idle as ever, I read very little. I was hopeless at skiing, due to my poor sense of balance (I have never been able to ride a bicycle). But I loved my first sight of Scandinavia, the mountains and the snow, and for the first time was attracted by a girl, the hotel receptionist, who was about my age. She suggested we should meet in Oslo, where she showed me round for a couple of days; I did not even dare to kiss her. This naivety in the presence of girls was typical of most public schoolboys of my generation who had no sisters; we just did not meet girls. Apart from a couple of weeks in Switzerland in 1935 as a Boy Scout, this was my first trip abroad. A Norwegian student told me in the cafeteria of Oslo University that he was a Nazi and that Hitler had no ambitions outside Germany. Fifteen months later the building in which we were drinking coffee was the Gestapo headquarters.

I left Wellington in July 1939 and went to stay in Paris with Dick, who had taken a year off from his medical studies at Cambridge to read French at the Sorbonne. (Peter had done the same in Switzerland; as a result, they both became fluent in French, which I was never to be.) Even by the standards of those days, Paris was unbelievably cheap; our bed and board in a pension on the rue Gay-Lussac, including a big and sunny double room, breakfast, and a splendid lunch and dinner, both including wine, cost us each five shillings (25p) a day. One could spend a whole evening drinking in a bar for half that sum, and I duly got drunk for the first time. After a few weeks I took the train south to join Peter at Avignon, where he was holidaying, and we drove south to St Tropez, then a quiet little seaside village where, even at the height of the season, one could get into any hotel. A few mornings later I was sitting on the front when a newspaper-seller appeared shouting something I could not understand. I bought a copy and read that Stalin had concluded a non-aggression pact with Hitler. We drove with thousands of other British tourists north to the Channel ports, and a few days later Hitler invaded Poland.

3

Oxford Poets in Wartime

Unlike their predecessors in 1914, the young men of Britain were not encouraged in 1939 to rush into the forces. In time, we were informed, we would be called up; meanwhile, those who had places at universities were encouraged to take them up. In my own case, there was the complication that I was, like so many of my generation, a committed pacifist. In my last year at Wellington I had joined the Peace Pledge Union, which involved signing a declaration that I would never take part in any war. It was natural in the late 1930s to embrace some 'ism', and for those of us who were not drawn to Communism or Fascism, pacifism offered an attractive alternative. So I went up to Oxford in October 1939 determined to register, when the time should arrive, as a conscientious objector. But it would be a year or more before the decision would be forced upon me.

I had decided to read English and, since the Christ Church tutor in that subject – the novelist Michael Innes – had left to do war work, I was allowed to choose from those at the other colleges. They were a distinguished bunch, including Edmund Blunden, David Cecil, J. R. R. Tolkien (not that many people outside the field of Anglo-Saxon studies had yet heard of him), C. S. Lewis, Nevill Coghill and M. R. Ridley, allegedly the original of Dorothy Sayers's Lord Peter Wimsey. I chose Blunden, mainly because I knew of him as the editor of Wilfred Owen, and mistakenly supposed him to have known him. I was very disappointed when he told me that they had never met. Blunden was then coming up to forty-three, and I remember my first sight of his tiny figure, 'like a chinchilla' as Edmund Gosse well described him, 'with his sharp nose and wonderful eyes . . . simple and ardent and responsive'. 'Well, now,' he said after a few minutes, 'we must fix a day and time for us to meet each week. Do you drink?' I confessed that I did. He consulted his diary. 'Shall we

say six p.m. on Tuesdays?' It seemed a strange time, but I nodded.
'They may have difficulty heating these rooms when it turns colder.
Do you know the Bear in Bear Lane?' So that was where I had my
tutorials for the next two years; they lasted until closing time, which
in those days was ten. After the first two or three weeks, he hinted
that it was unnecessary for me to bring an essay and thenceforth I did
very little work. Mostly at these drinking sessions we talked about
living poets, his friends such as Sassoon, Eliot and Graves, and the
younger ones, Auden, Spender, MacNeice, Day Lewis and Dylan
Thomas, all of whom he admired. Betjeman's star had not yet fully
risen. He mentioned another pupil of his who had been to his old
school, Christ's Hospital, and who he said was an interesting poet
who edited the university literary magazine, *Cherwell* (its rival, *Isis*,
had ceased publication on the outbreak of war). I should, he said,
meet this young man, Keith Douglas.

I duly bought the term's first issue of *Cherwell*, which had a distinguished pedigree. Since it had been founded in 1920, its undergraduate editors and contributors had included Robert Graves, Evelyn
Waugh, Graham Greene, Auden, Spender, MacNeice, Day Lewis,
Betjeman, Osbert Lancaster, Terence Rattigan, Blunden himself and
God knows who besides. It still carried the cover which Waugh had
designed in the mid-twenties. I submitted a poem, Douglas accepted
it, and I went to meet him at the *Cherwell* office by Folly Bridge.

Keith Douglas was then nineteen, lean and tough, a year older than
me but infinitely more mature. For one thing, he seemed to know
about girls, and as often as not had one on his knee as he sat at his
desk. He was not an easy person, cynical, abrasive and pugnacious.
Once I found him with a large piece of plaster on his face; when I
asked if he had had an accident, he said: 'No, a fight.' He returned
contributions which did not please him with sarcastic comments,
and frequently insulted individuals and institutions in his editorials
and reviews. One notice which he wrote of a revue at the Playhouse
was so abusive that the theatre withdrew not only *Cherwell*'s weekly
pair of complimentary tickets (their repertory company did a new
play every week), but also its weekly advertisement, for which I
seem to remember they paid 5s. 10d., almost the equivalent of
the sale of twelve copies. (When I became editor the following
autumn, I had to assure the theatre that our attitude would be less
aggressive before they would relent.) This abrasiveness of Keith's,
not surprisingly, concealed a raw sensitivity and great tenderness.
He published some splendid poems of his own in *Cherwell* during his

editorship. I remember especially 'Canoe', which perfectly captures the atmosphere of Oxford around the time France fell:

> Well, I am thinking this must be my last
> summer, but cannot lose even a part
> of pleasure in the old-fashioned art
> of idleness. I cannot stand aghast
>
> at whatever doom hovers in the background
> while grass and buildings and the somnolent river
> who know they are allowed to last for ever
> exchange between them the whole subdued sound
>
> of this hot time. What sudden fearful fate
> can deter my shade wandering next year
> from a return? Whistle, and I will hear
> and come another evening, when this boat
>
> travels with you alone towards Iffley:
> as you lie looking up for thunder again,
> this cool touch does not betoken rain;
> it is my spirit that kisses your mouth lightly.

Keith could hardly wait to join the Army and start fighting professionally. I never saw him after he went down that June, except once, in uniform across the floor of the Café Royal, entwined with a girl, not many weeks before he was killed.

I do not recall much of that first year at Oxford. There were the months of the Phoney War, when the two armies faced each other across the Siegfried and Maginot lines and we ignorantly supposed that the deadlock might last indefinitely. Then came the German breakthrough, the invasion of Denmark and Norway, the rout of the Allied armies and, finally, the newspaper posters in the High proclaiming the fall of France as we returned from cricket. Our peaceful life during those terrible months seemed totally unreal; whether one was going to fight or, like me, hopefully join some medical corps, one saw little prospect of not being killed. Any kind of study seemed pointless. Christ Church boasted various dons whom one saw around, too old to do war service or returning at weekends from their secret duties: Churchill's scientific adviser, F. A. Lindemann, later to become Lord Cherwell; R. H. Dundas, who occupied Lewis Carroll's old rooms, with a tiled screen painted with figures who were supposed to have inspired some of the characters in *Alice in Wonderland*; and four distinguished historians in Robert Blake, Frank Pakenham, Patrick Gordon-Walker and Hugh Trevor-Roper, then twenty-six but looking barely eighteen. But there was little contact between the dons and undergraduates at Christ Church, and the few I met I did so on the hockey or cricket field.

Nor, then or later, did I make many friends among my fellow-undergraduates in Christ Church, though I had plenty in other colleges. In 1939 Christ Church contained – I almost wrote 'was full of', for that was the impression they gave – many of the nastiest kind of Old Etonians, rich, loud and philistine. Some bore the names of families famous in English history. Had there been a revolution in England after the war (as some feared there might be, were Labour not returned in 1945), I should not have grieved to see them swinging from the lamp-posts. When I came back to Christ Church in 1946, they had been succeeded by similar types. They gave me a distrust of anyone with an Old Etonian tie which was only slowly eroded over the years. Their idea of a perfect end to an evening was to throw some harmless aesthete, never fortunately myself, into Mercury, the fountain in Tom Quad. Whether this type still exists, I do not know. I seldom revisit Christ Church, except to show friends around the hall and the cathedral. After the war I attended a couple of 'gaudies', or reunions, and searched in vain for anyone I was pleased to see. At one of them, doubtless owing to some confusion of identity, I was placed at a table with fifteen clergymen of my age. Never, even among scientists, have I found it so difficult to understand the jokes.

Keith Douglas had made me his sub-editor for the summer term of 1940, so that in October I succeeded to the editorship of *Cherwell*. Sales and advertisements had so declined under his editorship that the owners had in fact decided to cease publication, but my father guaranteed any loss the magazine might sustain. Otherwise I might not have met several of the remarkable generation of writers who came up in 1940 and 1941, and who were to shape my career towards authorship and away from acting. (I had chosen Oxford simply because I had joined my nurse in supporting Oxford in the Boat Race. Had I followed Peter and Dick to Cambridge I would not have met these writers. There were surprisingly few interesting ones at Cambridge during those early war years, and I would probably have continued with my intention to go on the stage.)

I decided that outside names were needed to promote interest in *Cherwell*. Although we could offer no fees, the response was generous. Contributions arrived from Cecil Day Lewis, C. E. M. Joad, Harold Laski, David Cecil, Blunden, E. M. Delafield, Naomi Mitchison, L. A. G. Strong, A. G. Macdonell, Clifford Bax, D. N. Pritt and my old Wellington teacher Cuthbert Worsley, by now a respected critic on the *New Statesman* and the author of a fine book about the Spanish war, *Behind the Battle*. More importantly, a number of remarkable undergraduate writers emerged. My contributors during my two terms of editorship included Sidney Keyes, Philip Larkin, John Heath-Stubbs, John Mortimer, Drummond Allison, Francis King, Michael Hamburger, David Wright and Michael Flanders, as well as Keith Douglas himself, who sent several poems from the Army. Iris Murdoch was up, but didn't contribute (or did she, and did I reject her? I see she published a poem in *Cherwell* in 1939). An editorial note in the issue of 28 November 1940 proudly recorded that 'sales for the first time in history touched the eight hundred mark'.

Keyes made the most immediate impact of all these, not only in Oxford but on the critics and the literary world at large, first through his contributions to *Eight Oxford Poets* in 1941, then with his two volumes *The Iron Laurel* and, posthumously, *The Cruel Solstice*, an impression that was strengthened when his *Collected Poems* appeared in 1945.

In the sixties, his star declined, mainly for two reasons. One was that when he was killed, shortly before his twenty-first birthday in 1943, he was praised for the wrong sentimental reasons by well-meaning non-combatants who, seeing him as representative of the younger generation that was dying to defend them, elevated or reduced him to the stature of martyr, resulting in a reaction which dismissed him as a new Rupert Brooke (though Brooke too was tougher and sharper than his detractors suppose). Another reason was the marked and oft-expressed hostility to his work by Philip Larkin, largely I believe for a reason which I will come to later. Larkin included only a single page of Keyes's poems in his *Oxford Book of Twentieth-Century English Verse*, compared with six pages for himself, and, according to Kingsley Amis in *Larkin at Sixty*, dismissed Keyes as 'a third-rate person', a judgement which I do not think anyone who really knew Keyes could conceivably have shared, whatever they may have felt about his work. Keyes remains for me a much deeper and broader-ranged poet than Larkin, and I have little doubt that posterity will rate him the bigger of the two.

One evening I came back very late to my rooms to find the usual pile of contributions awaiting me. I began to glance wearily through

them, and four poems, neatly typed, I remember, in contrast to most
of the others, jumped out at me: 'Elegy', 'Remember Your Lovers',
'Cervières' and 'Shall the Dead Return?' One did not need to be
perceptive to see that these were something out of the ordinary. I
asked the writer to come and see me, and he arrived in the middle of
a rowdy sherry party I was giving, mostly attended by my sporting
friends. I was filling glasses near the door when it opened, revealing
a slim, rather olive-skinned youth of about my own height in a grey
polo-neck sweater. I handed him a glass and asked his name, in that
order, and so our friendship began. I soon made Sidney sub-editor,
and he was very efficient at the job (and succeeded me as co-editor
with John Heath-Stubbs the following spring). Although Sidney was
impractical in some things (as who is not?), he was very clear-headed.
When my father met him, he said: 'Not my idea of a poet. I'd give
him a job any day.' He was a marvellous person for an undergraduate
editor to have around, for he had a stock of poems of varying length
(he wrote three or four a month), so that I could say: 'We're half a
column short', or four inches or whatever, and he would provide
something to fill the gap.

Sidney introduced me to three fellow poets, John Heath-Stubbs
and Drummond Allison, both in his own college, Queen's, and
David Wright of Oriel, a South African who had been stone deaf
since the age of seven but who could lip-read so perfectly that one
forgot his disability. All of these had come up the previous year, at
the same time as me, but I was unaware of their existence; perhaps
they had been among those whose efforts had been returned by Keith
Douglas with unflattering comments. Sidney also introduced me to
a friend of his from Tonbridge, Basil Taylor, a painter; but Basil's
critical instincts were stronger than his creative drive, and he was to
become instead one of the finest art critics of his generation. We soon
formed a tight group, meeting mostly in Sidney's rooms at Queen's. I
am ashamed to admit that I did not at first appreciate the poems of the
others, and it was only at Sidney's instigation that I published them.

Philip (who then signed his poems P. A. Larkin), John Mortimer
and Francis King were less unfamiliar to me in their style of writing,
as was Ian Bancroft, a fine poet who gave it up too soon to pursue
a distinguished career in the Civil Service, of which he ultimately
became head. Kingsley Amis, who came up in April 1941 after
I had retired from my editorship, records that Larkin in those
days was noisy, hard-drinking, and liked best to talk about jazz. I
remember him as very quiet and rather solemn; perhaps we others

were insufficiently interested in jazz. He already wore a curious air of middle age. The poems he published in *Cherwell* do not read very well today; they are technically quite accomplished but otherwise unremarkable, and he did not include them in his future collections. A later developer than the others, he looked very much at twenty as he was to at sixty, except that he still had most of his hair.

The dullness and heartiness of Christ Church had been relieved that autumn by the appearance of two eighteen-year-olds from Westminster of contrasting appearance and character, the one six feet four, an oarsman and a quarter-miler, the other small and bespectacled: Michael Flanders and Donald Swann. Swann did not write for us, but Flanders became a regular contributor, mostly with reviews of plays and films. I used to bring these fellow-writers along to the Bear to meet Blunden on Tuesday evenings, and there in the tiny front room we would drink with him until closing-time.

Michael Flanders had already decided to make the stage his career, and but for the disability which was shortly to strike him down he would surely have been one of the outstanding actors of his generation. He was the best student actor I have seen; tall and handsome, a fine mover with a superb voice and great intelligence, he had everything. I remember him as Brabantio in *Othello* and as Shawcross in Auden and Isherwood's *The Ascent of F6*, though sadly I was down with flu when he played Pirandello's Henry IV, by all accounts a remarkable performance. (That week away from Oxford also resulted in my missing Keith Douglas's twenty-first birthday party, for which he returned from the Army; in a letter he wrote to a friend asking him to organize it, I see Iris Murdoch's name just above mine on the guest list, so I missed meeting her too, and it was to be thirty years before I did.) During a vacation, Flanders also appeared as a professional at the Oxford Playhouse as Valentine the dentist in Shaw's *You Never Can Tell*. He had been one of a notable theatrical quartet at Westminster, since in addition to Swann he had been a contemporary there of Peter Ustinov and Peter Brook (not that anyone had yet heard of them), but when many years later I remarked that the dramatic performances there must have been something to see, he explained that drama in general had been somewhat frowned on apart from the annual Latin play, and that as none of them except Swann was any good at the classics, he, Ustinov and Brook had been little more than spear-carriers. Brook was to come up to Oxford the following year, when I was to meet him in bizarre circumstances.

Flanders was struck down by polio while in the Navy in 1943, and was confined to a wheelchair for the rest of his life. None of his friends could imagine what he would do, for writing had been very much a sideline to him. He played the clarinet, and arranged rather sad little musical evenings at his parents' home in Golders Green, his fellow instrumentalists including Gerard Hoffnung, a brilliant humorist who was to die young, on the tuba. After the war he wrote songs and lyrics for various revues; then, in 1956, I and his other friends received a printed note to the effect that he and Swann were to appear in a revue of their own, *At The Drop of a Hat*, at what would now be called a 'fringe' theatre, the New Lindsey in Kensington. It moved to the West End, where it ran for over two years and was still playing to capacity when they closed in order to take it to Broadway, where it was equally successful. Flanders married happily and had two daughters of whom he was hugely proud; I am godfather to the elder. But he still thought of the other career he might have had. The last time he appeared on a stage, in 1974, was in an entertainment I had devised which included a scene from *Hamlet*, and afterwards he said: 'Hamlet. There's a part I would like to have played.' Those of us who remember him as an undergraduate actor cannot but regret the performances we might have seen.

Drummond Allison was lean and fresh-faced, rather immature, outgoing, boyish and pleasantly garrulous, with a high, eager voice, and a passion for cricket which neither Keyes nor Heath-Stubbs shared, though Larkin, Flanders and I did, and Amis too. Heath-Stubbs was the most senior of us, having been born in 1918, which made him three years older than Allison and myself and four years older than Keyes and Larkin. Not surprisingly, he was also the most mature, with a breadth of reading in English poetry that humbled us all, even Keyes, who was himself exceptionally well read for an eighteen-year-old, in French and German as well as in English. Heath-Stubbs even contrived to give a fascinating lecture on 'Chaucer's Contemporaries' to some Oxford society; he could bring the most seemingly impenetrable poets to life.

John Heath-Stubbs was immensely tall and thin, and almost blind; at the age of fifteen, following an operation for glaucoma, he had been told that he would have to use Braille (though he never did), and was sent to continue his education at the Worcester College for the Blind. In the early sixties he was to lose his sight completely, and although he was still able to read as an undergraduate at Oxford he could do so only by holding the print an inch from his eyes; it made one feel slightly sick to watch him. He would often bang into lamp-posts when walking down the street, which he did rather fast with huge strides. But he took an active part in dramatics, both acting and directing, as well as writing at least one play. I particularly like one poem a'⌐out a plagiarist which he contributed to *Cherwell* and which for some reason he never reproduced in any of his published volumes:

SIMILE

Just as the cormorant (with stretched-out throttle
And glossed green plumage), shaped like a beer-bottle,
Flaps heavily across the qualmish sea,
With splay-feet dangling down; and just as she
Gliding among the little scaly fry –
Gulping them in, glints a sardonic eye,
Rises again, ruffling her ragged crest,
And sets her course towards her putrid nest,
Where with avidity her squeaking brood,
Befouled with their own excrement, squat, purblind, nude,
Stretch out for nutriment their craggy necks
(With petulant, fraternal little pecks),
Scramble for scraps of fish regurgitated
From her crammed crop, until their hunger's sated:
So you, my friend, emerged from that deep sea
Whose floods are the blue waves of poetry,
With your fat brain stocked full with what you've caught –
The newly spawned small fry of others' thought –
Belch out your reeking soul for callow eyes
And spew the half-digested words that are your prize.

Heath-Stubbs appeared in almost every issue of the magazine as a critic – usually of music or drama, or anyway of theatre, since for some reason which I can neither remember nor imagine, I sent him to the most unworthy of plays. The first four to which he applied his considerable mind were two musicals, *Me and My Girl* and *The Maid of the Mountains*, a trivial melodrama by Emlyn Williams called *The Light of Heart*, and a farce with Ralph Lynn, *Nap Hand*. Next term he got promoted to more serious stuff, covering *Hedda Gabler*, Strindberg's *The Ghost Sonata* (which he thought 'a very bad play') and Kotzebue's *Lovers' Vows*. He directed a production of Tourneur's *The Revenger's Tragedy*, and appeared as an archbishop confined in a concentration camp in a play by Keyes called *The Prisoners*, with Keyes himself as the camp commandant and Drummond Allison as another prisoner. The *Oxford Mail* records that Allison 'was unfortunately given an unintentionally hard blow in one scene and stood gesticulating with the blood running down his face and scarlet hands'. Of Heath-Stubbs's play *The Hall*, which completed the evening, the critic noted that 'the characters spoke with a charm of language but at too great a length'. The intervals were enlivened by piano music played by an undergraduate named Bruce Montgomery, who was to become famous as a thriller writer under the pseudonym of Edmund Crispin.

But Keyes was clearly the outstanding poet at Oxford then. He was an unusual mixture. By nature he was a country poet, a brilliantly precise observer of landscape and of bird and animal life in the tradition of Wordsworth, John Clare, Hardy and Edward Thomas. In a letter nine weeks before he was killed, he wrote: 'I think I should have been born in the last century in Oxfordshire or Wiltshire, instead of near London between two wars, because then I might have been a good pastoral poet, instead of an uncomfortable metaphysical without roots.' In fact this duality made him a much more interesting poet than if he had just been a recorder of nature. His interest in symbolism was precise and profound, not woolly, and his masters in this field were Yeats and, less fashionably, the German poets Hölderlin and Rilke, for the latter of whom especially he had a tremendous admiration. Their influence added to Keyes's work a dimension which none of his contemporaries or successors seem to me to have equalled. 'Death and the Maiden' is perhaps a good example:

He said, 'Dance for me', and he said
'You are too beautiful for the wind
To pick at, or the sun to burn.' He said,
'I'm a poor tattered thing, but not unkind
To the sad dancer and the dancing dead.'

So I smiled, and a slow measure
Mastered my feet and I was happy then.
He said, 'My people are gentle as lilies
And in my house there are no men
To wring your young heart with a foolish pleasure.'

37

Because my boy had crossed me in a strange bed
I danced for him and was not afraid.
He said, 'You are too beautiful for any man
To finger; you shall stay a maid
For ever in my kingdom and be comforted.'

He said, 'You shall be my daughter, and your feet move
In finer dances, maiden; and the hollow
Halls of my house shall flourish with your singing.'
He beckoned, and I knew that I must follow
Into the kingdom of no love.

One poetic form into which he breathed new life was the dramatic monologue, when he would enter into and evoke figures from the past who had fascinated him, especially poets such as Yeats, Schiller and, as here, Wordsworth:

No room for mourning: he's gone out
Into the noisy glen, or stands between the stones
Of the gaunt ridge, or you'll hear his shout
Rolling among the screes, he being a boy again.
He'll never fail nor die
And if they laid his bones
In the wet vaults or iron sarcophagi
Of fame, he'd rise at the first summer rain
And stride across the hills to seek
His rest among the broken lands and clouds.
He was a stormy day, a granite peak
Spearing the sky; and look, about its base
Words flower like crocuses in the hanging woods,
Blank though the dalehead and the bony face.

Personally I owe Keyes a particular debt, since I quickly realized that next to him I was no poet at all, and gave it up. In the same way, my friendships with George Orwell and Graham Greene, which began a couple of years later, cooled my ambition to become a novelist. Had I been a real poet or a real novelist, I am sure I would have continued. In the end I think I found the right niche.

Those were heady days, as we young poets met for coffee at the Copper Kettle in the High near Magdalen, or the Playhouse bar or the Bear, where Blunden's presence saved us from proctors, under-graduates then being forbidden to enter pubs unless with a senior member of the University. The huge events of the war thundered outside. Despite the Battle of Britain, disaster followed disaster; only the bombing of Pearl Harbor and the consequent entry of the United States into the war offered a glimmer of hope. My own attitude was uncertain. To be a conscientious objector had for the past five years been an article of faith, but my friends were getting killed, and one could not but wonder whether this was not, in fact, a different war to that of 1914, a matter of good, or anyway comparative good, against undoubted evil. I faced my tribunal, a traumatic experience, where fearsome old men poured ridicule on my so passionately held beliefs, and I was rejected. My appeal, before a less alarming board, was allowed, but by now I had lost my faith and volunteered for the RAF. So I waited to appear before a third board that summer of 1941.

I played hockey, once even for the University, and captained the combined Christ Church and Brasenose eleven, which for that autumn and winter contained what must have been the most intellectually brilliant forward line ever to have taken the field. Dons as well as undergraduates were allowed to play for their colleges in wartime, and our attack, at full strength, from right to left, ran: Blake, Waldock, Masterman, Gordon-Walker, Mortimer. All had, as undergraduates, won their 'Occasionals', which meant they had not been far off a Blue; Waldock had got his Blue and Masterman had played frequently for England. Robert Blake was to become the eminent biographer of Disraeli and Provost of Queen's; Humphrey Waldock was to be President of the International Court of Justice; J. C. Masterman was already a distinguished historian; Patrick Gordon-Walker, the brother of Robin, was to be Minister of Education and, albeit briefly, Foreign Secretary, and Bob Mortimer Bishop of Exeter. This illustrious line-up was sheepishly captained by me in goal. My pep-talks at half-time were far from authoritative.

Editing *Cherwell* left me no time for acting. I can remember only three stage appearances at Oxford: in my first term as the incompetent detective Plum in A. P. Herbert's *Two Gentlemen of Soho*, and later in the tiny part of a Merchant in *Timon of Athens* (when the director, Nevill Coghill, singled me out for public rebuke after the opening for being intolerably slow), and as Dogberry in a production by Glynne Wickham of *Much Ado about Nothing*, a role to which the *Oxford Mail* said I 'brought humour'. I never had any trouble getting a laugh on stage. This production took place in the Holywell Quad of New College beneath a large tree which rustled in the wind and drowned most of what we said. John Mortimer played one of the villains I had to arrest. After the final performance, we had a party on the river with strawberries, and as we climbed back over the wall into Christ Church, John insisted on striking a match to make sure that the roof of the bicycle shed, on to which there was a simple drop, was in fact beneath us. This match was seen in the black-out by the porter, who arrested us, and we were both fined £2, a large sum then. We took *Much Ado* to Winchester College, and a very sticky audience they were; I didn't get many laughs that afternoon, but the visit was not wasted for me, as I was put up for the night by Harry Altham, the great cricket historian, and talked cricket with him into the small hours. He was, with Crusoe Robertson-Glasgow, whom I met and played with the following year, the best talker on cricket I ever heard. I never, to my sorrow, met Neville Cardus, or C. B. Fry, both of whom I believe became something of a bore in their old age, but must have been rewarding when younger.

I also saw a good deal of theatre. My knowledge of serious theatre when I went up to Oxford was still minimal. For some reason I never visited the Old Vic until 1940, shortly before it was bombed, when I saw Granville Barker's great production of *King Lear* with Gielgud as the King, Cathleen Nesbitt, Fay Compton and Jessica Tandy as his daughters, Stephen Haggard as the Fool, Jack Hawkins and Robert Harris as Edmund and Edgar, Nicholas Hannen as Gloucester, Lewis Casson as Kent and Harcourt Williams as Albany. What a cast that was! Otherwise, apart from Saint-Denis's *Three Sisters*, Gielgud's *School for Scandal* and *The Importance of Being Earnest*, and two visiting productions by the Dublin Abbey Theatre – *Juno and the Paycock* and Lennox Robinson's *The White-Headed Boy*, which I managed to catch at the Golders Green Hippodrome and the Embassy, Swiss Cottage – my main source of stimulation had been the Westminster Theatre, where Michael MacOwan was in charge. He directed several exciting seasons there of Eugene O'Neill plays, *Anna Christie*, *Mourning Becomes Electra* and *Desire Under the Elms*, the last two containing magnificent performances by Beatrix Lehmann, for me the finest actress of that decade. I also saw there the first production of Eliot's *The Family Reunion*. Eliot, Priestley, Coward and the young Terence Rattigan were the only British playwrights of consequence in the thirties; and of the new American wave, Clifford Odets, Maxwell Anderson, Elmer Rice, Lillian Hellman and Robert E. Sherwood, I saw only Odets's *Golden Boy* and Rice's *Judgement Day* (not that any of those five writers have lasted very well). The West End was devoted to farces, musical comedies and novelettish melodramas. The only continental play I recall seeing before the war was Mauriac's *Asmodée*. Peter Godfrey was doing his best at the little Gate Theatre, but his seasonal lists do not read very excitingly today, largely I suppose because there were few interesting plays being written anywhere in the world then.

Oxford had two theatres: the New, a huge, cinema-like building which took touring productions; and the smaller Playhouse, with a repertory company which, like most provincial repertory companies then, put on a new play each week. The Playhouse had a fine company at that time, headed by two brilliant young talents, Cyril Cusack and Pamela Brown. There was also a very pretty girl who played small parts and whose mother was reputed to collect her from her dressing-room each night to make sure that she was not led astray. We all assumed she would remain briefly in the profession until some rich man married her, for she never seemed likely to be given a leading role; but we were wrong, for her name was Deborah Kerr. One of the directors was a very nice and modest man whose sole method of direction seemed to be to take the pipe out of his mouth occasionally and say: 'Jolly good.' He was rumoured to scribble verse plays in his spare time, but none of these ever got put on, so later in the war we were surprised to see one of them advertised in London. We were wrong about him too, for he was Christopher Fry. Among other things I saw my first Ibsen at the Playhouse, Pamela Brown as Hedda Gabler in January 1941. Her performance was acclaimed, not least by James Agate, who compared her in the *Sunday Times* to the young Sarah Bernhardt: 'As that great player must have been in her experimental years, so is this young actress now . . . the grace, the effortlessness, the alternating speed and languor, the ability to remain silent and hold the stage . . . the absence of compromise with or against her author, the complete understanding of and immersion in his intentions, the absence of any false notes and the preclusion of any such possibility.' Of the forty or so Heddas that I have seen in various countries since, Pamela Brown's remains the best. I think it was this production that first awoke my interest in Ibsen (I had partaken in readings of *The Wild Duck* at Wellington and *Peer Gynt* at Christ Church in the terrible old Everyman translations, and neither had made much impact on me). Pamela Brown was a superb actress whose career, like that of Madge Titheradge, was dogged by ill-health; I remember her also as a marvellous Nina in *The Seagull*, my first Chekhov play, and Cusack as an incomparable Christy Mahon in Synge's *The Playboy of the Western World*. How they managed to give the performances they did after a week's rehearsal amazes me, though we all took it for granted at the time. I was pleased to read in Alec Guinness's memoirs that Cusack is one of the two living actors whom he most admires, the other being Pierre Fresnay.

During the early part of 1941, Sidney Keyes conceived the idea of compiling an anthology to be entitled *Eight Oxford Poets*. My name appears on the title page as co-editor, but the choice was entirely his; I think he probably included me, both as poet and as 'co-editor', purely out of courtesy to me as the then editor of *Cherwell* (and perhaps in gratitude for my having published his work). The other six poets were Heath-Stubbs, Allison, Keith Douglas, Gordon Swaine, Roy Porter and J. A. Shaw. Those omitted included Larkin, John Mortimer and Francis King; Larkin never forgave Sidney for this. If I pressed for any of them, I cannot have pressed very hard, or Sidney would have yielded. Ian Bancroft should have been in; but perhaps he, like Larkin, had not yet written anything really good, though they were both better than me. The anthology was turned down by both T. S. Eliot for Faber, and John Lehmann, but was accepted by Herbert Read for Routledge. Sidney and I went to meet him in London; he was to prove a valued friend to both of us.

That June of 1941 I waited to appear before my RAF recruiting board. It sat in Balliol, and was presided over by the Master of that college, A. D. Lindsay. I had had to fill in a form stating my qualifications, including School Certificate credits (the equivalent of modern O-levels). I had truthfully written that I had credits in maths and physics, having secured pretty well the minimum required marks in each subject – fifty per cent or less, I think (and of course the knowledge needed for an exam taken at fifteen or sixteen was fairly elementary). When I appeared before the board, I was astonished to be asked if, in view of my scientific qualifications, I would like to be enrolled on a course to study radar, something of which I had barely heard. I said it sounded interesting, but expressed doubt whether I knew enough. 'You have Higher Certificate credits in maths and physics,' said Dr Lindsay (Higher Certificate corresponded to modern A-levels; one took them, if one did, which I hadn't, at eighteen). 'School Certificate,' I corrected him, but Dr Lindsay barked: 'It says here Higher Certificate,' and I was told my name would be submitted to another tribunal.

In due course I came before this second tribunal, presided over by C. P. Snow, with Harry Hoff, later to become a well-known novelist under the name of William Cooper, as secretary. Exactly the same thing happened. I was informed that I had Higher Certificate credits in maths and physics, and was sharply corrected by Snow when I tried to put the matter straight. I was told that I would return to Oxford for another year to study radar; in the meantime, since it was a couple of years since I had taken Higher Certificate, I might take private tuition to brush up my memories of calculus and so forth, since a high standard was expected on the course I was to follow.

I did not even know what calculus was, so I hastily found a private tutor, a vast and splendid man who had played rugby for the New Zealand All Blacks, and together we did our best to squeeze two years of mathematical study into three months. I learned the rudiments of calculus and, more importantly, lost my virginity to his daughter, a pretty girl a year older than me, borrowing my brother Dick's flat in Bloomsbury for the purpose. That October of 1941 I returned to Oxford, to undergo the most humiliating year of my life.

I found delightful digs in Bath Place off Holywell Street, where two sisters, the Misses Walklett, owned a couple of seventeenth-century cottages, at £2 12s. 6d. a week, including breakfast. The radar course, presided over by a Wadham don named Keeley, comprised lectures and practicals. Everyone else on it had a degree in maths or physics, or at the least had won a scholarship in one or the other. At the end of the first week I went to Mr Keeley and told him I thought I had better not continue as I had not understood a word that had been uttered. He looked me up in his card index and said:

'That can't be true. You have Higher Certificate credits in both maths and physics.'

'No, School Certificate.'

'School Certificate? It says here Higher Certificate.'

I explained.

'Good heavens, this must all be miles beyond you.'

I assured him that it was. He then astonished me by saying:

'You mustn't leave us.'

'Why not?'

'We're having great difficulty in getting people screened for this course because they want everyone for the forces. If they find someone's slipped through the net, it'll cause the most frightful trouble. I'll arrange for you to have tuition. Stay and pick up what you can. At the end of the year there's an exam which no one fails.

You won't get very good marks and probably won't be given an important job.'

I expressed the fervent hope that I would not; the prospect of being placed in charge of the radar defences of Liverpool or Coventry did not attract me. So I was sent to a pleasant Christ Church don named Collie for tuition. However, I could not understand him any more than the lectures and practicals. Eight hours a day, for three terms, I sat or, in the laboratories, stood, while a flood of unintelligible information swept over me. In the world outside, disasters continued to plague the Allied cause. The *Prince of Wales* and the *Repulse* were sunk; Singapore fell. The Eighth Army was driven back into Egypt. Unlike most English cities of its size, Oxford was never bombed; rumour had it that the black-out there was so bad that the German aircraft preferred to use it as a navigational guide.

Comfort arrived in October in the shape of advance copies of *Eight Oxford Poets*, a nicely printed paperback of eighty-four pages in a red cover, priced at half a crown. It was published on 2 November. One S. Gorley Putt dismissed it in a single sentence in *Time and Tide* ('I cannot pretend that by next week I shall be able to recall a poem or distinguish between the authors'), but Edwin Muir in the *New Statesman* found that 'all the contributors show a distinct literary aptitude', and declared Keyes to be 'obviously a poet of original talent. All his poetry has shape, significance, and a fine precision of imagery.' Sidney had written a short foreword, attempting to trace

certain elements common to the work of us all. We seem
to share a horror at the world's predicament, together with
the feeling that we cannot save ourselves without some kind
of spiritual readjustment . . . We are all, with the possible
exception of Shaw, Romantic writers, though by that I mean
little more than that our greatest fault is a tendency to floridity; and that we have, on the whole, little sympathy with
the Audenian school of poets.

An anonymous reviewer in the *Times Literary Supplement* felt that this 'claim to be "Romantic" writers is hard to reconcile with so much watchfulness of feeling, not to say such "debunking" of traditional romance as is found in a poem like [Allison's] *The Remnant*. But each poet expresses the different balance in his own way, Mr Meyer [!], Mr Shaw and Mr Keyes coming nearest perhaps to the simplicity which combines the opposites in due proportions' (the only instance of my poetry having been praised in print by anyone anywhere). No other leading newspaper or journal noticed the book and not surprisingly it enjoyed only a modest sale. I hear that a second-hand copy in good condition now fetches £2,500; I wonder what mine, signed by all the contributors except Douglas, is worth?

Sidney Keyes left Oxford in March 1942 and joined the Army the following month. To my surprise, he found military life quite tolerable. 'I keep thinking of you in the fleshpots of Bath Place and grinding my teeth with envy!', he wrote to me from Omagh in Northern Ireland on 26 April. 'But Omagh isn't at all bad. The work is extremely hard – up to Commando standard, I'm told, and can believe it! – but we get a good deal of time off and people are, on the whole, a decent lot. . . . I've written two short poems since I came here and am preparing a longish one.' In May he moved to Dunbar, 'a bleak stony town with few enough attractions', and on 10 June sent me my share of the advance on *Eight Oxford Poets*: £1 9s. 5d. On 4 July he posted me a copy of his first collection of poems, *The Iron Laurel*, a forty-eight-page paperback containing twenty-two poems and priced at half a crown. 'Here . . . is the *Laurel*', he wrote, 'with best wishes to its author's first great patron. May it be said that as Burke was to Crabbe, so Meyer is to Keyes! I can't find an appropriately insulting inscription just now, but will perhaps do so before we meet.' He had hopes that he might be transferred to the Intelligence Corps, which would have meant returning to Oxford that winter. 'If so, our positions will be exactly reversed!'

Sidney had a sharp sense of humour, which especially manifested itself in his account of the inanities of Army life, such as 'the Trolley Torpedo':

> I don't know who invented it, but it must surely be the silliest weapon in the world. It consists of an anti-tank mine attached to a small wooden trolley; behind the trolley is a drainpipe containing a curtain-rod, which is forced forward by a charge of HE (High Explosive) tied on the back. Rather like this. [Sketch] You light the fuse, the charge explodes, drives the rod forward, which pushes the trolley away at a speed of about 30 mph. What happens then is very obscure – presumably it will run into a tank or something if you aim right and the ground is completely flat. This senile contraption is made entirely from old boxes, pipes, electric fittings etc., and is probably the British Secret Weapon. So please

don't communicate this information! It was shown to me in
all seriousness. Perhaps it would do to fire against Keble on a
dark night.

He also wrote much about his unreciprocated love for Milein
Cosmann, a brilliant young German painter who was studying at
the Slade School of Art, now temporarily evacuated to Oxford.
'She is worth any trouble or pain whatever; but perhaps I am not
strong enough to achieve it, though I thought I was . . . At the
moment, I'm almost without feelings on this subject; the passionate
need that I felt for three months has suddenly stopped, as if a string
had snapped on an instrument, or a muscle that gave me pain had
parted . . . There is a kind of love so destructive that it cannot be
borne.'

In July he came to stay with me at Bath Place, inscribing my copy
of *The Iron Laurel* with a sentence he had found in a letter written
by William Blake to B. R. Haydon: '. . . our excellent and manly
friend Mr Meyer'. That visit to Oxford proved fateful, for during
it he started an affair with a fellow-student of Milein at the Slade,
Renée-Jane Scott. One night he did not return to Bath Place, and
next day I found a postcard awaiting me: 'I am spending tonight
also with Renée.' On 31 July he wrote to me from Dunbar: 'The
days at Bath Place were some of the most pleasant and eventful I've
ever spent . . . Renée is absolutely wonderful in every way and we
are genuinely and deeply in love with each other . . . You will note
that now I've done what you have been urging me to do for months;
the only conclusion is that you know better than I do about myself
as well as about sex in general!' (I was in fact very unsophisticated
in sexual matters, and in a state of considerable confusion myself.
What was it that I had been urging him to do for months? Find
another girl?)

One morning during that summer of 1942 there was a knock on
my door in Bath Place and a small boy – I cannot describe him
otherwise – peered timidly round the door. He looked only about
fourteen, though he turned out to be just seventeen. He explained
that he was hoping to stage *A Midsummer Night's Dream*. Would I
consider playing Bottom? I was by now the senior member of OUDS
in residence, excluding dons. Was this for OUDS, I asked? No. For
the College? No, he was just hoping to get a group together. Even
by Oxford standards, this sounded wildly unpromising, especially
considering his barely adolescent appearance. I declined but, feeling

sorry for him, offered him a glass of sherry, which he gratefully accepted and sipped sitting on the edge of a chair. Once he had got over his nervousness, he turned out to be highly intelligent. His name was Peter Brook. Others whom he approached evidently shared my first doubts, for he never directed a single stage production while he was at Oxford, only a film of Sterne's *Sentimental Journey* which he managed to get set up and which was shown at the Union after I went down; I remember Basil Taylor reporting to me: 'It is frightful beyond measure and in every possible way.' Apart from everything else, I believe the celluloid itself was of poor quality, so that everything looked scratchy.

So I turned down the lead in a Peter Brook production. Two years later in 1944 I was queueing at the New Theatre in London for seats for the great Olivier-Richardson season when I heard myself hailed from the back of the queue and saw Peter standing there (I must be one of the few people to have seen him sitting nervously on the edge of a chair and standing at the back of a theatre queue). When we had got our tickets, I invited him for a cup of tea at the Arts Theatre Club across the way. I asked what he was doing, and he said: 'Directing plays at the Birmingham Rep.' I suspected that he was probably stage-managing, but politely asked which plays; he named among others Ibsen's *The Lady from the Sea*. 'We've got one marvellous young actor,' he told me. 'He's going to be the new Olivier.' 'What's his name?' 'You won't have heard of him. A chap called Paul Scofield.' I thought no more of this until the following year when I read with astonishment that Sir Barry Jackson, the founder and still head of the Birmingham Rep, had agreed to run the Shakespeare Memorial Theatre at Stratford-upon-Avon and was taking with him his brilliant young nineteen-year-old director Peter Brook, whose productions at Birmingham had won such local acclaim. That summer of 1945 he did a marvellous *Love's Labour's Lost* at Stratford with Scofield, then twenty-three, as Don Armado, and both their careers were launched.

At the other end of the age scale, I became acquainted with the oldest don in Oxford, W. N. Stocker of Brasenose. Through cricket, I had become friendly with the Principal of Brasenose, W. T. S. Stallybrass, and occasionally dined with him at High Table. Stocker was by now well into his nineties; he had been elected a fellow the year young Oscar Wilde had come up to Magdalen as a freshman, and for twenty years had been a fellow don of Walter Pater. He smoked a cigar more thoroughly than anyone I have seen, sticking a pin into the butt and continuing until the glowing end actually entered his luxuriant white moustache, which for some reason it never ignited. He had a good memory and said everything twice. Once I asked him what kind of person Pater was. 'Rum chap, rum chap. Didn't say much, didn't say much. Never stayed long after dinner. Never stayed long after dinner.' At first I was disappointed, but afterwards I thought he had given a vivid picture of Pater. Stocker remembered watching them building Holborn Viaduct, and told me that when sitting his scholarship to Oxford he had finished his last paper early and walked up to Keble to watch them finishing work on the chapel. His uncle had vivaed Gladstone for a scholarship to Christ Church. He was still a great walker, and carried a pedometer so that he could record how many miles he had covered each year. He hated anyone walking behind him and would startle undergraduates, who politely slowed down so as not to rush past him, by whipping round and barking: 'Stop following me, damn you!' He had been elected a fellow in the days when all such elections were for life, but even in wartime, he no longer tutored, which was just as well, since his subject was engineering.

Stallybrass told me that until Stocker was over ninety he remained only the second senior don in the University, due to the continued existence of one Canon Payne Smith at Christ Church, whom nobody had seen for years but who was known to be still alive. One morning the *Oxford Mail* printed a brief notice, for the news was of no interest to anyone else, that the Canon had died. At High Table that evening there was a pre-arranged silence, and Stallybrass said: 'Stocker, I see in the paper that Payne Smith is dead.' Stocker nodded and took a few more mouthfuls of soup; then the news penetrated, he put down his spoon and a slow smile came over his face. Noticing the silence, and feeling that some comment was expected from him, he muttered: 'I never bore him any malice, you know.' One morning his 'scout' found him lying in evening dress on the floor of his bedroom; he had fallen and was unable to get to his feet. Amazingly, he was unhurt, but was spluttering with rage. He might well have achieved his century had he not been knocked down and killed by a motor cycle in the High.

As the end of the summer term approached at Oxford, so did my dreaded radar exam. I had been assured by Mr Keeley that nobody ever failed it, but when the paper was put before me I literally did not know what any of the questions meant, let alone the answers. Everyone else was scribbling away like mad. I had arranged with a man called Timpson to look at his answers, as we reckoned that invigilation would probably be slack, and indeed the invigilator seemed immersed in a book. So I edged close to Timpson and began copying his, to me, incomprehensible equations. But by bad luck, almost at once the invigilator looked up and with a friendly smile said: 'Nothing implied, but would you mind sitting just a little further apart?' My fate was sealed; I sat wretchedly for the remainder of the three hours, then miserably handed in my half-sheet of paper.

A few days later, Mr Keeley summoned me to his office. 'You're the lad who shouldn't have been here, aren't you?' he said. 'We don't usually fail anyone on this exam, but you got nought.' 'Yes,' I said. 'I never understood anything.' Mr Keeley was astonishingly sympathetic. 'We'll try to fix you up with something,' he said. I could not imagine what this might be, for what, in any way connected with radar, could I possibly understand? I suppose he was still fearful that the screening error might come to light.

I waited gloomily at home. 'If lucky, you may be forgotten for months,' Sidney wrote from Dunbar. '. . . My advice is to do *nothing* until things look very menacing indeed . . . don't give any information to anyone; and above all, DON'T SIGN ANYTHING, however cunningly disguised, in the nature of an Army Form. As an old soldier with 5 (nearly 6) months' service, I would say that it is very important to keep out of the Army if you possibly can. It is a collossal [*sic*] waste of time . . . Our Platoon Commander and I have reached a pass where he habitually refers to me as "that fu . . . g halfwit Keyes" and I to him as "that pissing swine Harding". Yesterday he threatened me with Court Martial.' Sidney suggested that I go up to Dunbar to visit him, 'for as long as you like', but I never did, just as a few years later I never managed to accept George Orwell's repeated invitations to stay with him on Jura, two missed opportunities that I have never ceased to regret.

That September I met my first Great Writer, apart from Blunden and the occasional visiting speaker at Oxford (Walter de la Mare, sweet and gentle; James Agate, who was neither). One day I went to my father's office and found him in conversation with a large man in plus-fours whom he introduced as his insurance agent, Mr Clench.

'Ah,' said Mr Clench. 'I hear you're a writer. You've probably heard of Bernard Shaw.'

I confessed that I had.

'I handle his insurance,' said Mr Clench. 'I can visit him any time. Would you like to meet him?'

'Of course.'

'When would suit you?'

'When would suit *me*? Any time would suit me – when would suit him?'

'Shall we say Tuesday?'

After he had left, I said to my father: 'He must be out of his mind', but father confirmed that Shaw was so interested in any form of making or saving money that Mr Clench had only to phone him and say he had a new insurance scheme and Shaw would put anyone off to see him.

So on Tuesday I found myself standing outside the door of Shaw's house at Ayot St Lawrence with Mr Clench and his wife, who had both turned out to be very nice. We were greeted by Mrs Shaw, then eighty-five, a year younger than her husband, a sweet little apple-cheeked lady with a shining brass ear-trumpet. 'G.B.S. is resting,' she explained. 'He's been chopping wood all morning.' We waited with her and Shaw's secretary, Blanche Patch, in that curiously unattractive house which, as several observers have remarked, seemed mainly to be furnished with busts and portraits of himself. After some while Mrs Shaw said: 'I wonder why he's taking so long,' and on cue, as though in a bad play, and just the kind of thing he would never have allowed in one of his own, he entered. The first things that struck me were his tallness, the straightness of his back and the warmth of his smile. He was dressed in a Norfolk jacket with a pair of pince-nez spectacles clipped to the lapel, and shoes with large tongues hanging over almost to the toe like thirsty dogs. Miss Patch brought tea, and instead of us all gathering round a table Mrs Shaw thoughtfully seated him and me in a corner, so that for about twenty minutes I had him to myself. Instead of tea he drank milk, for some reason out of a cardboard container from which she had removed the lid.

I had expected to find him hard and brilliant, and prepared myself to listen to an entertaining monologue, but he was extraordinarily kind, and kept asking me questions so as to make it a conversation ('What do young people today feel about . . .?'). Perhaps this was a habit of his generation, for later I was to find it in Max Beerbohm, and Beerbohm told me that it was a characteristic of Oscar Wilde. He spoke of H. G. Wells, and how he, Shaw, would suddenly receive abusive letters from him for no reason that he could imagine, followed by a charming one as though the previous letter and the reason or supposed reason for it had never existed.

'Once he accused me of being a homosexual' (I shall never forget Shaw's precise enunciation of the word, the first syllable of which he pronounced to rhyme with 'dome'). He then told an anecdote about the premiere of *Heartbreak House* at Birmingham, when the recorded sound of bombs during the last scene failed to materialize until Barry Jackson began his curtain speech, when they started to explode one after the other. Once Mrs Shaw called severely: 'G.B.S., you're not drinking your milk', and he took an apologetic draught. Then she deposited a large piece of plum cake on his plate, at which he looked in some alarm.

We got on to the subject of revolutions and, remembering something Arthur Koestler had written in *Darkness at Noon*, which I had just read and which I suspected Shaw had probably not, I thought I might make an impression by quoting it as my own. 'Don't you feel, sir,' I said, 'that every revolution always ends in a tyranny that is often worse than the tyranny which caused the revolution?' He looked at me with a little twinkle, and said: 'That's a penetrating observation, my boy. It's odd you should make it, for I remember Tolstoy writing to me and putting a very similar point of view, forty or fifty years ago.' It was a charming put-down, the gently implied rebuke being softened by the information that I had said something which Tolstoy had said to the same person. I had brought a book of his in my pocket for him to sign, but when the time came to leave I was so fearful he might refuse that I lacked the courage to ask him. When, on the way home, I mentioned this to Mr Clench, he said that of course Shaw would have signed it. So there was another opportunity missed.

That autumn I was summoned to the office of a tremendously high-powered scientist in the Air Ministry. He was a knight, but I forget his name; a genial old gentleman.

'Oh dear,' he said, perusing the letter before him. 'You didn't do very well, did you?'

'I'm afraid not, sir.'

'What can we do with you? It'd be a pity to waste someone with all your training. So many people don't show their best in exams. I suppose you don't know anything else that might be of value to the war effort apart from maths and physics?'

As he was so friendly, I ventured a little joke. 'All I did at Oxford was write poetry and edit a literary magazine.'

He became inexplicably excited. 'You're the man we're looking for.'

'Gosh. How?'

'Sir Arthur Harris, the head of Bomber Command, complains he can't understand the reports his scientific section gives him, and wants us to send him someone with a degree in English or history, which you have, and an advanced knowledge of maths and physics, to translate them into layman's language.'

'But, sir, I haven't a knowledge of maths and physics.'

'Nonsense,' he said, pointing to the letter. 'You have Higher Certificate credits in both.' So, in October 1942, I was posted to Bomber Command Headquarters outside High Wycombe in Buckinghamshire as technical assistant in the Operational Research Section at a salary of £250 a year.

5 With Nanny

6 Aged 3

7 Family Group

8 *Above* Aged 5 with Nanny At Frinton

9 *Right* 1937, before my nose was broken at cricket

10 *Below* Robin Gordon-Walker with the History Sixth at Wellington, 1939

4

Some Writers of the Forties

The three years I spent at Bomber Command were only marginally less humiliating than my radar course at Oxford, though there was, thank heavens, no examination. Everyone else in the section, apart from a few clerks and an administrative officer, was a scientist even more formidable than my companions at Oxford. I was given the job of preparing the night-raid reports. Every morning I had to collect data about the raids from the scientists who had analysed the various aspects. Apart from the weather, these analyses were no more intelligible to me than they had been to Sir Arthur Harris. I asked their authors to explain them to me in layman's language, but none of them could. I decided that the only thing to do was to play around with the wording, dress it up with a few layman's phrases and hope for the best. The result seemed to please everyone. The scientists read them through and said: 'Excellent', and I never had any complaint from Sir Arthur. Occasionally some horrendous error would be spotted weeks or months later by one of the scientists when consulting them, such as my putting a nought too few or too many, but the retribution that I daily feared never materialized.

Occasionally I felt that I ought to be engaged on something more useful, but I could not really imagine what, and at least I was not actively damaging the war effort as others of my acquaintance seemed to be doing by their incompetence. When, years later, Harris published his memoirs, *Bomber Offensive*, he included a special chapter paying tribute to the invaluable work of the Operational Research Section. So that was how I won the war. When I read subsequent analyses of the role played by Bomber Command, I sometimes wonder about the statistics they quote, culled from my night-raid reports.

At first I was billeted in a pub called the Plough in a tiny village called Speen near High Wycombe, run by Ishbel Macdonald, the daughter of Ramsay Macdonald. Since he was already a widower when he became Prime Minister, she had been First Lady at Downing Street. After his death, she had caused a sensation by marrying a barely literate farm-labourer, Norman Ridgley. He was an ugly man with a huge wart by his nose, who now did nothing but drink; he told me that he usually managed twenty pints a day. One of my fellow guests was the Army liaison officer at Bomber Command, Charles Carrington, who had survived the Somme and had written one of the best books about it, *A Subaltern's War*, under the pseudonym of Charles Edmonds. A peppery but fascinating man, he was later to become director of Chatham House and to write an excellent biography of Kipling; he is still alive as I write, in his nineties. We became good friends. But the Plough, though ancient and picturesque, was squalid even by wartime standards. When I told Ishbel that my room was full of large black beetles, she expressed no surprise but simply put down a poisonous powder, which proved cruelly slow in its effect, for when I woke next morning the floor was covered with scores of them on their backs and kicking their legs. When a few nights later I found several in my bed, I decided it was time to move, and found a much pleasanter billet in the vicarage at nearby Hughenden, in the grounds of Disraeli's old home. A bus to the camp passed the gate at 8.30 am, but I soon found I had no need to catch this. At 8.40 I could thumb a lift from junior officers in their cars, at 8.50 from squadron-leaders and wing-commanders in more comfortable cars, and one morning, well after 9, having overslept, I even managed a lift from Sir Arthur himself in his Rolls. As I should by now have been at my desk for some twenty minutes, I feared the worst, especially as he was notoriously choleric; but he was geniality itself, though the most alarming driver I have ever travelled with, shooting along the winding country lanes as though they were one-way autobahns. I remember that he issued a complaint around that time that officers and men were not saluting his car; all we had time to do was fling ourselves into the ditch as it approached, invisible anyway behind a cloud of dust.

I had little in common with my fellow-workers (I almost wrote 'fellow-scientists') in the Operational Research Section, admirable though I am sure they were. Fortunately, the public relations department of the HQ comprised three men of letters: John Lawrence of *The Times*, Hugh Massingham and Arthur Clutton-Brock. They were attended by a macabre lance-corporal clerk, Brian Howard, the part-original of Anthony Blanche, the aesthete in Evelyn Waugh's *Brideshead Revisited*. He had been at Eton with Orwell and Robert Longden, and was the most unpleasant person I have ever met, by a short head from Tom Harrisson, the founder of Mass-Observation, an ex-Member of Parliament and media man, who is still alive. I have never met such concentrated venom in a human being. He seemed to have a compulsion to enrage people. John Lawrence told me how, as the Dunkirk evacuation was nearing its end, Brian entered a pub in Dover where exhausted survivors were sitting and said loudly in his campest voice: 'Well! That wasn't very clever of you all, was it?' He became a sad, hated figure, and finally took his own life. I once asked Harold Acton, the other part-original of Blanche, if Brian had ever been likable, and Harold said that when young he had had a certain attractiveness which made his extravagances tolerable.

I spent my weekly day off in London, going to a theatre or cinema in the evening and then drinking in a pub next to Selfridge's until closing-time before walking back through the black-out to my father's flat. One evening I hesitated between a film in Leicester Square and another at the Paramount in Tottenham Court Road, chose the latter and consequently ended up at another pub in Soho. My choice of film saved my life, for a few minutes before closing time a bomb scored a direct hit on the pub by Selfridge's and killed everyone in it. One accepted the air-raids as a part of life; at first one assumed one would be killed, then, gradually and equally illogically, one assumed that one would not.

Sidney wrote regularly, from various camps in Scotland, about his problems with Renée and the tedium of Army life. 'I am in process of direct transfer to the Intelligence Corps,' he informed me happily on 7 February 1943, but through some bureaucratic inefficiency, which was to cost him his life, the transfer was delayed. We managed to meet several times in London, and once I went to stay with him and his stepmother in Ripley in Yorkshire. We shared a bedroom, and talked late into the night. He told me more about himself than ever before. Next morning I could remember little of what he had said, something for which I have never forgiven myself, for it was the last time we met. His next letter to me, on 26 March 1943, came from Algiers: 'I have now gone into semi-permanent and not very honourable exile among the Berbers; but have left behind a sort of posthumous child in the form of a new collection of verse called *The Cruel Solstice* (Routledge 6/- in autumn). John [Heath-Stubbs] will show you the MS – though you've read them all before . . . I consider myself 8 Oxford Poets' front line!' A month later he was killed, still a few weeks short of his twenty-first birthday. His runner in that battle, James Lucas, tells that Sidney and one of his men were last seen 'standing shoulder to shoulder firing Tommy guns at the oncoming German paratroopers', to cover the retreat of his patrol into the company square; all of them except these two were taken prisoner and survived the war.

That summer Herbert Read sent me an advance copy of *The Cruel Solstice*. I remember coming back from work and settling down to glance through it, my legs over the side of one of the vicarage armchairs (why do I remember that?), and my astonishment at the quality and maturity of the poems it contained. Contrary to what Sidney had said, many of them were new to me. *The Iron Laurel* had been impressive enough, but everything in that had been written before March 1942, when he was still nineteen.

The Cruel Solstice was acclaimed even more than *The Iron Laurel*, and Herbert Read asked me to edit and introduce Sidney's collected poems. I still do not know why he asked me rather than John Heath-Stubbs, who had been in much closer touch with Sidney and knew more about his creative process; and John's eyesight was still good enough for that kind of work. But John was agreeable to my doing it, and gave generously of his help. I did most of it in my office at Bomber Command, to the annoyance of the senior scientist, a Cambridge geologist, who shared it with me; he even reported me, fortunately to no effect. Routledge paid me £25, which was rather small even for those days. But the *Collected Poems* had a big success when they appeared in July 1945, going into a third printing within eight months, and gave me an entry into the literary world which my own writing would not have earned.

Sidney's was one of a disproportionate number of deaths among my friends during those last two years of war. Rowland Hill had been killed in a flying accident in 1941; then eighteen months passed without any more casualties in my closest circle, and hardly a month went by without one or more of them coming to stay with me in London on my day off, which I was able to take any time in the week to fit in with them. Even those in the RAF seemed miraculously blessed. Then, beginning with Sidney, they all went: Charles Ruck-Keene and Andrew Tod in accidents, Drummond Allison killed in Italy, Keith Foottit and John Williams on bombing missions, Keith Douglas in Normandy soon after D-Day, Alan Sykes needlessly in yet another accident the same month, and Claud Raymond in Burma in March

1945. Suddenly, none of my best friends were left except Michael Flanders in his wheelchair.

I gained some measure of compensation by acquiring several friends of an older generation. Herbert Read lived at Seer Green, a village only a couple of stations down the line from High Wycombe, and I visited him and his wife frequently for supper. Graham Greene has described him as the gentlest of men, and he was. His voice was very soft and retained some Yorkshire vowels; he was tall, slim and always neatly dressed, often with a bow-tie, which was less usual then than now. He was a wonderful publisher for a young man to have, creatively helpful and never obtrusive, with a modesty which I was to find in all the First World War poets I met – Blunden, Graves and Sassoon, men who had continuously looked death in the eyes. Like them, he had won the Military Cross, and also in his case the Distinguished Service Order (and, like them, he had beautiful handwriting). His short memoir *In Retreat* is as fine an evocation of the Western Front as anything by his fellows. Occasionally I would help to bathe his three small children, Sophie, Benedict and Piers Paul.

Herbert was an old and close friend of Eliot, but I never met Eliot at their house, though I was to do so later elsewhere. Leonie Cohn, a young German refugee who lived with the Reads, told me how she had begged Herbert to invite Eliot down. At last he came, but it proved an unrewarding evening. Eliot and Herbert were both air-raid wardens, and soon after Eliot's arrival an argument developed between them concerning the way to use a stirrup-pump, a device used for extinguishing incendiary bombs. Things became quite heated, appropriately, considering the topic, and they went out into the garden with Herbert's pump to demonstrate their different theories. Neither could convince the other, and they kept returning to the subject throughout the evening, despite the attempts of Herbert's wife, Ludo, and Leonie to divert the conversation to art and literature. Leonie and Ludo both told me that it was one of the most disappointing evenings they had ever spent. Another, for Ludo though for nobody else, had been when the painter Mark Gertler had come to dinner. Herbert told me that Gertler was the most fascinating talker he had known; he had also told Ludo, who begged him to let her meet him, and eventually he, like Eliot, came to dinner. Ludo was a fine cook and put herself out over the stove that afternoon, with the unfortunate result that immediately after dinner she fell asleep and awoke only as Gertler was leaving. She never met him again, and Herbert made things worse by telling her that Gertler had talked more brilliantly that evening than he had ever heard him.

I once asked Herbert about Virginia Woolf. 'Remarkable,' he said, 'but the cattiest woman I have ever known.' He died in agony, from cancer of the tongue, but with astonishing calm and courage; as Greene has written of him, 'he looked at death with the same clear, shrewd, gentle eyes he turned on a friend'.

Vernon Watkins was a similarly gentle spirit, a splendid Welsh poet who worked, seemingly content, as a bank clerk for all his adult life except the war until not long before his death, when his reputation won him visiting professorships in America. Sidney Keyes much admired Watkins's collection *The Ballad of the Mari Lwyd* when it appeared in 1941, and as a result of my writing to Watkins and telling him this we became good friends. He was a literary perfectionist such as I have never known, working on even short poems for years. When in 1951 I was arranging an exhibition of twentieth-century poetry and asked him for some corrected drafts, he replied:

> I'm sorry I haven't a manuscript copy of 'The Mummy'.
> There must have been about sixty, but they were all burnt
> . . . I have the whole manuscript (the 30th, I should think),
> of 'The Broken Sea', but that's too long . . . If you wanted
> successive versions I could send you a bundle (by parcel post)
> for any one of about ten poems of the last five years . . .
> I have some of 'After Sunset', but only two or three out
> of over fifty, I should think. The poem took 4 years to
> get right.

As a result, his output was comparatively small; but it was powerful and distinguished, and his reputation has remained steady since his death in 1967. 'Intimate and sensitive links with individuals, silently expressed, are all one hopes for,' he once wrote to me. 'For reputation I care nothing.'

In 1943, through an Oxford friend who was courting his daughter, a dancer (without success, but nobody did better; a few years later she became a nun), I met Hugh Kingsmill. He was a vain and peppery man who felt he had never received his true recognition as a writer but, as long as you shared or pretended to share his own opinion of himself, kindly and generous and a fascinating talker. The truth was that his writing was much less good than his conversation. He was one of the best raconteurs I have known, and he seemed to have known everyone in the literary world over the previous thirty years. He had been a friend of Conan Doyle and Arnold Bennett. Doyle, he said, had gradually taken on the persona of Sherlock Holmes himself. Kingsmill's real name was Lunn, and once when they were sitting together Doyle said to him: 'You are the brother of Arnold Lunn, are you not?' Kingsmill nodded. After a long pause, Doyle said: 'And Arnold Lunn is the son of Sir Henry Lunn – am I right?' Kingsmill confirmed that this was so. Doyle pulled at his calabash pipe for several minutes; smoke filled the room. At length, he removed the pipe from his mouth, pointed it at Kingsmill, and said: 'Then you, too, are the son of Sir Henry Lunn.'

Kingsmill said Bennett could be very difficult. One evening they were fellow-guests at somebody's house, and the main course was followed by a savoury. Bennett, with his stutter, asked: 'Wh-where's the pudding?' The hostess said: 'I thought we'd have a savoury instead.' Bennett replied: 'I like a pudding', left the table, and took a taxi to the Savoy Grill, where he ordered and ate one. Of Bennett's appearance, Kingsmill said that he suffered from a rush of teeth to the head.

It was Kingsmill who, early in 1944, introduced me to Graham Greene. I had discovered Greene during my first year at Oxford, through buying a Penguin copy of *It's a Battlefield*, and when I expressed admiration for his work, Kingsmill said: 'Young Greene? You like his novels? Care to meet him?', and invited us both to dinner. Greene was then just coming up to forty, but looked, as he always has since I have known him, at least ten years younger. I was surprised by his youthful appearance and unpretentiousness, and shocked by his irreverence for various sacred cows. *King Lear* was mentioned, I think with reference to Donald Wolfit's rightly acclaimed performance, and Greene expressed doubts as to whether it was really such a good play. (Two years earlier, in *British Dramatists*, he had accused Shakespeare of not being able to portray madness convincingly: 'The mad Lear is no more mad than Hamlet, only distraught, and Ophelia and her flowers is a pretty conceit that might have come from one of Greene's novels' – Robert Greene's, not his own.) I don't think I had ever heard anyone question the validity of any Shakespeare play before. Our acquaintance would probably have ended that evening, but by good fortune he and I left together and had a lengthy wait on High Street Kensington station for the next train; they were infrequent in wartime. Kingsmill, as was his boisterous wont, had done most of the talking in his flat. But on the gloomy Underground platform I found Greene, in his shy way, warm and easy, and when he got out at his stop he said: 'Let's meet again. Give me a ring.' So in due course I invited him to lunch with Orwell, and thereafter we met fairly frequently, though it was not until the mid-fifties that our relationship became close.

My editing of Sidney Keyes's poems brought me into touch with various writers who admired him. Vita Sackville-West invited me down for a day at Sissinghurst Castle. The recent publicity given to her love-affairs with Virginia Woolf and Violet Trefusis has created the impression of a formidable predator, but I found her warm and direct, and greatly liked her. Her swarthy complexion betrayed her gipsy ancestry, for one of her grandmothers had been a celebrated Spanish dancer, Pepita d'Oliva; decades later, when writing a life of Ibsen, I discovered that Pepita's success at a theatre in Christiania (now Oslo) in 1861 had helped to bankrupt the rival theatre which the young Ibsen was managing.

I committed an unfortunate gaffe at lunch. It ended with apple pie and cream – a luxury which I had not seen since the beginning of the war – served in a curious antique silver jug, thin and twisted. I helped myself to what I calculated to be about one-third of the cream; Vita gave me the slightest of glances, and took only a drop. I supposed she might be on some kind of diet. She offered me a second helping of the pie but not of the cream. Not knowing when I might see that commodity again, I reached for the jug, to find that it was empty. It had a false bottom. I was so embarrassed by this that I never dared to contact her again.

Another admirer of Sidney was Rosamond Lehmann. I visited her often in the Berkshire village of Aldworth, where she lived with Cecil Day Lewis. She was then forty-two, tall, with premature grey, almost white hair, which somehow enhanced her beauty. Although we later became distant, I still think of her as one of the most magical people I have known; she radiated an extraordinary repose, the more extraordinary since I slowly came to understand how tormented, possessive and even predatory she was. She had then just published *The Ballad and the Source*, one of her finest novels. 'It took me nearly two years,' she wrote to me, 'and it was mostly like a struggle in the dark, underground, with a Laocoon. At the end I wondered if I had produced a monster.' The protagonist, Sybil Jardine, is a dominating and destructive woman, very unlike the romantically attractive characters of her early books such as *Dusty Answer, Invitation to the Waltz* and *The Weather in the Streets*, and when I met her I wondered how she could have conceived such a character. It was some time before I realized that it was a self-portrait.

Day Lewis and she seemed completely happy, like young lovers. He was married, but neither seemed in any doubt that in due course he and Rosamond would legalize their relationship. He took me to dinner at the Savile Club, the first time I entered that place which was to prove so important in my life (among other things, it was through a conversation here that I became an Ibsen translator), and I remember him telling me how he longed to marry Rosamond but how essential he felt it was that he and his wife should not divorce until their sons had finished school. He was a great charmer, though vain and rather touchy. He had a beautiful tenor voice, and loved to sing ballads such as 'The Earl of Moray', with Rosamond accompanying slightly stiffly on the piano.

I used to look forward to those visits to Aldworth, but they aroused mixed emotions in me. I was very insecure and easily embarrassed, as witness the incident with the cream jug, but that was nothing to the social solecisms that I was made to feel I had committed with Rosamond. A glance from her would make me realize that I should not have taken that extra potato, or said what I had said. It was not until years later that I learned that Rosamond made all her guests feel similarly uncomfortable. She and Cecil shared a curious bitchiness which occasionally manifested itself. One evening they took me to visit two old ladies who lived in the village, sisters of the poet Laurence Binyon, who wrote the famous epitaph on the dead of the First World War which begins 'They shall grow not old as we that are left grow old.' (I had once, when at Wellington, been taken to hear him give a talk at Reading; an impressive, Blake-like figure with loose hair and wild eyes.) I found them enchantingly naive, sitting among a quantity of small polished brass objects in a tiny room, thrilled at the presence of the (as they seemed to them) young poet and novelist, and asking childlike questions. On the walk back along the darkened lanes, Rosamond and Cecil poured scorn on them, mockingly quoting things they had said. Later I realized that this was an echo of Bloomsbury, of which Rosamond had been a fringe member. In time I was dropped. I could not understand why until someone else who had been a fellow-guest with me there, I think

Laurie Lee, said: 'Rosamond dropped everyone.' But that may have been characteristic of her only during the uncertain period towards the end of, and after, her relationship with Cecil. After the break-up she wrote a good novel about herself and him, which she originally called *The Buried Day*. Collins, her publishers, persuaded her to alter the title (can she have been unaware of its secondary significance?) to *The Echoing Grove*. A few years later Cecil used her first title for his autobiography. Her novels went out of print and she seemed to have been forgotten, but when she was eighty Virago reprinted them, and she was rightly acclaimed as one of the finest novelists of her generation.

A more lasting friend was Mervyn Peake. He had not yet embarked on his remarkable series of Gothic novels, and was known only as an artist and poet. Like Vernon Watkins, he was a quiet and modest man of great charm. He had been a fine athlete in his youth, having played wing three-quarter for Kent Schoolboys when at Eltham College. Once, after the war, we played cricket together at a village in Hampshire; he was then nearly forty, but still a swift runner and a beautiful fielder in the deep. Almost every white surface in his house except the ceilings bore one or more of his drawings, executed directly onto the paint. One found them on the wainscoting by the floor, and in unexpected places in the lavatory. He did these at extraordinary speed. When I asked him to sign my copy of *Titus Groan*, he filled the flyleaf with a detailed illustration incorporating two of the book's characters in less than a minute. His end was tragic, for in his late forties this handsome man developed Alzheimer's disease and spent his last years in a home, looking twenty years more than his age, his face a cruel caricature beneath a mane of white hair.

Alys Russell belonged to an older generation. Almost eighty when I first met her, she had been the first wife of Bertrand Russell, who was a few years her junior, and the sister of the essayist Logan Pearsall Smith. She was a remarkable link with the past, for in her childhood she had met Whitman, Emerson and Tennyson. Her father had been a famous evangelist preacher in America, and Whitman was a frequent visitor to their house. He would drop in, she said, ostensibly for tea and would stay for days and even weeks. She remembered that he spent an inordinate amount of time in their only lavatory, at great inconvenience to the large family. Once her mother was giving a dinner party and asked her husband if he could lend Whitman a coat, since she was pretty sure he had arrived in only trousers and a sweater. When Mr Smith suggested this to Whitman, the poet replied: 'I've got a coat', and duly came down to dinner wearing his overcoat, which he kept on throughout the meal. Alys and Logan often visited Whitman. He received them in his study, which was ankle deep in press cuttings. The children would ask: 'Has there been anything nice about you in the papers lately, Uncle Walt?', and Uncle Walt would say: 'There was a complimentary piece in the *Baltimore Sun*', reach for a spiked pole like the ones park-keepers use, which he kept by his chair, spear a cutting and read it out to them. She said he obviously knew where the best ones were.

Her father took her to tea with Tennyson, whom she remembered as very gruff. As they were about to leave, Mr Smith asked the poet if he might beg an autograph for his children. Tennyson waved his arms. 'Everyone asks me that,' he growled. 'Why can't people think of me as an ordinary human being?' The Reverend Mr Smith apologized, whereupon Tennyson said: 'However, they seem well-behaved children, so for once – ', bent down and opened a cupboard at floor-level. Alys, being tiny, could see past him a considerable pile of photographs of himself. He pretended to grope, took the top one and signed it for them.

I asked her if she ever went to the theatre. She said not.

'You'll think me an old fogey, but I don't think the actors today are what they were when I was a gel.'

'Irving?' I suggested.

But she said: 'No, I thought he was a ham. The one I admired was Salvini.'

Salvini was the great Italian actor whose Othello had been the subject of a memorable essay by George Henry Lewes in 1875.

I said: 'Alys, you *couldn't* have seen Salvini.'

But she said: 'Yes, when I was six he came to act Othello in Philadelphia, and father took Logan and me to see him. I've never forgotten it.'

'Was his English good enough for you to follow the plot?'

'Oh, he spoke it all in Italian.'

'But it must have been very difficult for you if it was all in Italian.'

'Oh, no,' she said. 'He was the only one who talked Italian. Everyone else spoke English.'

It seemed that Salvini toured alone, each town would assemble what professional and amateur actors they could, and he would slot into the production like a modern opera star.

I met T. S. Eliot a couple of times. He praised Keyes. 'Good poet,' he said forcefully. I said: 'He thought you were good too.' 'Well,' said Eliot, 'that showed admirable judgement on his part.' He struck me as the nicest kind of bishop, a little inclined to weighty observations but kind and shyly humorous. Forty years later his widow told me that as my Ibsen translations appeared, Rupert Hart-Davis, who published them, sent them to Eliot, and she and her husband read them aloud together, taking the various parts. I should have liked to have heard his Brand and Borkman, and the final act of his Peer Gynt.

Basil Taylor, who had been one of my sub-editors on *Cherwell*, had become a talks producer at the BBC, and early in 1945 he suggested that I should review books for them. The prospect terrified me; I was plagued by a nervous sniff and cough when I tried to speak in public (though not when acting); once I had returned to Oxford to address a literary club and had made an embarrassing hash of it. But he persuaded me that I could, something for which I have always been grateful; apart from all else, I could never otherwise have accepted the lectureship in Sweden which was to shape my life. My first talk dealt with recent novels by Maugham and Joyce Cary and one by an unknown Bulgarian writing in German, Elias Canetti's *Auto-da-Fé*. This last had been sceptically received in Britain, but it greatly excited me, and I extolled it at the expense of the other two. This earned me an invitation to tea with Canetti in Hampstead. A squat, shock-haired man, he seemed childishly grateful, and played me a record of animal and bird noises recorded in the jungle which we both thought remarkable. He remained largely unrecognized in Britain; thirty years later, when I was elected to the Royal Society of Literature, I was astonished to find that he was not even a Fellow, and nominated him unsuccessfully to be a Companion, an honour they grant to supposedly outstanding writers. The following year he was awarded the Nobel Prize for Literature.

These new acquaintances were a lifeline to me as the friends of my own generation were killed one by one, while I sat in my Nissen hut fabricating my night-raid reports and surreptitiously editing Sidney's poems. In the evenings at the Plough and later at the vicarage I did more reading than I had ever done at Oxford, mostly of the great classical novelists. I soon stopped writing poetry; I wrote scarcely a line after leaving Oxford. Had I moved among actors rather than writers at this time, I am sure my early wish to make that my career would have revived. But I knew none except, slightly, Rosamond Lehmann's sister Beatrix; all my new friends were writers. One in particular, eighteen years my senior, became close to me.

5

Memories of George Orwell

I first met George Orwell in April 1943, through an odd character named Tambimuttu, the Sinhalese editor of *Poetry, London*. Tambi was a tremendous scrounger and a moderate poet, of the scruffiest imaginable appearance even by wartime Soho standards; but he had a curious charm, and somehow managed to persuade almost every British poet of note to contribute to his magazine, from Eliot downwards. Orwell was known and respected at this time, but not the outstanding figure he was to become two years later with the publication of *Animal Farm*. I expressed admiration of *Down and Out in Paris and London* to Tambi, who said: 'Would you like to meet him? I'll tell him you'll be writing to him.' Even more than most of Tambi's promises, this seemed unlikely to bear fruit, but when a few days later I did write timidly to Orwell asking if he would lunch with me, I received a courteous handwritten letter of acceptance on BBC notepaper (he was in the midst of what he was later to describe as his 'two wasted years' in that organization).

We met, as so often later, at the Hungarian Czarda in Dean Street. I remember being surprised by his great height and thinness, his staring pale-blue eyes and his high-pitched drawl with its markedly Old Etonian accent, so out of keeping with most (not all) of what he wrote. I recall little of our conversation at that first meeting except that he asked: 'Isn't that an Old Wellingtonian tie?' (what on earth could have made me choose that for a meeting with Orwell?), and talked of the single term he had spent there in 1917 before moving on to Eton. He had found Wellington terrifyingly spartan, and the only pleasant memory he retained was of skating on the lake. I see from the College Register that he was a contemporary there of Tyrone Guthrie.

When we parted he invited me to come and have supper with him, and a week or so later I visited him in his small flat in Mortimer Crescent, off the junction of Maida Vale and Kilburn High Street. His wife Eileen was a pretty brown-haired Irish girl (I write 'girl', for that is how she struck me, but I find she was then thirty-eight, only two years George's junior, though she looked much younger). Although he was born Eric Blair she called him George; the only person I ever heard call him Eric was his sister. Somehow our conversation got on to H. G. Wells, and they told me the sad story of how their brief friendship with him had ended. Some time earlier Wells had offered them the use of a flat above the garage of his house in Regent's Park. They had been very happy there until one day Wells read a critical essay that George had written about him in *Horizon* and ordered them to leave immediately. A few months later the Orwells thought they would try to patch things up, so they wrote to Wells inviting him to dinner. Wells replied at once with a warm acceptance and expressed wonder at their having left the flat he had lent them so suddenly and without explanation. He turned up full of amiability and began by warning them that he had diabetes and could not eat anything rich. 'Oh dear,' said Eileen. 'I've cooked a curry.' 'I mustn't touch that,' said Wells. 'Just give me a very little.' He ate well none the less, drank plentifully and chatted away in excellent form. After dinner the poet William Empson arrived. It transpired that he had not eaten, and the curry was finished, so Eileen said: 'All I can offer you is some plum cake.' 'Plum cake,' said Wells, overhearing this. 'I don't think I could manage that.' 'I'm not offering it to you, it's for Bill,' said Eileen, but when it appeared Wells observed that it looked uncommonly good and took two slices. Around midnight he left in the best of spirits, and as he drove off he cried: 'Don't lose touch with me for so long again.' They congratulated themselves on having repaired the friendship, but a week later they got a furious letter from Wells, saying: 'You knew I was ill and on a diet, you deliberately plied me with food and drink,' etc., and declaring that he never wanted to see either of them again. Apparently Wells had been taken violently ill later that night; obviously they had conspired against him in revenge for (he now remembered) the trouble over the flat.

Such was George and Eileen's account of the evening. Inez Holden, a friend of theirs who arrived after dinner, gives a slightly different record of the occasion in her diary (quoted in Bernard Crick's biography of Orwell, pp. 293–4). In two letters published in the *Listener* in February and March 1972, querying this account as given by me in a volume entitled *The World of George Orwell* which had appeared the previous year, she denied that the Orwells had ever lived in Wells's garage flat, but Rebecca West wrote to me on 14 March that year confirming that they did and adding some interesting details of why they were ejected:

There were actually several reasons why the Orwells were asked to leave the garage flat. One of H.G.'s closest friends, who had a great influence over him, was always complaining about them; the flat was in fact needed for members of the Wells family who lived in the country and were finding it very difficult to get rooms when they came up to town; and there was some idea of putting a nurse in the flat – and at any rate the Wellses, not unnaturally, feared a time might come when they did not want strangers on the premises. The whole household *did* find (I am not speaking of H.G., but of the family, particularly Marjorie Wells) that the Orwells were slow about leaving when they were asked to, but probably they did not realize how hard it was for the Orwells to move in wartime. I think it highly probable that H.G. did not know exactly when and how the Orwells left, for there were several weeks when he was acutely ill with influenza and pneumonia, just about that time.

In the same letter, Rebecca questioned what I had quoted about the cake: 'H.G. had diabetes (badly) and an obscure intestinal disorder . . . He could not eat cake at all. A slice of it would have sent him into a coma within minutes.' But Inez Holden in the *Listener* (24 February) wrote: '. . . on this particular evening he said that he enjoyed the plum cake but knew that his doctor would think that he should not have any of it'. How difficult it is to ferret out the truth even about comparatively recent events.

Once when I visited George in the winter of 1943–4, he outlined the plot of a short book he was writing, a 'kind of parable' to remind people of the realities of Stalinist Communism, which he felt were in danger of being forgotten because of sympathy for Russian resistance to the Germans. Like so many writers, he was hopeless at telling the story of any of his books. His summary went something like this. 'There's a farm, and the animals get fed up with the way the farmer runs it, so they chuck him out and try to run it themselves. But they run it just as badly as the farmer and become tyrants like him, and they invite the humans back and gang up with them to bully the other animals.' 'Yes?' I said encouragingly, and George said: 'It's a kind of parable, you see.' It sounded desperately unpromising, and I was hardly surprised when a few months later George said: 'That damned fool Victor Gollancz has turned my book down. He doesn't want to publish anything anti-Russian.' Each time I visited him I heard of some new publisher who had rejected it. Jonathan Cape liked it but, unfortunately for him, mentioned the project to a friend in the Ministry of Information who told him not to touch a book that might damage good relations with Russia. 'It would be less offensive,' Cape wrote to George's agent, Leonard Moore, 'if the predominant caste in the fable were not pigs. I think the choice of pigs as the ruling caste will no doubt give offence to many people, and particularly to anyone who is a bit touchy, as undoubtedly the Russians are.' T. S. Eliot, in his capacity as a director of Faber & Faber, turned it down on the extraordinary ground that, as he wrote to George: 'We have no conviction . . . that this is the right point of view from which to criticise the political situation at the present time.'

Billy Collins, chairman of the publishing firm that bears that name, was not worried about the political implications, but said he could see no market for a novel of only 30,000 words. Bernard Crick, in his biography (p. 216n), queries this, saying 'there is no record of this in the firm, nor memory either'. But I was a good deal at Collins in 1950–1, when they accepted and then published my one novel, and it was common knowledge in the firm then. My first informant was Milton Waldman, their senior literary adviser, and the rejection was confirmed to me recently by Waldman's fellow-director Mark Bonham-Carter, who added that he was 'far from surprised' that no record existed in the Collins archives. Billy Collins was, to put it politely, one of the least generous of publishers, except to his best-sellers, and it is pleasant to know that he lived to see *Animal Farm* achieve sales exceeding, I have been told, that of any other book in English except the Bible.

There seemed no hope of the book finding acceptance, and George felt so strongly about the need to get its message over quickly that he even considered publishing it at his own expense as a twopenny pamphlet. Luckily Fred Warburg, who had published George's *Homage to Catalonia* five years previously, was not afraid of the Ministry of Information, and his decision transformed the fortunes of that distinguished but, until that point, always struggling little firm. I remember when *Animal Farm* appeared I saw a copy in an Oxford Street bookshop before there had been any reviews. I didn't much look forward to reading it after George's description and all the rejections, but I thought I would help George by forking out five shillings. So I bought it, took it home and was staggered by its brilliance. Never can a book have been so much better than its author's account of it.

In June 1944 the Orwells were bombed out of Mortimer Crescent, and that autumn they moved to a flat in Canonbury Square in Islington, then by no means the fashionable quarter it has since become. I visited them often there, for tea or dinner; the tea was always very black and strong, with large leaves floating on top, poured by George from a huge metal pot which must have held the best part of a gallon. He was very proud of his skill at carpentry, which in fact was minimal. There was a dreadful chair which he had made himself and in which one had to sit. It was impossible to be comfortable in it in any position. One day he told me that he wanted to make some bookshelves but couldn't get hold of the wood because of wartime restrictions. I mentioned this to my father, who took the hint and procured him several lengths of the most beautiful cherry-wood. George was delighted and grateful, and a few weeks later asked me along to see the finished product. It was awful beyond belief. He had whitewashed it, a criminal way to treat cherry-wood, and had not put in sufficient supports so that the shelves curved like hammocks. I am glad my father never saw them.

George spoke much about his early life. His literary earnings up to the war, he told me, had averaged a pound a week. He talked of an unpleasant school where he had briefly taught for some pathetic salary (I think, though I am not sure, that he got £80 a year plus his keep during term-time). The headmaster had been a monster and, some years after leaving, George had been pleased to read in the *News of the World* that the man had been jailed for messing about with the boys. The judge, in passing sentence, had observed that a particularly bad feature of the case had been that the headmaster had also been the school Scoutmaster and had put the boys on their honour as Scouts to say nothing about it. Homosexuality was something for which George always expressed a particular revulsion, curious in one so liberal; he mentioned with distaste various attempts that had been made on him at one time or another.

Speaking of the novelists he admired, he surprised me by naming Somerset Maugham and praising the unadorned simplicity of his style. In an autobiographical note which he wrote in 1940, after naming 'the writers I most care about and never grow tired of' as 'Shakespeare, Swift, Fielding, Dickens, Charles Reade, Samuel Butler, Zola, Flaubert and, among modern writers, James Joyce, T. S. Eliot and D. H. Lawrence', he concluded: 'But I believe the modern writer who has influenced me most is Somerset Maugham, whom I admire immensely for his power of telling a story straightforwardly and without frills.'

Early in 1944 I found that Graham Greene, whom I had by now got to know, had never met George, and thought it would be fun to bring them together, so I told George that Graham admired him, which was only partly true, since Graham had reservations about George as a novelist (this was before he had written *Animal Farm* and *Nineteen Eighty-Four*), and Graham that George admired him, which was likewise only partly true, and invited them both to lunch on my twenty-third birthday, 11 June 1944, at the Czarda. They got on extremely well, as one might have expected with two such modest and likeable men, though I was disappointed that for most of the time they talked politics rather than literature.

I felt very small beside them, physically as well as intellectually, as Graham stood six feet two and George six feet three. George happened to mention his fondness for the Edwardian novelist Leonard Merrick, and Graham asked if he would like to write an introduction to one of Merrick's works for a series of forgotten classics called the Century Library which Graham was editing for Eyre & Spottiswoode. George said: 'I'd jump at it', and suggested *The Position of Peggy Harper*; but although he wrote the introduction later that year, Graham had by that time left Eyre & Spottiswoode, and Douglas Jerrold, the firm's chairman, cancelled the series.

They conversed so eagerly that when the restaurant closed we continued in a pub across the road called The Crown and Two Chairmen, and when that shut George suggested that we should both lunch with him the following week at a restaurant named the Elysée. This was in Percy Street, opposite another Cypriot restaurant, the Akropolis, which George had ceased to patronize because of a quarrel with the proprietor, who had asked him to replace his jacket when George had removed it on a particularly hot day. George had deliberately chosen the Elysée as his new haunt so that the proprietor of the Akropolis, who had the habit of standing in his doorway, could see him going in and out. A week or two later Graham stood us both a lunch at Rule's, where the claret arrived at, as he pointed out to the waiter, the temperature of warm bath-water.

After the first of these meetings, George borrowed *The Power and the Glory* (which he had never read) from me; but he did not like it, any more than he did Graham's other religious novels – though he allowed it some merit, which was more than he did to *The Heart of the Matter*, of which he wrote a very hostile review for the *New Yorker* two years later:

> The central idea of the book is that it is better, spiritually higher, to be an erring Catholic than a virtuous pagan . . . It is impossible not to feel a sort of snobbishness in Mr. Greene's attitude, both here and in other books written from an explicitly Catholic standpoint. He appears to share the idea, which has been floating around ever since Baudelaire, that there is something rather *distingué* in being damned; Hell is a sort of high-class night-club, entry to which is reserved for Catholics only, since the others, the non-Catholics, are too ignorant to be held guilty, like the beasts that perish . . . This cult of the sanctified sinner seems to me to be frivolous . . . If he [Scobie] believed in Hell, he would not risk going there merely to spare the feelings of a couple of neurotic women.

This review struck me as insensitive when I first read it, for *The Heart of the Matter* was a bigger success with both critics and public than anything Graham had previously written, but in time Graham inclined towards George's view of the book. 'The scales seem to me too heavily weighted,' he was to confess in *Ways of Escape* (1980), 'the plot overloaded, the religious scruples of Scobie too extreme.' And in an interview broadcast a few years later, he said that on reflection he thought that he should have written it as black comedy rather than as tragedy; that he had intended Scobie as an example of the sin of pride, but that critics had taken him for a saint.

George had something of a blind spot where religion was concerned; he thought it an evasion of the world's problems, and disliked Eliot's *Four Quartets* for the same reason. He was interested in the leftness of Graham's politics. 'You refer to him as an extreme Conservative, the usual Catholic reactionary type,' he wrote in 1949 to Tosco Fyvel, who had succeeded him as literary editor of *Tribune*. 'This isn't so at all, either in his books or privately. Of course

71

he is a Catholic and in some issues has to take sides politically with the Church, but in outlook he is just a mild Left with faint CP leanings. I have even thought that he might become our first Catholic fellow-traveller, a thing that doesn't exist in England but does in France.' Another of George's blind spots was philosophy; like so many distinguished creative writers, Ibsen for one, he had little patience with abstract thought.

Late in 1944 the Olivier–Richardson season opened at the New Theatre (now the Albery), and when they introduced the two parts of *Henry IV* into the repertory George remarked that one ought to take the opportunity to see both parts on the same day. I discovered a day when Part One was being performed in the afternoon and Part Two in the evening, and booked a couple of tickets. We finished lunch in north Soho rather late and I walked him fast the five hundred yards or so to the theatre, where we arrived after curtain up. I remember the dreadful whistling heaviness of his breathing for fully five minutes after we had taken our seats, and my shame at having forgotten the state of his lungs. What a production that was, by John Burrell. I shall never see a greater Falstaff than Richardson's, or a finer Hotspur than Olivier's, though I did not share the general admiration for Olivier's Justice Shallow; like all his comic performances, it seemed to me self-conscious and a caricature. At the end of Part Two, George and I had a Chinese dinner at the Hong Kong restaurant in Shaftesbury Avenue; we were both so exhausted by the seven hours of Shakespeare we had seen that we ate, for once, in virtual silence.

In May 1946 George moved into Barnhill, the remote farmhouse he had rented on Jura in the Hebrides, and wrote to me in Oxford asking if I could get him some black powder and percussion caps for his gun; but the shop in St Aldate's told me I would have to show a gun licence to buy the powder, and when I asked George to post me his he replied that he didn't have one as there was no policeman on the island.

> I'm just settling in here – up to my eyes getting the house
> straight, but it's a lovely house . . . Only difficulties at pres-
> ent are (a) that I can't yet get a jeep (hope to get one at
> the end of the month) & am having to make do with a motor
> bike which is hell on these roads, & (b) owing to the drought
> there's no water for baths, though enough to drink. How-
> ever, one doesn't get very dirty here. Come & stay some-
> time. It's not such an impossible journey (abt 48 [!] hours

from London) & there's plenty of room in this house, though of course conditions are rough.

A later letter (14 August) added the discouraging information that after reaching the island by a combination of train, boat, bus, another boat and a hired car as far as the owner would allow it to travel, my journey would end with a six-mile walk. He concluded: 'I did no work at all for 3 months, then recently I've started on another book . . . Lord knows when it will be finished, perhaps some time in 1947 and 1948, but the great thing is to get it started, which I couldn't when I was writing three articles a week.' This was *Nineteen Eighty-Four*.

I asked if I could come in late August, but he replied that they were full then with '7 or 8 people, which is about our full capacity' and suggested mid-September, but the difficulty of making contact with him on Jura ('. . . there are only two posts a week here . . . a telegram doesn't get here any quicker than a letter') meant that his reply did not reach me in time, and when I tried again in 1948 (1947 was a busy year for me, starting a new job in Sweden), the only time I could manage, in August, was no good for him ('We have . . . prospectively, 8 adults and 3 children . . . some of them are overflowing into tents'). He added some sad details about his health.

I have spent since last November in hospital (T.B.), and only came out 10 days ago. I was really ill most of last year, having I think started off in that horrible cold winter of 1946–7. I'm much better now, but I've still got to live an invalid life probably until some time next year. I only get up for half the day and can't manage any kind of exertion. However, it's a great pleasure to be home again, and I am getting on with some work . . . I have got quite used to working in bed . . . I was supposed to finish a novel [*Nineteen Eighty-Four*] by the beginning of this year, but as it is I shan't finish it till about Christmas.

Later that month he wrote to me optimistically: 'Next year I trust I shall be more or less normal.'

That winter of 1948, however, George's health so declined that he was removed to a sanatorium at Cranham in Gloucestershire. 'I began to relapse last September', he wrote to me on 12 March 1949, 'and should have gone for treatment earlier, but I had to finish that beastly book which I had been struggling with for so long. It is a great bore, my health breaking up like this. I cannot resign myself to leading a sedentary life, which I suppose I shall have to from now on. I shall at any rate have to spend the winters in some get-atable place near a doctor, perhaps in somewhere like Brighton.' He gave me a good piece of advice about the novel I was trying to write, which has served me well ever since, namely, to finish the book, however badly: 'If you once have a draft finished, however discouraging it is, you can generally pull it into shape. I simply destroyed my first novel after unsuccessfully submitting it to one publisher, for which I'm rather sorry now.' He added as a postscript that he had been 'rereading some of Hardy's novels, after very many years, and was agreeably surprised'.

I did not see him when I came to England that summer. I was hoping to do so when I returned for Christmas, but one afternoon in January I opened the evening paper and read that he was dead.

I remember him as, not merely the most courteous, kindly and lovable man I have known, but the one of all my friends with whom, if I could today, I would choose to spend an evening. I have heard people describe him as taciturn; Michael Ayrton, a brilliant talker, once referred to him as 'gloomy George'. I never found him gloomy. He had a weak voice, doubtless due to his tuberculosis and his having been shot in the throat in Spain, and could not raise it to make himself heard above a loud adversary or a general conversation. Once he took me to one of the weekly lunches which he, Anthony Powell and Malcolm Muggeridge used to hold at the Bourgogne Restaurant in Soho, and I remember him several times trying to contribute to the discussion and abandoning the attempt halfway because of the noise. Another time I took him to dinner with the politician Patrick Gordon-Walker, one of my Christ Church hockey forward line, a nice man but inclined to hold forth in a powerful voice. I had much looked forward to hearing them debate; but after a few unsuccessful efforts to get a word in, George quietly and with perfect courtesy became a silent auditor like the rest of us. Bernard Crick's otherwise excellent biography suggests a much more sombre man than the one I knew, and hints at a streak of cruelty in him which I never came across. Once he punched Rayner Heppenstall; but Heppenstall could be extremely tiresome.

George was a shy man, but if one prompted him and listened, he was a most rewarding conversationalist. Above all, he was the best informed and most illuminating talker on politics I have ever heard, with the possible exception of Arthur Koestler; how I wish I could have heard them together. His conversation was like his writing, unaffected, lucid, witty and humane; and he was, even to those of us who were young and brash, the kindest and most encouraging of listeners. Apart from the odd paranoiac like Wells, I wonder if he died with a single enemy.

6

Post-War Oxford

In May 1945, Eyre & Spottiswoode started a monthly magazine, the *New English Review*, edited by Douglas Jerrold, with Hugh Kingsmill as literary editor. One day Kingsmill telephoned me at Bomber Command to ask if I would care to be their drama critic. I said I knew nothing about the theatre, but he said nor did anyone else when they started, so I accepted. I did not have to cover every new production and knew I could wangle enough free evenings a month to see most things that might be worth reviewing. It proved an illuminating experience for me, if not for the readers. Most of the plays and performances I saw were so unrewarding that when anything occurred that was not a complete waste of time I overpraised it, partly from relief and gratitude and partly because I was so glad at last to have something that I could recommend the readers to see. I soon realized how difficult it must be for a daily critic, who sees four or five productions a week, to maintain his or her artistic standards.

Kingsmill was not very happy with my reviews; he wanted me to be more elegant and less colloquial, and was always rebuking me for using slang. Somehow I survived for fifteen months before he sacked me for writing a hostile notice of Laurence Olivier's *King Lear*. Kingsmill, who had been a schoolmaster in his time, wrote me a schoolmasterly letter.

I gave well over an hour some months ago to telling you
that you must read more, and explaining why slang is not
witty, graceful or telling. There is no evidence that you have
been reading more, or that my remarks meant anything to
you . . . I only wish I could have made you understand
that there are other factors in your work of ultimately greater

importance, even from the standpoint of success, than those
on which you have concentrated.

To my protest that five minutes' work could have put right the details
of which he complained, he replied:

You forget that I had a long talk with you in the Authors'
[Club] and that I did my best to explain my point of
view about slang . . . I am afraid we are antipathetic, and
that much more patience is required on both sides before we
could have co-operated in reasonable harmony. However, we
may meet again in mellower humour, and meanwhile I
wish you more than the kind of success you will undoubtedly
achieve, and are at present aiming at.

I think we must eventually have met again, for a year later,
congratulating me on my appointment at Uppsala, he wrote: 'Either
you or Uppsala, or, I suppose, both, have, in the inscrutable workings
of destiny, deserved each other. It would be very pleasant to see your
much-enduring smile once again . . . Come round for a drink.' I
remain grateful to him, partly for the many good evenings I had
at his home before we fell out, partly for giving me my first paid
literary work apart from editing the Keyes poems, but mostly for
introducing me to Greene.

Halfway through my stint as drama critic, after the end of the war,
I had transferred from Bomber Command HQ to the Air Historical
Branch off Knightsbridge. This, though mercifully non-scientific,
was scarcely less boring than the Operational Research Section, and
after a few months, in the spring of 1946, I managed to get released
to return to Oxford on the pretext of working for a postgraduate
degree. Oxford in 1919 was supposed to have been a place of
particular delight, but in 1946 I found it scarcely less dispiriting
than it had been in wartime. Most of the old restrictions remained,
apart from the black-out; food and clothes were still rationed, as was
fuel, and at twenty-five I felt no desire to become a student again.
Nor did I act at all; I wonder why? And there was a surprising
paucity of good undergraduate writers, especially compared with
1940–1. I spent most of my time playing games. I kept goal
at hockey well enough to get into the University Final Trial; if
the incumbent Blue, John Woodcock, had been injured, I might
have played against Cambridge. I also played number four for the

university at real tennis, which would mean a Half Blue today, but the University Match was then only two a side; and a lot of coarse cricket for the Christ Church Warrigals, who invaded local villages at week-ends.

Blunden, who had left Oxford, suggested that I might take as the subject for my thesis a minor Romantic poet named Lord Thurlow. I was allotted as my supervisor Lord David Cecil, a delightful man. He tended to arrive rather late for our tutorials, and sometimes found an excuse to leave early, so that I rarely had anything like my supposed hour, but such time as I did have with him was always rewarding. I soon deposed Thurlow in favour of Thomas Hood, who seemed to me, and to Cecil, deserving of a new biography, though as things turned out I never got down to it.

Before I abandoned him, Thurlow provided me with one of the strangest weekends I have ever spent. Blunden told me that Siegfried Sassoon was interested in Thurlow and suggested that I should drop him a line, adding that if I mentioned that I played cricket Sassoon might invite me to stay. Sure enough, on notepaper simply and impressively headed: 'Heytesbury House, Wiltshire', he replied, 'Bring your bat, as you will have to play for Heytesbury v. Devizes at 2.30! Our ground is in good condition, but every ball arrives at a different height – usually either a shooter or at nose-level, owing to the weeds which have accumulated.'

Heytesbury House is a grand and very beautiful Georgian building in its own grounds, which then included a cricket field. A housekeeper greeted me formally: 'Captain Sassoon is expecting you', and ushered me into a room to wait for him. It was an unusually hot day, but the inside of the house was freezing; the whole week-end resembled a visit to a sauna. After some minutes Sassoon entered. At sixty, he was still a magnificent figure of a man, tall and lean with broad shoulders and a spare waist; I have read that twenty years later he was still able to tie his shoelaces without bending his knees. Keeping his eyes away from me, he shook my hand and, speaking faster than anyone I had met, said: 'You're the young man Blunden wrote about you're interested in Thurlow I've got the 1813 volume and the 1821 volume there are some poems in the 1813 volume which aren't in the 1821 some in the 1821 which aren't in the 1813 not a bad poet a bit tame but quite charming are you married?'

'No.'

'That's wise I married late I don't regret it she gave me a son

78

George he's at Oundle quite a good cricketer but he plays back
to everything you can't play back to everything if the ball's short
you play back if it's pitched up you play forward you're a cricketer
you know he plays back to everything my wife doesn't understand
about writers you're a writer she puts her head into my study and
says about lunch I say don't interrupt me now she says it's a question
of the meat I say beef lamb pork chicken I don't mind she says it's
beef do you want it roast or boiled I say roast boiled grilled fried
what you like . . .'

All this was delivered in a toneless machine-gun natter with his
eyes fixed on the wall to my right. It went on and on. The prospect
of a whole week-end of this appalled me. The housekeeper announced
lunch and we went into a dining-room where the most exiguous meal
was provided even by 1946 rationing standards: half a tiny bowl of
clear soup followed by a single scrambled egg. As soon as we sat
down Sassoon's talk ceased and was replaced by a Trappist-like
silence. I could not get a word out of him; to my questions he
would either nod or shake his head. When lunch, if you could
call it that, was over, we returned to the library and sat in further
silence. There seemed no point in asking more questions. At length
he muttered what sounded like: 'Let's pull bracken' and strode out
through the front door clapping a deerstalker hat on his head.

I supposed I must have misheard him, but I had not. He led me to
a large patch of bracken not far from the house and began to uproot
it ferociously. I was clearly expected to help. He had no trouble in
bending, but even as a young man I was never able to touch my toes.
Within five minutes, my back was breaking, the sweat was pouring
off me – the hot sunshine was intolerable after the icy conditions
inside the house – and my hands were bleeding. After half an hour
of this futile and silent exercise, which made little impression on the
mass of bracken, he strode back towards the house, pausing only to
pluck a peach from a tree and hand it to me as a reward – the only
decent food I had all week-end, if hardly hunger-appeasing.

He then took me for a drive. This proved an alarming experience,
for as we approached a bend on the narrow twisting lanes he would
turn his head to point out some interesting architectural or rural
feature which we had just passed. I have never been so frightened in a
car. Fortunately there were few other motorists about. After another
desperately inadequate meal, I asked him about Wilfred Owen. He
bent down and rummaged in a cupboard, muttering inaudibly, then
threw on to the table a small bundle of papers tied with ribbon.

These, when I unfastened them, turned out to be Owen's letters to him from the Western Front. They read curiously similarly to the letters I had been receiving from my friends on active service over the past few years, except that now and then Owen would say: 'Wrote something last week. Don't know if it's any good', and there would follow one or another of the greatest poems of the century. As I read these, and reflected that Owen had been killed on a totally unnecessary and, through no fault of his, botched mission seven days before the Armistice, I could not refrain from thinking: 'Why didn't he live instead of this chap?' Immediately, Sassoon swung round, fixed me with his piercing blue eyes, and said: 'I know exactly what you're thinking.' I shook my head feebly, but he put a hand on my shoulder and said: 'You're thinking it could have happened to me.' I nodded eagerly, and so that crisis was past; I had, unjustly, risen in his estimation.

I asked him what Rupert Brooke, whom he had known at Cambridge and who had been his junior by a year, would be if he were alive, and Sassoon replied: 'He'd be Provost of King's.'

Next day came the cricket. Sassoon did not bat, for we declared before he was due in. After half an hour's fielding, he walked silently towards the pavilion. Our skipper, a shepherd (I do not lie) named Clodd, signalled to a spectator to 'take the Captain's place'. This was evidently no uncommon occurrence. I assumed he must have left to relieve himself, but instead he stalked round the boundary three or four times, apparently deep in thought, then, in the middle of an over, returned to his place at mid-off as silently as he had left, whereupon the spectator returned to his bench. No one commented on this; apart from everything else, Sassoon owned the field.

That evening, Sassoon showed me Thomas Hardy's letters to him, and told me that the second Mrs Hardy had told him that Hardy was still sexually potent in his eighties; his final will, indeed, makes allowance for the possible birth of a child. He began to relax somewhat, signed my two volumes of his poems and gave me an inscribed copy of *The Old Century*. We parted cordially, and the next summer I wrote asking if I might come again, but he replied (3 July 1947):

With extreme regret I am unable to welcome you here this month, though I was hoping for a repetition of last summer's week-end. The reason is that I knocked myself up last winter and spring by my frantic efforts to get my Meredith

book printed (combined with the appalling winter conditions
in Feb and March, and various domestic worries). Have had
nervous indigestion and the doctor says that the only way
to get rid of it is by complete rest. So I have had to deprive
myself of all visits by friends (and haven't had a bat in my
hand all summer).

I had another friendly letter from him that December, mainly
about his son.

I am very much involved in minding George during his
Xmas holidays . . . He has been given an enormous Accordion and a printing press, of which I enclose his prospectus.
You can imagine the Ink performances, and the Accordion
makes clear thinking difficult. However, all that he does and is
continues to delight my soul . . . My *Collected Poems*
have sold out their 6,000 edition. Some rather sniffy reviews
by the clever boys, who find my later work dull.

I should have pursued the relationship, for since then I have met
people who found him charming and rewarding. But I don't think
any of them were closeted alone with him for two days. Blunden's
wife Claire told me that she found him difficult ('He made Edmund
bowl at him in the net for ages and only asked him to bat when it
had begun to rain'), and the possibility of another weekend like the
first daunted me. Which mood would I find him in? When, four
years later, I needed to write to him in connection with a poetry
exhibition I was organizing, I tactlessly began my letter 'Dear Captain
Sassoon', and received a justifiably cool reply beginning 'Dear Meyer'
and ending 'I really don't quite comprehend what sort of things you
are asking for'. He was a lonely and unhappy man, and I was too
young and self-preoccupied to sense it.

Soon after my return to Oxford in January 1946, I received an
invitation from an undergraduate in Magdalen telling me that he
was planning to restart *Cherwell*, which had ceased publication in
1942, and would like to discuss things with me. I found a very thin
eighteen-year-old with a marked stammer who looked and dressed
like a parody of an aesthete, living in Edward VIII's old rooms, as
unprepossessing in his way as the young Peter Brook had seemed
four years earlier. But I soon realized that he was no less remarkable.

Kenneth Tynan was the illegitimate son of a North Country

industrialist, Sir Peter Peacock. He was uncommonly widely and deeply read in literature, perhaps the most brilliant English scholar of his time at Oxford, and took an active part in university dramatics, both as director and as actor. I saw him as Bishop Nicholas in Ibsen's early play *The Pretenders*, when he was not untalented in an extravagant off-beat way; he directed various plays, including *Samson Agonistes* in the University Church and the Quarto version of *Hamlet* with Peter Parker as the Prince, Robert Hardy as Claudius and John Schlesinger and Lindsay Anderson successively as Horatio. Parker remembers Ken as 'splendidly flashing and funny, and courageous . . . superbly young, but eerily never amateurish about what he *wanted*'.★ I did not see any of these (the last two occurred after I had gone abroad); the only production of his I saw was Leopold Lewis's Victorian melodrama *The Bells* at the Bedford Theatre in Camden Town in 1950. It was a curious mixture of inventiveness and amateurism, made memorable by Frederick Valk's tremendous performance as Matthias, Henry Irving's old part. Ken knew the XYZ of direction, but not the ABC; his desire to shock, which he kept under a certain amount of control as a critic, made him as a director go for effect, and the cumulative result of this was counter-productive. I think, too, that he was impatient of the nitty-gritty of direction, the attention to small tiresome detail which marks all good, never mind great, directors. Valk, who liked Ken and was grateful to him for championing him, later told me that he thought him, though indeed imaginative, an absolute amateur as a director. I dare say that Ken might have agreed with this, for the same year, following the success of his first book of theatrical essays, *He That Plays the King*, he abandoned directing for dramatic criticism.

Ken made many enemies at Oxford and throughout his life by his precociousness and sharp tongue. He remained to the end of his days an *enfant terrible*. When he was around forty, he demanded at a January party that everyone should say something which the rest of us had to decide was true or false, and began the proceedings by announcing: 'I've masturbated twelve times this year already', which interested no one very much. (My contribution was: 'I once performed a solo dance of thanks before an audience of two hundred head-hunters', and nobody guessed right about that.) I have always supposed that all this and his stammer were caused by his feelings about his illegitimacy.

★In a letter to the author.

I liked Ken greatly, but I am not sure that I would have done so had I been an actor or a director, for he had a wounding pen, and I am glad that I nearly always met him privately when he did not feel compelled to shock. He was, in my view, the best dramatic critic who has ever written in English, better even than Shaw, Montague or Agate. Shaw was so anxious to promote the new drama that he was unfair to almost everything and everyone else (one would never guess from reading *Our Theatre in the Nineties* that Irving was worth much), and Agate's reviews of such as Ibsen and Chekhov, though he admired both, do not read very perceptively today (and he was frequently lazy and bitchy, especially in later years). Ken possessed pretty well every requirement of a dramatic critic. He was very widely read, had practical experience as both actor and director (that he was not talented as either matters no more than the fact of a director having been a poor actor, as most directors notoriously are); he had also, unlike Shaw, a surprisingly wide range of sympathy, wrote brilliantly and, above all, was extremely perceptive. He knew bogus flashiness when he saw it, in either writing or acting. Above all, he had that rarest of gifts of being able to convey why a play or a performance had excited him. Agate had this in his early days, Montague throughout his career, but neither was Ken's equal, and he demonstrated it when he was still a schoolboy and an undergraduate in the reviews which were to form the substance of *He That Plays the King*.

Ken's chief fault as a writer was that he could not endure to be bored, and this meant that, apart from his collections of reviews and profiles and the short *Bull Fever*, he never wrote a book, though he planned several. That kind of extended effort was beyond his patience. Even the longer general essays with which he complemented his reviews when they appeared in book form are inferior to the reviews themselves. But the reviews remain as vivid and, in most cases, valid as when he wrote them. I have always regretted that he accepted the post of dramaturge to the National Theatre, though I appreciate that he must have felt he could hardly refuse, having pleaded for the establishment of a National Theatre for so long. It constrained him to defend some performances about which I suspect he felt strong reservations.

He once said sadly: 'I was at my peak when I left Oxford', and in a sense that was true. Although he did not decline, he did not really develop; even the best of his later work is no advance on the best in *He That Plays the King*. He shared my enthusiasm for cricket; once I played with him, and to my surprise, for he looked the most unathletic of men, he proved to be a stylish and obviously well-coached left-hand batsman.

I still had no clear idea of what I wanted to do. Having written a radio play about eighteenth-century cricket called *The Hambledon Men*, which had been (very badly) performed, I was thinking vaguely of trying to join the BBC as a features writer and producer. I would have been a colleague there of the likes of Louis MacNeice, Douglas Cleverdon and Stephen Potter, and have been able to work with some of the best actors in the country. Then, one afternoon in the bitter winter of 1947, at the real tennis court in Magpie Lane, an Irish friend of mine named Guy Jackson said: 'Would you like to come and ski in Sweden at Easter?' 'Why Sweden?' I asked, to which he replied that he had been there before the war and had liked it. That and a chance meeting on a train were to determine my ultimate career.

We skied at Riksgränsen in the extreme north of Sweden, well inside the Arctic Circle, just over the border from the Norwegian port of Narvik. I left there three days before the others to visit a friend of my father's, a timber merchant in central Sweden, a journey of some seven hours by rail. The train left Riksgränsen at 9 a.m., and not until the guard came round did I learn that no food was available, nor would I have time to get any at stops. By mid-afternoon I was ravenous. Then a stout middle-aged lady entered my carriage and opened a hamper which contained enough to feed several people. I explained my plight and asked if she could spare something, which she did. She turned out to be a teacher from the small town of Lidköping, and when she heard that I had a degree in English, she said: 'When you get to Stockholm, look up my friend Miss Burgess in the British Council and she will arrange for you to come and lecture to Anglo-Swedish Societies.' I thought no more of this until, walking along a Stockholm street after my stay with the timber merchant, I saw some blown-up photographs in a window, crossed to look at them and saw the words British Council on the door. I remembered the name Burgess and, it being noon, thought I might manage to cadge a drink.

Miss Burgess received me amiably and gave me a sherry. After we had been talking for a few minutes another lady in the room, a Mrs Cameron, suddenly said: 'Would you like to be Lecturer in English at Uppsala University?' My first thought was that should I land such a job I could abandon my thesis; I had done hardly a

11 At Oxford

12 Keith Douglas at Oxford

13 Sidney Keyes at Oxford

14 Michael Flanders at Oxford

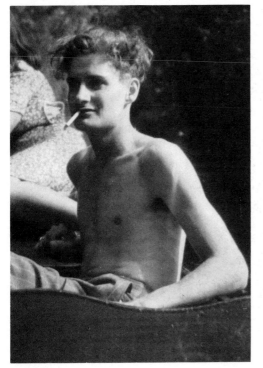

15 Edmund Blunden

16 Herbert Read

17 Mervyn Peake

18 George Orwell

stroke of work on it and would probably fail to satisfy the examiners. They explained that although the Uppsala post had been advertised in Britain, Professor Liljegren at Uppsala was reluctant to take anyone whom he had not personally met, since the Council had once sent him a lecturer with a strong Manchester accent, with the result that many of the students from that particular year spoke like him. (Later I met one of them and he did.) I knew no Swedish, of course, but this was not required. So I took the train to Uppsala, and was left with the impression that I had landed the job.

I returned to Oxford for the summer term of 1947, but the weeks passed and I heard nothing. I wrote twice to Professor Liljegren but received no reply. Then a Swede in pebble spectacles and white gym-shoes appeared in my college rooms and explained that he had been asked by the Professor to look me up and tell me more about the job. I said I had heard nothing; he assured me that the appointment had been posted on the university notice-board. A third letter to the Professor was greeted with silence, so I telephoned Miss Burgess in Stockholm from the coin-box in Meadow Buildings and in due course received confirmation. This was the first hint I had of the eccentricity of Professor Liljegren, from which I, like my predecessors, was to suffer over the next three years.

That August, on a hot, still evening, I found myself trying to persuade the receptionist at the Hotel Hörnan in Uppsala that a room had been booked for me. He knew no English and simply said: 'Full. Full.' At last he took me upstairs to a bedroom in which sat an old gentleman with his wooden leg standing in the corner. He knew English, he proudly told me, having been a sea-captain, and explained everything satisfactorily. I remember shutting the door of my room, opening the window and looking out over the little river that ran by the hotel, wondering what this country held for me.

7

A Love Affair with Sweden

Uppsala is now big, bustling and industrialized, but in 1947 it was about the size of modern Cambridge, with a fine Gothic cathedral, insanely covered outside during the last century in red brick, and various handsome old buildings. The university, sited on a hill, dates from the fifteenth century. The city wore two quite different aspects, according to the seasons. In spring and summer it was a place of delicate colours – the mellow ochre of the eighteenth-century wooden houses, the pastel greens and pinks and yellows of the modern blocks of flats with their bright balconies and awnings, the blood red of the domed mediaeval castle standing sentinel on its hill, the gunmetal blue of the river Fyris running Venetian style down the main street. In winter it wore a bridal dress of white, the trees and wooden houses groaning under their weight of snow, and bearded icicles dangling from every gutterpipe. The river hung motionless over the weir, a wall of combed ice, and the people moved shapeless under their layers of winter clothing, silent as ghosts.

I have always been drawn to the north, the way most people are to the south. Being red-haired and fair-skinned, I could never lie for long in the sun; even an afternoon's fielding in an English July turned my face and arms the colour of a ripe strawberry. To this day, I feel a greater thrill travelling north than south, even in Britain. Perhaps the instincts of old Brody Meyer and his Polish ancestors have surfaced in me. My three years in Uppsala, and the year that followed in Stockholm, enabled me to discover who I was in a way I might never have achieved had I stayed in England.

Perhaps most importantly, it sorted me out sexually. At the age of twenty-six, I had had only two affairs with girls, neither of which had been really satisfactory. Like so many of my generation who had been to public schools, I had flirted with homosexuality, but that had not worked out either. But in Uppsala I had the good fortune to be seduced by a schoolgirl of eighteen. I put it that way because although, like everyone else in the town, I found her attractive, I would never have dared to make the first move. She was happily promiscuous, and I was only one among several lovers. The first time we made love I had a leg encased in plaster of Paris (a city in which she later became a successful fashion model). Feeling that I needed someone more faithful, she procured for me one of her classmates, a virgin, with whom I was very happy until shortly before I left; then, in the brief time that remained, I met a married woman a year older than me, a sophisticated lover who taught me much. I still correspond affectionately with the first two; I wish I knew what had happened to the third.

It is difficult for a modern generation to realize the difference that existed then between sexual attitudes in England and Sweden. I remember telling the Scandinavian Society in Oxford in about 1950 that most girls in Sweden wanted a lover, not necessarily you or me, but someone, whereas most English girls, and those in America, wanted a husband. Nobody at the Oxford meeting challenged this view. Also, I was by no means unique in having had only two heterosexual affairs by my mid-twenties, or in supposing myself to be homosexual when in fact I was not. Though I sometimes wonder: had I enjoyed a successful homosexual relationship, might I have continued that way?

At first I could make little contact with my pupils at the university, though I was scarcely older than they, and some were my age. There was no tradition of question and answer, of an exchange of views; they obediently noted down my opinions. I tried to institute seminars, but even here it was difficult to persuade them to think for themselves. At the end of a frustrating first term I returned to London for Christmas and told my father that wild horses would not drag me back for a second year. But gradually the students' reserve was dissolved, I met my schoolgirl and things changed. I even began to learn the language. French had been one of my worst subjects at school, and like so many of my generation I regarded modern languages as a kind of élite mystery, like advanced mathematics, which only a chosen few could master. Nowadays to speak a foreign language is accepted as something that any reasonably intelligent human being can cope with, like cooking or driving a car. I shall never forget my astonishment when I opened the local paper one morning and found that I understood more than I didn't.

Equally importantly, I escaped from the influence of my father. I do not mean to suggest that he imposed his ideas on his sons; on the contrary, he encouraged us to be individuals. Whereas Uncle Monty took it for granted that his two sons would enter the family firm, my father said it had been fun for him and his brother to start it, but that if we wanted to do something else that would be fine. Thus, Peter entered the firm and became a distinguished French translator, Dick became a doctor and later a psychiatrist, and I, eventually, a writer. But my father was such a brilliant and magnetic person that I felt irretrievably inferior to him. It was unthinkable to me that I should take any important decision without asking his advice and abiding by it. When I returned to live in England after my time in Sweden, I at once returned to this state of vassalage, and it was not until his death in 1955, when I was thirty-four, that I found my independence and individuality for good.

My years in Sweden greatly broadened and deepened my knowledge of the theatre and cinema. In addition to my Uppsala duties, I gave two lectures each week at the Stockholm High School, shortly to become Stockholm University. For each lecture I received thirty crowns, about £2, which was enough for a meal and a ticket to the Royal Dramatic Theatre. Dramaten, as it is known, was then in a golden period; the company was the strongest and most versatile that I have seen anywhere, then or since. In addition to a mighty quintet of senior players – Lars Hanson, Märta Ekström, Tora Teje, Anders Henrikson and Inga Tidblad – a brilliant young generation was emerging, several of whose names would become familiar abroad through films: Ulf Palme, Per Oscarsson, Jarl Kulle and Anita Björk (Mai Zetterling, arguably the most talented of them, had just left to start a successful career in Britain). In between, there was a strong thirty to forty age group, and several splendid old actors to play supporting roles. Any of these players would have been a star in any country, and here they were gathered in a single company. And unknown to me, in the drama schools, or about to enter them, were the young men and women whom Ingmar Bergman was to make famous: Bibi Andersson, Max von Sydow, Harriet Andersson, Ingrid Thulin and Gunnel Lindblom. Dramaten also possessed two of the greatest stage directors in Europe: Olof Molander and Alf Sjöberg. Molander was then in his fifties, Sjöberg in his forties, so that both were in their prime.

Apart from the excellence of its company and directors, Dramaten had a much broader and more international repertory than any theatre

in Britain at that time. In addition to such European classical dramatists as Goethe, Racine, Schiller and Calderon, it presented modern
playwrights such as Brecht and Anouilh; one had no chance to see
the work of any of these writers, old or new, in London. The first
production I saw at Dramaten was in the spring of 1947, on my way
back from my skiing trip; my father's friend, seeing in the newspaper
that they were performing Shakespeare's *Richard III*, had telephoned
to book me a seat. On reaching the theatre I was surprised to find
the rest of the occupants of the stalls in evening dress, and even
more surprised when the curtain rose to see that the play had been
set in ancient Rome. It seemed to have been rather freely adapted,
and it was not until the interval that I discovered that I was in
fact attending the premiere of Racine's *Britannicus*. My ignorance
of Swedish did not prevent me from realizing that in the role of
Agrippina I was watching an actress of a different calibre from any
I had seen in England.

I saw Tora Teje many times over the next twenty years, and
she still seems to me the greatest actress I have seen, just as the
German Frederick Valk was the greatest actor. Once, later, I was
dining at the Theatre Grill next to Dramaten and among the smart
guests sat a drably dressed and rather plain little old lady eating a
rissole by herself. It was not until she walked past me on her way
out that I recognized her as the regal performer whom I had so
often admired in the theatre across the street. She was equally at
home in comedy, as in Giraudoux's *La Folle de Chaillot*, but it is in
tragedy that I remember her best, as an incomparable Mrs Alving in
Ibsen's *Ghosts*, as Agatha in Eliot's *The Family Reunion*, and as the
Judge's Wife in Strindberg's *Advent*. She had a marvellous stillness
and power and unforced pathos; and, as with Valk, the word 'acting'
never crossed one's mind until after the final curtain had fallen.

Märta Ekström, who many said was her equal, was a dying
woman when I saw her, but one could recognize the embers of a
splendid talent. Inga Tidblad was a superb classical comedienne with
infectious high spirits. Once she did a programme of four classical
roles from Shakespeare – Portia, Rosalind, Viola and Juliet – and
although I did not greatly like her Juliet, I have never seen anyone to
touch her in the other three parts, except perhaps the young Vanessa
Redgrave as Rosalind. How I wish I could have seen her play the
roles in their entirety. She was also a brilliant Lady Cicely in Shaw's
Captain Brassbound's Conversion. Tragedy was not really within her
range. I disliked her Cleopatra, Mrs Alving and Miss Julie, nor did

I share the general admiration for her as the drug-addicted wife in O'Neill's *Long Day's Journey into Night*; but even in the wrong part, she could bewitch an audience. My father used to speak in similar terms of Ellen Terry, and I imagine that Inga Tidblad's quality must have been close to Terry's.

Lars Hanson was the giant of the Swedish stage then; but I never liked his acting, powerful and accomplished as it was. I found him mannered and selfish, in the sense that he never seemed able to act a relationship. He gave grand solo performances, which were fine if the character he was playing was the kind of person who has no contact with those around him. He was ideally cast as James Tyrone in *Long Day's Journey*, and as the Pope in Peter Weiss's *The Representative*. Anders Henrikson, a fine, precise, amply powerful actor, was much more to my taste. I remember him as a wonderful Hummel in Strindberg's *The Ghost Sonata*, and as Relling in Ibsen's *The Wild Duck*; I do not expect to see either role better played.

But my favourite actor in that company was Ulf Palme. Filmgoers who are acquainted with Alf Sjöberg's great screen version of Strindberg's *Miss Julie* will recall his performance as the valet, Jean – a perfectly judged combination of sexuality and servility. A bull of a man, by no means classically handsome, he could act pretty well anything, but he excelled as split, guilt-ridden men such as Hjalmar Ekdal in *The Wild Duck*, Strindberg's epileptic *Erik the Fourteenth*, and the Captain in *The Dance of Death*. Palme followed his Jean with two more magnificent film performances in films by Sjöberg: Barabbas in an adaptation of the Pär Lagerkvist novel of that name, and Göran Persson, Erik the Fourteenth's evil counsellor, in a version of the Strindberg play in which he had, on stage, played the King. But for some reason his film career never took off – Bergman, I think, used him only once – and in early middle age he virtually abandoned the live theatre.

Strangely few of that gifted younger generation fulfilled their promise. Three at least became alcoholics, a fourth left the stage to write indifferent novels, a fifth spent his best years playing musical leads in commercial theatres, a sixth married a commercial director and devoted her best years to light comedy, a seventh concentrated, even more incongruously, on revue. Two of the best actresses gave up acting for directing. It was different with Bergman's young players on the west coast; his films brought the best out of them, and with each new film their talents blossomed and their reputations grew. But that brilliant Dramaten group largely vanished from the serious stage, and no one has quite taken their place.

The fact that I at first knew no Swedish, and picked it up slowly, for I am not a natural linguist and can learn a language only from the printed page, no doubt hampered my full appreciation of the performances I saw, but it did not prevent my sense of wonder. Not having to listen to the words means that your eyes notice more than they otherwise would. Dramaten's standing was such that few pupils in its famous school, where Garbo had once studied, had any further ambition than to enter the company on leaving and stay there until they died. The consequent near-permanence of the company had two disadvantages: one seldom saw a new pairing of players who had never previously acted opposite each other, and roles sometimes tended to be allotted by seniority rather than suitability. Thus, Inga Tidblad played Miss Julie and Gunn Wållgren played Nora when they were both approaching fifty. This did not bother the Swedish public, any more than it would in opera, but it bothered me. On the other hand, the system made for wonderful ensemble playing; one did get the feeling that married couples, or the inhabitants of a small town in a Chekhov play, had known each other for years.

But the most important revelation for me was Dramaten's productions of Strindberg. When I came to Sweden in 1947 I had seen only one Strindberg, that inadequate and confusing *Ghost Sonata* at Oxford during the war. I had read some of his plays in the dreadful old Edwin Björkman translations, and had been further confused. I could not relate Strindberg's characters or stories to life as I knew it. But Dramaten presented several Strindberg plays every year, so that in addition to *Miss Julie* I saw his best historical drama, *Erik the Fourteenth*, his one-acters *Pariah* and *The Stronger*, his first great play *Master Olof*, his final play *The Great Highway* and, in due course, *The Ghost Sonata*, *A Dream Play*, *Gustav III* and such rare items as *Advent*, *Charles XII*, *Sir Bengt's Wife*, *Comrades* and *The Pelican*. How that company could act Strindberg, especially when Molander or Sjöberg was directing them! They presented the plays not as impossible nightmares but as real life, lived in that border country where sanity and insanity merge, a no man's land which all of us enter at some stage in our lives, driven by love, hatred or jealousy or a combination of the three, and which Strindberg mapped as no dramatist had done before him. I learned to see his plays not as fanciful imaginings but as mirrors, and those evenings at Dramaten were unforgettable experiences, immensely broadening my understanding both of life and of what a dramatist and a director might accomplish on a stage.

In the cinema, my horizon was similarly broadened. In London, although foreign classics were occasionally shown at film societies or at the Everyman in Hampstead, it was virtually impossible to see any contemporary European films except a few from France. But Uppsala offered a wide cosmopolitan repertoire. I remember a Russian film about the Crimean War which showed the British as cowardly scoundrels, hiding behind trees and stabbing honest Russian soldiers in the back. A British friend and I enjoyed ourselves greatly at this, hissing our villainous compatriots to the embarrassment of the Swedes all around us, who took us for Communists. The most enterprising cinema was a tiny one called Fyris; it had only one projector, so that there had to be an interval while they changed the reels. Most exciting, though, was the sharply realistic work of a young Swedish director in his late twenties whose shoestring films, written by himself, were unlike anything else I had seen. On a visit to London I met the owner of the Everyman at a party and suggested that he might have a look at these, but he replied that there would be no market for Swedish films, and when I offered to subtitle them for nothing he turned away. The combination of an unknown director and an unknown translator must have seemed doubly unpromising. It was not until several years later that Ingmar Bergman made his breakthrough in Britain with *Sawdust and Tinsel*. Bergman also wrote plays, flawed but interesting. I translated one of these, *Rachel and the Cinema Usher*, on spec, the first translation I had done since school, but no English theatre was interested. When Bergman became famous, enquiries began to come in, but Bergman then said, not unreasonably, that he thought his plays poor and did not want them to be performed.

Alf Sjöberg, who had directed Bergman's early script, *Frenzy* (known in the United States as *Torment*), was also making films. I thought him then, as I do now, a deeper artist than Bergman, and without the coldness which permeates every film Bergman made until *Fanny and Alexander*. Bergman's films have the advantage for people who do not know Swedish that they assume the subtitles to be flat versions of something brilliant in the original, just as for the same reason Somerset Maugham was for years more highly regarded abroad than in Britain. In reality Bergman's dialogue often declines into glib paradox. But Sweden was so short of good dramatists and novelists that he had no alternative but to write his own stories;

he has always insisted that he can only make films about Swedes
because they are the only people he really knows. (Ibsen, despite
spending most of his working life in Italy and Germany, continued
to set his plays in Norway for the same reason.)

Sjöberg came to Uppsala to take part in a debate; we met, and
became good friends. He was as inspiring a person as I have known,
a visionary whose technique matched his imagination, and the most
generous of men, seemingly without envy and ever encouraging to
the young. A director of superb authority and panache, he always
regarded himself as the interpreter of a dramatist, unlike Bergman,
who would mould a play to fit himself. Bergman is a fine stager of
Strindberg, with whom he is able to identify without qualification,
but a quirky director of anyone else, as I was to find twenty years
later when I worked with him on Ibsen's *Hedda Gabler*.

Curiously, although several good film directors – such as Bo
Widerberg, Jan Troell and Mai Zetterling – were to emerge in
Sweden over the next few decades, Molander and Sjöberg, and
for that matter Bergman, have had no successors of distinction on
the stage. The recent standard of production in Sweden has been
disappointingly low; even the best contemporary film directors such
as Widerberg have not been good in the theatre.

I was very happy at Uppsala. I liked the lecturing and, after that
first lonely term, developed a full social life. I was only five or six
years older than my students, and soon broke down the barrier which
they assumed must exist between themselves and any teacher; it was
evidently a new experience for them to have a lecturer who regarded
himself as one of them. My salary after tax was 664 crowns (about
£40) a month, plus £2 for each weekly lecture in Stockholm. On
this I lived pretty comfortably; my rent of two good rooms with a
shared bathroom was £13 a month. Even an *extra smörgåsbord* at the
Hotel Gillet, comprising smoked salmon, smoked eel, various ways
with herring and as much besides as even I could eat, set me back
no more than 4.50 crowns (30p). With my colleagues I had less in
common. The pedantry in the language and literature departments
amazed me. People spent up to ten years writing theses on the most
recondite subjects, such as the difference between 'shall' and 'will', a
problem that holds an inexplicable fascination for Swedish academics.
I would meet men and women of nearly forty still struggling to
complete one of these enormous and useless projects. One term

a man named Danielsson, later to become Professor of English in Stockholm, shared with me the correction of examination papers. He complained to Professor Liljegren that I seemed unacquainted with some of the laws of English grammar, as laid down by a Dane some decades previously, and listed various errors which I had missed. My protestations that what the students had written would be regarded as legitimate by most living writers fell on deaf ears. The Danish primer was the Bible. Professor Liljegren, who by now had taken against me as against most of my predecessors, pinned up a notice warning students that any of them who joined my courses 'will, because of Mr Meyer's incompetence, do so at their own risk'. He tried to terminate my contract but was overruled by the Vice-Chancellor, and wrote me a series of paranoiac letters. When, thirty years later, I started to write a biography of Strindberg, I found myself in familiar territory.

During my last eighteen months at Uppsala, I wrote a novel, *The End of the Corridor*. Like most first novels, it was thinly disguised autobiography. I needed to get my childhood and adolescence out of my system, and for my narrator I created an imaginary portrait of what I thought I might be like at forty, a self-indulgent and dilettante bachelor of private means. It turned out to be not far from the truth, except that I stopped being a dilettante in my middle to late thirties. Ibsen described the character of Brand, in his play of that name, as 'myself in my best moments', and my narrator now seems to me, as Ibsen might have described Peer Gynt, myself in my worst moments.

As the end of my third year at Uppsala arrived, I wondered whether to apply for a renewal of tenure. Professor Liljegren was about to retire, and his successor, Henry Donner, wanted me to stay. I was very tempted. But my novel had been accepted in England, I wanted to make a career as a writer, and I knew that although others managed to combine that with teaching, I could not. Looking at my fellow dons, some of them admirable men and women, I saw what I would be like at their age, contributing the occasional article to learned journals or spending ten years on a book that should take two. Moreover, my father, to avoid death duties, had generously settled enough on my brothers and me to make us financially independent. This could have been the ruin of me; as things turned out, it enabled me to spend twenty-five years translating and writing biographies of Ibsen and Strindberg, which I would otherwise not have done. But such thoughts were far from my mind as I walked down the long hill from my rooms to the station one sunny morning in late May, 1950. I left Uppsala with sadness, for I had discovered myself there as I never had at Oxford. There was an idyllic quality to my life there which I sensed I would never find again; and I never have.

8

First Steps as a Writer

David Higham, who had expressed interest in becoming my agent when I was editing *Cherwell*, thought *The End of the Corridor* might be difficult to sell because of a scene describing a boy's first homosexual experience, and asked if I knew any publisher personally. I was about to reply no when I remembered that, playing in 1947 for a team of writers (heaven knows how I got invited) against the publishing house of Collins in an annual cricket match they held at Marlow as part of their staff outing, I had scored eighty including a six over the trees off Billy Collins, the chairman, eliciting from him the splendid *non sequitur*: 'Magnificent shot. You must write a book for us.' When I told David this, he said it was just the kind of thing that Billy would remember, and sure enough when my manuscript arrived Billy did remember and told his reader: 'We must publish this chap if we can.' He did not read it himself until it was in proof, when I gather he expressed grave doubts, for Collins regarded themselves as a very respectable firm. But it appeared in March 1951. It was condescendingly noticed in the two main Sundays, the *Sunday Times* and *Observer*, by C. P. Snow and Lionel Hale, respectively, but got several good reviews elsewhere. John Betjeman, in a generous piece in the *Daily Telegraph*, summed it up as 'a picture of the strange stirrings which adolescents have when they discover poetry and love and music and sex and logic, and mix them all up', and later named it as one of his books of the year.

Collins printed 5,000 copies, of which they sold 4,500. This seemed to me rather satisfactory, but Collins regarded it as a failure. The head of sales, John Ford, shook his head gloomily when I looked in after a few months to ask how it had gone. 'Very disappointing, I'm afraid, Michael. Very disappointing indeed. We've had a good quarter otherwise.' He listed the sales of their best-selling authors, Agatha Christie, Nigel Balchin, Alistair Maclean and half a dozen others. Whether this was intended to cheer me up I do not know, but it made me feel very despondent. I had let Billy Collins down. I had not lived up to the promise of my six at Marlow.

1951 was the year of the Festival of Britain, and Herbert Read asked if I would collect material for an exhibition of twentieth-century poetry which he wanted to present at the new Institute of Contemporary Arts, of which he was a co-founder. I had only ten weeks in which to do this, and only my ignorance of the amount of work involved led me to accept, but all the poets I approached, and the heirs of those dead, responded promptly and generously. Many of them, especially the heirs, let me rummage through their boxes; the most interesting items were often those they didn't know they had. I made several new friends as a result, notably Wilfred Owen's brother Harold, Edward Thomas's widow Helen, Sir Edward Marsh and John Hayward, the crippled bibliophile with whom T. S. Eliot shared a flat.

Harold Owen was a painter, a small, shy and extremely charming man who lived in a remote part of Oxfordshire. I have never known a house more difficult to find; after explaining that the village named at the head of his notepaper was 'miles out of your way', his instructions, which occupied a page and a half of his letter, ended: 'Look for an obscure opening in the hedge, this is the entrance to my drive – you will not see the house . . . but will find it some three hundred yards up this rather rough drive.' This letter was written entirely in neat capitals; it was, he explained, the only form of writing he could manage. When I remarked that at least he must sign cheques in the ordinary way, he said that this was not the case; upon his bank manager protesting that a signature in capitals would be easy to forge, Harold had convinced him that his capitals would in fact be especially difficult to imitate. 'I have been at work', he wrote in his first letter to me, 'upon a sort of biography of W. O. and his family for some time, it has spread itself into some two hundred thousand words, I still have the last few years of his life to do.' When I visited him I saw this enormous pile of typescript on a table. Who on earth, I thought, will want to publish that in anything like its present form, especially since the most important part of Wilfred's life would surely bring the whole up to nearer three hundred thousand words? But the result was the wonderful trilogy *Journey from Obscurity*, one of the great memoirs of this century, and its fine sequel *Aftermath*.

Helen Thomas had written an equally remarkable account of her life with Edward Thomas in two brief and deeply moving books, *As It Was* and *World Without End*. She was still living, as she had done ever since her marriage, in considerable poverty outside Chippenham with her daughter Ann and the latter's small child, whose father was the novelist Henry Williamson. Unlike Harold Owen, Helen had the most illegible handwriting I have known; it took an age to decode even her shortest letters. She was a twinkling little old lady, and she spoke of Edward Thomas with the same simple eloquence with which she had written about him. 'I am nearly 74 and Edward would have been 73', she wrote to me in one of her letters, 'but to me he is eternally young and eternally the same as when he left me.'

Sir Edward Marsh, friend of Rupert Brooke, editor of the Georgian poetry anthologies and sometime Private Secretary to Winston Churchill, lived in a tiny flat in Walton Street, Chelsea. He cannot have been well off on his pension, for his collars were always very frayed, but he had a fine collection of modern paintings which overflowed into his bathroom, covering its walls like stamps in an album, and of personally inscribed books which reminded one that the Georgian volumes had included not only those traditional poets whom Ezra Pound so despised, but also D. H. Lawrence, Robert Graves and some fiercely anti-war poems by Sassoon. Marsh also showed me a letter written to him by Graham Greene, when the latter was an undergraduate at Balliol, asking him to consider some enclosed verses; unluckily Marsh had just discontinued the series, otherwise Greene too would probably have appeared as a Georgian, though his poetry now strikes one as being ultra-Imagist. Marsh lent me the original of the famous Harvard Thomas drawing of Brooke, which nearly came to a sticky end. One evening as I was working with the exhibits scattered over my desk I saw a large blob of ink gather on the nib of my fountain pen immediately above the Brooke drawing which lay in front of me. Before I could do anything, the blob fell, by good fortune an inch away from the portrait. Had it landed on it, I think I would have had to have a tracing made of the drawing and hope that Marsh, by then very old, would not notice the difference.

Several other prized items nearly met with disaster. Father Corbishley of Campion Hall lent me a number of manuscripts and drawings by Gerard Manley Hopkins. Six months after the exhibition, I was driving half the Hampstead hockey team (of which I was goalkeeper) back from a match at Cambridge when our left half, Peter Moon, subsequently an ambassador, said from behind me: 'Is this a drawing of you?' and handed me a small pen-and-ink sketch which I recognized as being a self-portrait by Hopkins. This had apparently slipped down the back of the rear seat, where it had remained all this time, fortunately undamaged.

Then there was the business of the David Jones painting. I visited

Jones, the author of that great record of life in the Flanders trenches, *In Parenthesis*, in his flat at Harrow, and as well as his manuscript he offered me a painting by him which hung on the wall. In my ignorance I did not know that Jones was as celebrated a painter as he was as a writer, and, not having much of an eye for art, I accepted it with polite though I hope concealed indifference and shoved it in the boot of my car. A couple of days later I happened to mention this to my brother, who almost expired in horror. I retrieved the painting from the boot and it occupied pride of place in the exhibition.

Unlike Harold, Helen and Eddie, John Hayward could hardly be called genial. He was one of the most alarming persons I have known. When a boy at Eton he had been permanently crippled by polio, not merely in his limbs but also facially, so that his lower lip hung hideously outwards. He was tiny, fiercely autocratic and very quick-tempered. Even the most important people would be commanded to push him outside for a breather in his wheelchair, and he and Eliot were a common sight as spectators at the Burton Court cricket ground which lay near their block. But he could be highly rewarding, for he was a fine scholar and a considerable wit. He lent some splendid exhibits, including several rare items which Eliot had given him. When Eliot entered upon his second marriage, Hayward had to find new accommodation; the break brought out the worst in him, he never forgave Eliot and they remained estranged.

Other links with the past whom I met included James Elroy Flecker's widow Hellé, a little bespectacled old Greek lady; Harold Monro's widow Alida, full of brisk energy; and Dorothy Wellesley, the close friend of W. B. Yeats, who much admired her work. Although long separated from her husband Gerald Wellesley, she had never divorced him, and when he became Duke of Wellington on the death of his nephew she took, and thereafter always used, the title of Duchess, much to his annoyance. She gave me a bad fish lunch in Tunbridge Wells and then took me to her nearby home, at which Yeats had been a frequent visitor. After tea she announced that she would retire to rest, and emerged an hour later very drunk. It was sad to see this once beautiful woman raddled and hideous.

The exhibition was a great success. Edith Sitwell opened it in her grandest style. She behaved like the most gracious kind of royalty; one felt privileged to have shaken her hand, and only afterwards did the effect seem slightly ridiculous. Auden was there, together with Spender, Dylan Thomas, Wyndham Lewis, Arthur Waley and many others. It was the only time I met Thomas; he was cold sober and enchanting. I remember being surprised how small he was, and by the bright blueness of his eyes. Our star items were Hopkins's notebooks and sketches, the prompt copy of Yeats's play *At the Hawk's Well* with corrections by both himself and Pound, Housman's own copy of *A Shropshire Lad*, Wilfred Owen's rough drafts of 'Apologia pro Poemate Meo' and 'Strange Meeting', Rupert Brooke's last letter, an early draft of Eliot's 'Little Gidding' with manuscript corrections, and Hardy's manuscripts of *Wessex Poems* with his own illustrations. Roy Campbell let me keep his contribution, a page from an old army notebook bearing on one side a couple of manuscript poems, two drawings of a picador and one of a fish, and on the other:

GRENADES

Corp. Rambanya   best in the platoon
L.Corp. Aloysius   excellent

Priv. Asim	O.K.
Bambata	O.K.
Bottle	O.K
Njimp	O.K.
Wata	O.K
Whiskey	O.K.

These others need a great deal of instruction: some of them are dangerous.

The Wanderobo
Boni minor
Epaloni
Pangapanga (very dangerous)
Muganda
Christopher
Trevor
Aboudu
Neta
Absalom
Maji
Motomoto
Elijah
Sam
Nduku

These are only fair

Sixpence	F
Denis	F
Tambala	F
Malambula	F
Shitehawk	F
Boni	F
Msilo	F
Nwele	F
Abdulla	F
Rihambo	F (nervous)

This bunch cannot learn to throw with a straight arm. They need practice. This is my suggestion – to send them to get round stones the size of grenades out of the Weru-weru river which is full of them and make them throw all day, backwards and forwards, till they learn a bit more.

I never discovered what all this referred to.

I was in England only briefly for the publication of my novel and this exhibition, for on leaving Uppsala the previous summer I had found myself unable to settle into any kind of a life in London. I felt little in common with the new writers of the fifties who were beginning to emerge, such as Kingsley Amis, John Wain and Philip Larkin. Most of my friends were dead or belonged to an older generation. After six months I returned, not to Uppsala but to Stockholm. Returning to Uppsala seemed to me rather like going back to teach at the school where one has been happy as a boy, always a dangerous recipe. My girlfriends there would have found new lovers, and I did not like the idea of living close to the university and not being a part of it. Stockholm was more cosmopolitan, and I had many friends there. I rented a small and shabby two-room apartment at Jarlaplan near the city centre. It had no bathroom, so that like many of the city's inhabitants I had to use the public baths, and my toilet was so small that when I washed at the tiny basin I had to stand with one foot on the lavatory seat. But I felt a sense of belonging, which I didn't in London, acquired a Finnish girlfriend, and that summer wrote a play to get Uppsala out of my system as I had written *The End of the Corridor* to lay the ghosts of Wellington. I set it not in Uppsala but in an unnamed remote town in the extreme north of Sweden. It had five characters, and the interweaving themes were: the difficulty, especially for a woman, of wrenching oneself off the rails on which circumstances or other people have set one; the peculiar problem of the female artist, because of the different significance which children have for women; and how some people can only find happiness through the unhappiness of others. It arose from a poem which I could not get out of my head, and a chance remark I heard about a certain custom practised in France.

The poem was Sidney Keyes's 'Death and the Maiden', which I have quoted on page 37. The previous autumn I had tried to write a novel based on the significance that I thought this poem possessed for me, called *The Sun Through Dark Glasses*, but it would not come.

That summer of 1951 a French friend asked if we in England ever ate ortolans. I said that as far as I knew we did not, and that I had never heard of them. She explained to me that they were small birds, and that in her part of France, the Landes district, there was a special way of breeding and killing them. This consisted in keeping the bird in a small box, holding a packet of grain to a hole in the box, and then shining a light through the grain. The bird, desperate to get at the light, pecks at the grain. This goes on for several weeks. Then, when it has eaten itself so full that it cannot stand or see, they drown it in cognac. Gourmets regard it as an exceptional delicacy.

This picture seemed to me to complement the poem and the result was the play, which I called *The Ortolan*.

At the end of 1951 I returned to live in London, hoping to establish myself there as a playwright. But my agent, David Higham, warned me that in his experience it took even a subsequently successful play by an unknown dramatist six years to reach the stage. There was no real venue for minority plays then unless they were verse dramas for the Mercury Theatre in Notting Hill Gate, which had launched Christopher Fry and Ronald Duncan. Peter Hall had not yet started his regime at the Arts Theatre, nor George Devine at the Royal Court, and the 'fringe' as we know it today did not exist at all.

A few people showed interest in *The Ortolan*. Terence Rattigan, who had liked *The End of the Corridor*, asked to read it and wrote to me that he thought it a big advance on the novel; he 'liked the characters, motivation and dialogue, and found it all convincing', though he felt it needed cutting. He took me to lunch at the Caprice to discuss it, and gave me much excellent advice. Among other things, he said: 'Never forget that the spoken word is not twice nor three times, but five times as potent as the written word, so that what would occupy a page in a novel should take up only five lines in a play.' He recommended *The Ortolan* to a couple of directors, but they rejected it. A German play publisher thought it would be 'of great interest to the German-speaking countries', and wanted to publish it in Germany, but this never happened. A friend who represented the great French actress Edwige Feuillère in Britain sent it to her, but her lover and agent Pol Quentin, though finding it 'a first play which gives proof of great talent and augurs well for its author's future', felt that it was not for her. A director at the Gothenburg Stadsteater, Åke Falck, wanted to stage it there, but the head of the theatre said no. Peter Glenville, then one of the most successful directors in London, summed up the general reaction when writing that he found it 'extremely interesting and most intelligently written, but too special and unsympathetic to appeal to any sort of general audience'.

So *The Ortolan* gathered dust, and I did not follow it up as I ought to have done. A different kind of publisher from Billy Collins might have helped, but neither he nor anyone else in the firm, pleasant as some of them were, was the kind of midwife I needed. Other writers would have shown more resilience, but I stopped believing in myself as a dramatist or novelist just as I had ceased to believe in myself as a poet, and retired, sulking, into the tent of translation.

Billy had been sent a Swedish novel about the Vikings, *Röde Orm*, by Frans G. Bengtsson, a brilliant essayist and historian who before the war had written a fine life of Charles XII, the eighteenth-century warrior-king on whom Dr Johnson wrote a famous epitaph. Billy asked me to read it for them; I recommended it strongly. But the translation fee that Billy offered, 10s. (50p) a page, was so wretched that all the recognized Swedish translators (not that they were many) turned it down; the book was over six hundred pages and obviously difficult to translate. So I was asked to do it. I was not sure whether my Swedish was good enough, but I had nothing original that I wanted to write and thought this might be an interesting exercise. It took seven and a half months, and I got £350, which worked out at under £11 a week.

A bad translation of the first half of the book had appeared in America during the war and had fallen dead from the press, so I suggested to Billy that if it now succeeded – if, say, it went into paperback – he might grant me an additional fee. He assured me that in such a case I would not find him ungenerous. The book appeared under the English title of *The Long Ships* and got handsome reviews, as did I. Within two years it had sold 27,000 hardback copies in England and 15,000 in the USA, and subsequently went into repeated paperback editions in both countries. Thirty-five years later, it still sells steadily. But I never saw another penny from Billy.

Bengtsson was one of the finest talkers I have ever heard. Physically, he bore a striking resemblance to Dr Johnson, and he talked as Boswell tells us Johnson did, forcefully and pithily, even in English. He was widely read in at least seven languages, and continually amazed me by his knowledge of the backwaters of English, French and American literature. I met him only twice, but received many letters from him while I was working on his book, in vigorous if sometimes eccentric English; they, like his conversation, were an education.

At about this time my father had developed valvular disease of the heart, and was not expected to live long, though in the event, and against the predictions of the doctors, he survived another four years. I had been living with him since my return from Sweden; the flat in Portman Square was large enough for me to feel reasonably independent. Our relationship was now very close and remained so until his death. I took up hockey and cricket again, keeping goal for Hampstead, a useful side, and playing cricket for two pleasant wandering clubs, the Jesters and the Bushmen. The Bushmen had been founded during the war to provide exercise for the BBC Overseas Services, then as now based in Bush House in the Strand, and contained several distinguished figures. Graham Greene's younger brother Hugh and Patrick Gordon-Walker, later to become Director-General of the BBC and Foreign Secretary respectively, turned out regularly for us, as did my old tutor Edmund Blunden and the great West Indian cricketer Learie Constantine, a regular and valued broadcaster who once hit fifty in under three overs for us against a Buckinghamshire village. I rarely got many runs, but did well enough at hockey to earn a Middlesex trial. But Middlesex then had two international goalkeepers, Day and Archer, so I never played for the county.

I also joined the Savile Club, to which I had been taken during the war by Cecil Day Lewis and Edward Sackville-West, and found it very stimulating. Its membership was catholic, in that it was open to men of all professions, though with a bias towards writers. In the past, Thomas Hardy, Robert Louis Stevenson, Henry James, Herbert Spencer, Rudyard Kipling, H. G. Wells, W. B. Yeats, Max Beerbohm, E. M. Forster and Lytton Strachey had been members. Founded in 1871 with the stated purpose of offering a less expensive membership fee and subscription than other clubs so that more young people could join, and with communal tables for meals so that members could converse as they ate and not read alone at little tables, it had maintained the tradition that nobody, however important, behaved grandly. You talked to your neighbour on equal terms. One senior member when I joined was Viscount Maugham, the elder brother of Somerset Maugham and a former Lord Chancellor. He was only one of several who had been elected in Queen Victoria's reign; it was not uncommon to find oneself chatting to people who remembered James and Hardy. Wells, who spent a lot of his time there, had died only four years before I joined.

The Savile was unlike other London clubs in its informality and its willingness to include mavericks. The level of tolerance was high, and I can recall only two instances in which serious action had to be taken. The most notorious occurred during the war and concerned John Davenport, a choleric and sometimes violent writer who was the more dangerous by reason of his having won a boxing Blue while at Oxford. He had been, and may still have been, a Communist at the time. On this occasion he drank heavily at the bar for some time before proceeding upstairs to dinner. As he sat drinking his tomato soup, his eye was caught by a white waistcoat and tails worn by an old and eminent gentleman dining opposite him. 'You're dressed up,' said Davenport, to which the old gentleman replied that his granddaughter was celebrating her twenty-first birthday and he was going to her party. 'Drinking champagne, I suppose?' said Davenport. The old gentleman beamed and nodded. 'You bloody swine,' said Davenport. 'People are being killed all over the world and you doll up and drink champagne,' and he threw the remains of his tomato soup over the white waistcoat. For this he was ordered out of the dining-room.

Davenport returned to the bar and drank for a further hour. Then, needing to visit the lavatory, he walked through a room known as the 'sandpit' (because of the colour of its walls) in which several elderly members were listening to the news on a wireless set. The main item concerned an advance by the Russians, prompting one member to remark that these Reds had something in them. Davenport halted in his tracks. 'You bloody old bastards! When they were trying to build a decent country you did all you could to stop them, and now they're dying for your sake all you can say is they've got something in them. You're not worthy to listen to the news of their victories', and he yanked the flex out of its plug so fiercely that it broke and the transmission could be heard no more. Davenport then proceeded into the hall, where the third and most controversial event of the evening took place.

The Savile members were in general a liberal-minded lot, but we included one dreadful Fascist, a Major Pollard, of whom Raymond Postgate once remarked that he had not merely flown Franco into Spain in 1936, but boasted of having done so. Major Pollard was an expert in ballistics. If anything was fired up, he was the man to tell you where it would come down. His intolerance knew few bounds; years later, on being asked where he lived, he named some suburb, adding: 'It's not the most convenient, but it has one advantage. There aren't any niggers there', and when his questioner said: 'Don't you like black people?', Major Pollard shouted for the whole room to hear: 'I hate 'em.' Nobody in the Club could stand him, but he had been elected long before anyone had heard of Fascism, and we had to put up with him.

During the war Major Pollard worked at some ministry, from which he would patriotically walk each evening after work (we were all exhorted not to use public transport if we could avoid it), take up a position against the mantelpiece in the bar and deliver a detailed and boring account of his day's work, with many a reminder of how secret it was ('You'll understand I can't go into details about this'). On this occasion, he happened to enter the Club at the precise moment when John Davenport was passing through the hall on his way to the lavatory. Unpopular as Major Pollard was in the Savile, by no one was he hated more than by John Davenport. As Major Pollard came through the door, no doubt looking forward to describing his day to the members eagerly awaiting his appearance, he was confronted by the gorilla-like figure of Davenport, who said: 'You're the worst of the bloody lot', advanced on him and threw him out into the night.

But Major Pollard had not been a soldier for nothing. He carried a swordstick, in case he should be attacked in the black-out. This he now unsheathed, and the porter was treated to the unusual sight of a member entering the Club with a drawn sword and advancing on a fellow-member who disarmed him easily, broke the sword over his knee and threw him a second time into the night. Major Pollard did not attempt to force a third entry. This action of Davenport's was generally approved, but his earlier behaviour was not, and he was asked to resign.

Then there was the unfortunate incident concerning Gilbert Harding and Hubert Clifford. Harding was the most celebrated television personality of the fifties, a reputation which he had built mainly through rudeness. He was famous for insulting people, limiting himself to those who were unimportant and timid; waiters were his particular target, as they were to Evelyn Waugh. Soon after I had joined, he picked on me as a whipping-boy; his first remark to me, on my second or third entry into the Club, was: 'You look a very conceited young man. You must be either very rich or very important. Which?' I replied that I was neither, whereupon he continued his attack in terms which I have forgotten. When some months later a good review of my novel appeared, his attitude changed, and thereafter he was genial and excellent company. On one occasion he reverted to his former rudeness, but by this time I was less timid, and emptied a glass of beer over his head, which quietened him immediately.

Harding was homosexual but, he explained to everyone, impotent. He was an unhappy, impossible, yet often endearing man. One evening he came to the Club with two young male guests, one of them an American, and sat drinking with them in the bar. Hubert

Clifford, a portly red-haired Australian of about Gilbert's age, who was head of music for the BBC Light Programme and was fairly drunk, took it into his head to walk up and down in front of Gilbert and his guests with a glass of brandy in his hand, saying loudly: 'I am normal.' Gilbert, who for once was not drunk, endured this for a while, then said: 'By normal, I take it you mean pacing the pavements of Piccadilly pawing the soiled smalls of prostitutes.' At this, Clifford threw his brandy into Gilbert's face and rushed at him, and the two grossly overweight men rolled locked on the Club floor.

An ex-colonel named Edward Crankshaw, who wrote with distinction for the *Observer* on military and other matters, tried to separate them but, being small, failed, and was rolled by them on to the brandy glass, which broke and cut him badly so that he bled on to the carpet. At this the young American panicked, ran to the phone, dialled 999 and asked for the police. When he got them, he said: 'Come quickly. There's a terrible fight.' 'Where?' 'It's a Club.' 'What Club?' 'I think it's called the Savage.' The police promptly sent a carload of constables to the Savage Club in Carlton House Terrace, which proved to be empty except for four elderly members playing bridge. Meanwhile, at the Savile, a large Alsatian which belonged to another member and had been left tethered in the hall got loose, wandered into the bar and began lapping up Edward Crankshaw's blood. Somehow Gilbert and Hubert were separated, and Gilbert went into the street to find a taxi; but Hubert pursued him there, held him against the Club railings and began kicking his shins. For this, Hubert was suspended from membership for six months.

Such incidents were, however, the exception rather than the rule. It was in general the most civilized place, and a splendid introduction for a young writer to the literary and artistic world of London. On my first visit as a member I found myself urinating in the Club lavatory next to an old gentleman named Sir Ernest Pooley, whose wife's first husband had had a pass made at him by Oscar Wilde. As we stood side by side at the urinals, he turned to me and said: 'Emerson once observed that every major pleasure known to man except eating and drinking consists of one form or another of emission.' I began to think this was a place I might find congenial.

9

A Mixed Membership

One of the doyens of the Savile was Compton Mackenzie, who had been a member since 1912. I was anxious to meet him, since Rosamond Lehmann had named him as the most brilliant talker she had heard, as well as being a skilled mimic of the great men he had known, such as Henry James and D. H. Lawrence. Mackenzie was a vain, kindly old man, but by the time I met him, he had become a monumental bore. He no longer conversed, but held forth, and that repetitively; even if you were alone with him, he addressed you as though you were a hundred people who had paid to listen. His talk was punctuated by enormous pauses while he sniffed at and mused over a cigar before lighting it, or merely mused. Usually one can escape from aged bores because they have to go out fairly often to relieve themselves, but Mackenzie had even found a way of stopping you from doing that. Once, when I was closeted with him in an otherwise empty bar, he was in the midst of some interminable story. 'And then – now this will interest you, my boy – Her Majesty . . .' (enormous pause, while he savoured his drink). 'What was I saying?' 'Queen Alexandra, Sir Compton.' 'Ah, yes. Her Majesty turned to me, and said – ' He touched my knee and rose. 'Just a moment, my boy.' And off he went to the gents. How could one not be there when he returned?

On another occasion, when staying at the Club, I returned late one night to find it empty except for Compton Mackenzie and Gilbert Harding engaged in an extraordinary dialogue. Conversation is hardly the word, for what they said could have been printed as an example of how not to write a play. One held forth at leisure while the other made no pretence of listening; then the speaker would pause, to retrieve a match from the floor or squirt some soda into his whisky, at which as though by some prearranged agreement the listener would begin speaking and the speaker fall silent, rather like 'hand-out' at squash. They were still at it when I went to bed half an hour later.

Somebody told me that the secret of getting the best out of Mackenzie was to turn the conversation, or rather his monologue, from himself to the people he had known. Next time I found myself next to him at lunch, I said: 'You knew Henry James well, did you not, Sir Compton?' 'Indeed I did. He admired my novels.' My heart sank. However, he continued: 'I remember the last time I met Henry. Not long before he died, I went down to have luncheon with him at Rye. We had an excellent luncheon – he had a very good cook – and afterwards we drank coffee in the garden in the sun.' This is gold, I thought; how could I have found this man boring? 'And I remember, I said to him: "Of course, Henry, the difficulty with your novels is . . ."' And for the next half hour he told me what he had said to Henry James, none of it remotely interesting or original. Not a word that Henry James had said, if he had got one in, was quoted.

Still, I reflected, it had been shortly before James had died, and they had been sitting in the sun after a good luncheon, so perhaps James had in fact not said anything. I tried to think of someone else Mackenzie had known who could be relied on not to have remained silent. 'You also knew D. H. Lawrence well, did you not, Sir Compton?' 'Ah, David was completely different.' My spirits rose. This would be worth listening to. 'I remember once I was staying with David and Frieda on Capri, and David and I went for a walk. David was a wonderful person to go on a country stroll with. He would talk about animals and birds, and trees and flowers, and you really felt he was closer to them than to other humans.' 'Yes, yes?' 'Well, we were walking through an olive grove – I can see it to this day – and I said to him: "Of course, David, people are always going to say about your writing . . ."' And the next half hour was occupied by what he had said to Lawrence. When I at last escaped, he had not told me a single word that either James or Lawrence had uttered. I regard this as the most wasted hour of my life, when I think what he could have told me.

Another tedious member was the Irish poet W. J. Turner, author of the splendid 'Romance', about Chimborazo and Cotopaxi ('When I was but thirteen or so . . .'). He was tall and spidery, and had a way of turning across you as he sat beside you on a sofa and grasping your lapel, so that there was no means of escape. My father suggested that I should have a special coat made with detachable lapels, so that I could slip away leaving him still clutching one of them in his hand. What made it worse was that the poor man had very bad breath. However, he was, like Mackenzie, a kindly man, so that one could not be brusque as one would have been had the offender been Major Pollard.

Even more boring than either of these was a rich American named Everts Scudder. He lived in splendour in the Nash terraces and did nothing. A large man, who claimed to have won a tennis Blue at Oxford (but I looked him up in the records, and he was not there), he was notoriously mean. He persuaded the wine committee to lay in some very cheap Chilean wine which nobody else could stomach; it existed only in full bottles and, as Scudder could not manage a full bottle alone, he would waylay new members at the bar and suggest that they went up to lunch together. Such an offer could not politely be refused and, once seated, Scudder would say: 'They have an excellent Chilean red here. Care to join me in a bottle?' When they went to the cashier's desk to pay, Scudder would say: 'Split the wine between me and Mr . . .'

One summer evening, Scudder invited the novelist Winston Graham to stroll back with him to his house, ten minutes' walk. Winston agreed, and when they arrived was surprised to hear Scudder say: 'Care to come in for a nightcap?' Nobody could remember Scudder having offered anyone a drink before. Glancing at the bookshelves while Scudder poured a small whisky, Winston noticed a slim and faded volume bearing the title *Poems*, by Everts Scudder. Before he could stop himself, Winston said: 'I didn't know you were a poet, Everts.' 'Sit down,' said Scudder. 'I'll read some to you,' and proceeded to read aloud the entire volume; slim indeed, but not that slim. At length it was finished but, Winston told me, it was one of those evenings when words come out of one's mouth before one can stop them, and he heard himself saying: 'How very splendid. Was that your only book?' 'No,' said Scudder, and reached up to the shelf. Desperately, Winston said: 'Everts, are you sure your voice isn't getting tired?' 'A little, perhaps,' said Scudder, and handed the book to Winston. 'You read them to me.' And Winston found himself reading Scudder's poems to Scudder.

Denys Kilham Roberts, the Secretary-General of the Society of Authors, wrote him an epitaph while he was still alive:

Stranger, spare a passing shudder
Over the bones of Everts Scudder.
Here Greek meets Greek on equal terms;
The worms bore him, he bores the worms.

Arguably the worst bore ever to enter the Savile, for he contrived on a single visit to drive the entire membership, or anyway all those who were present, to distraction, was not a member but a guest, a Swedish novelist named Vilhelm Moberg. The publisher Max Reinhardt telephoned me one day to say that he was issuing one of Moberg's novels and asked if I would care to join the two of them for lunch at the Club. Moberg was a fine novelist of working-class origins who had achieved a success in America with two books, *The Emigrants* and *The Immigrants*, about a nineteenth-century farmer who had gone with his family to seek his fortune in the New World, though the flat journalistic translation had hindered their appreciation in Britain. A huge man with a powerful voice, he reminded one of that eighteenth-century Methodist preacher George Whitefield who, we are assured, could comfortably be heard by crowds of twenty thousand people. After a few minutes, Max mentioned in some context or other the word 'university'. 'University!' roared Moberg. 'I've no time for universities. I tell you a story. In Sweden we have a university called Lund. Last year they write and say they wish to do me the honour of making me a doctor *honoris causa*. I say, why do I wish to be a doctor, I am a famous novelist and playwright – I write plays too, Mr Reinhardt – my works are translated into many languages, I have won many prizes. But if you wish to make me a doctor, O.K. But then' – and now he began to roar so as to render any other conversation in the bar virtually impossible – 'the university Chancellor, a Mr Thomson, not a professor, not a scholar at all, a civil servant, he tell them: "You must not make this Mr Moberg a doctor *honoris causa*, because he is a republican." What do you think of that?'

Max and I agreed that this was disgraceful, and escorted him upstairs to lunch, where Max cleverly seated him at the head of the long table. This pleased Moberg, as did the steak he ordered, which he spread liberally with mustard before cutting it. During the meal, however, Max made the mistake of asking him whether he had ever visited Oxford or Cambridge. 'No,' said Moberg. 'I've no time for universities. I tell you a story. In Sweden we have a university called Lund . . .' And the whole table heard the story a second time.

We repaired to the bar for coffee and brandy, both Max and I resolved not to mention universities again. But some pretext arose, I cannot remember what, and for the third time the assembled membership heard the story of Vilhelm Moberg and Chancellor Thomson. When Moberg at last left, a very old member named Wallis, who chaired the wine committee and (unlike Mackenzie) enjoyed reminiscing about Henry James, came over to Max and me as we sat recovering in our corner like boxers, and said: 'I haven't the faintest idea who Chancellor Thomson was, but in my opinion he was perfectly right to refuse that man an honorary degree.'

Eva Tisell, who was Moberg's play agent, told me that he behaved similarly at a lunch which Ingrid Bergman and her then husband, the impresario Lars Schmidt, gave for him in France. Ingrid Bergman had invited some distinguished guests to meet Moberg, including Cocteau, but none of them got a word in because Moberg repeatedly told them how his latest play had been refused by the Stadsteater in Malmö. A few years later the poor man committed suicide, swimming out into a lake and leaving a note behind him.

Our touchiest member, apart from Major Pollard, was probably J. B. Priestley. Behind a mask of overpowering *bonhomie*, he was quick to take offence, even with old friends. Ralph Richardson, with whom he had shared several considerable successes in the theatre, told me that when, after lunching together, they went to the desk to pay, the cashier asked: 'Shall I charge the wine to you, Sir Ralph, or shall I split it?' As was the custom when members ate together, Ralph said: 'Split it.' At this, according to Ralph, 'Jack went red in the face, didn't say a word over coffee, and I had to take him out and buy him a pound of his favourite tobacco, which set me back eight quid.' On another occasion, having purchased a new car, he invited Ralph for a drive and, once out in the countryside, asked Ralph what he thought of it. Ralph praised it highly, but ventured a small criticism of the wood used for the dashboard. Priestley said: 'I asked you out to enjoy yourself, not to criticize,' turned the car round and headed for home.

I once told him about my weekend with Sassoon. 'I knew Sassoon,' said Priestley. 'He was a funny chap. A few years ago he published a book about George Meredith.' 'Extraordinary,' I said. 'I suppose he thought some people might be interested in him.' 'No, no, no,' said Priestley angrily. 'You've missed the point completely. I'd written a very good book about George Meredith.' He was incredulous that anyone could regard his as anything but the last word on the subject.

Priestley had less sense of the ridiculous than anyone I have known, with the possible exception of the actor Donald Wolfit. When my Ibsen biography won the Whitbread Award in 1971, Priestley was chairman of the judges, and on my arrival at the ceremony I was presented to him. We had not met often, and he had excusably forgotten me. The person in charge said: 'Mr Priestley, this is Mr Meyer, the author of the Ibsen biography.' Without any prefatory remark, Priestley said: 'I did more for the art of dramatic exposition than Ibsen.' Stephen Potter told me that, during the fifties, some of the Savile members were discussing in the billiards room what they would do if they got a hundred thousand pounds, at that time a small fortune. Priestley rolled in like a galleon, and Stephen said: 'Jack, what would you do if you got a hundred thousand pounds?' 'I've got a hundred thousand pounds.' 'But what would you do if you got another hundred thousand pounds?' 'I've got another hundred thousand pounds.'

Another member with little sense of the ridiculous as far as his own work was concerned was C. P. Snow. Although kindly and encouraging to young writers, he resented any criticism of his own fiction. John Morris, who ran the Third Programme and had climbed Everest, came into the Club one Sunday when Snow's latest novel had been damned in the *Observer*. Morris commiserated with him. Snow replied: 'It's annoying. But one rides these things, because one knows one will be read in two hundred years.' Even this confidence was surpassed by John Braine, author of a best-seller called *Room at the Top*. Some of us were discussing which were the ten greatest novels of the twentieth century. The obvious ones were named, and some less obvious; then Braine, who had hitherto been silent, said: 'You've all forgotten one pretty obvious candidate.' When pressed to name his choice, he said: '*Room at the Top*', and when we laughed, said: 'I'm not joking.'

Our two most distinguished actor members were Ralph Richardson and Robert Donat. Of Ralph Richardson I shall write later. Robert Donat was reputed in the profession to be neurotic and awkward to work with. Ralph told me how when they were young unknowns at the Birmingham Rep, the director, H. K. Ayliff, had addressed Donat somewhat brusquely, as was his wont. Donat did not turn up for rehearsal next morning, and Ralph was sent to see if he was ill. He found Donat in bed, vowing that he would never work again with Ayliff. Ralph had great difficulty in persuading him. But as a fellow-member Donat was delightful and very accessible;

he frequented the Club a lot, especially when he lived in a small flat which the Club owned in the mews behind. He had been born in Manchester, the son of a Polish immigrant and a Yorkshire mother; he remembered how his father had tried to dissuade him from speaking in a thick Manchester accent. Once I was chatting with Walter Greenwood, the author of *Love on the Dole*, that fine working-class novel about the depression of the 1930s. Walter had the broadest of Manchester accents. Donat came in, and was talking at the bar in his usual aristocratic voice when Walter spotted him and said: ''Ullo, Robert.' Robert turned, cried: ''Ullo, Walter!', sat down with us and without affectation dropped into his own natural accent which was identical with Walter's, and equally broad. I could barely understand much of what they said.

Another actor member who was rewarding to listen to was Esmé Percy, who had made his London début as Romeo in 1905. He had studied for the stage in Paris, where he had even acted with Sarah Bernhardt. He gave a vivid and, I was told, lifelike impression of how she declaimed her lines. Once I asked him if he had seen Edith Evans's legendary début as Cressida for the Elizabethan Stage Society in 1912, when she was still a milliner. 'See her, my boy? I acted opposite her.' 'Were you Pandarus?' I asked without thinking, for in his old age Esmé's appearance was slightly grotesque. There was an enormous pause. 'I was Troilus,' he at length replied. 'I was rather beautiful then.'

Stephen Potter, the author of *Gamesmanship*, practised that science and Lifemanship with remarkable success, even though we were all on our guard against him. When I made some general remark about Swedish national characteristics, Stephen said: 'Not in the south, surely.' 'You're right,' I said. 'I didn't know you knew Sweden that well.' 'I don't,' said Stephen. 'But if anyone generalizes about any country, it's usually safe to say: "Not in the south".' On another occasion I was playing in a snooker doubles against him after lunch. He was by far the best player in the Club, and my task was never to leave him an opening. I was succeeding pretty well. Stephen began to glance at his watch, played several hurried strokes, and muttered to his partner that he had an appointment at three. The rest of us began to play more quickly, I made an error which let him in for a break of fifty and they won, whereupon Stephen sat down with a newspaper in the reading-room until tea-time. Once I had to play him in the final of the Club competition. It was the best of three frames; I had won the previous year and was twenty years his junior. Before we started, he said that he had promised to take his wife to dinner at the Garrick; should the match go the full distance, would I be his guest there and play the final frame afterwards? How could I refuse? At one all, he took me to the Garrick and dined and wined me well, then drove me back to the Savile, where I offered little resistance.

Stephen was one of the wittiest men I have known. As with Frank Muir today, Stephen's wit was of the best and rarest kind in that it arose naturally from the subject under conversation, instead of consisting of anecdotes produced on flimsy pretexts. This was equally true of one of the most legendary of English wits, Max Beerbohm, whom I was lucky enough to get an introduction to from the thriller writer Selwyn Jepson and whom I visited at Rapallo in 1953. I was driving round Italy with a girlfriend, foreign currency was still limited, and we found ourselves very short as we turned back towards France, where we had some francs waiting for us. I thought we might be able to borrow a few lira from Beerbohm. I phoned, and was answered by Lady Beerbohm, a German lady who had formerly been secretary to Gerhart Hauptmann. She greeted my request to drop in very suspiciously, but at length agreed. When we arrived, she said she was sorry if she had sounded unwelcoming, but 'So many English people try to borrow money off Max. You would not believe it.' So there was no question of raising that subject. Max, however, was enchanting. He was very shy as he sat with his bulging eyes and plump beringed little fingers clasped on the table before him. I asked if any of the people he caricatured had taken offence, and he said yes, two: Rudyard Kipling and King Edward VII. Kipling, of course, he had cruelly savaged, but I asked what had particularly vexed the King. 'I drew him in a kilt. And what was very naughty, I made him fill the whole frame. In profile.' 'What was so wrong about that?' 'I made the drawing twice as wide as it was tall. His Majesty was very displeased.'

He spoke of Oscar Wilde, saying that although everyone only wanted to hear him talk, he would bring all those present, even the mousiest, into the conversation, so that all felt that they were taking part. Remembering my own similar experience with Shaw, I wonder if that may have been a characteristic of that generation. Perhaps the greatest tribute to Wilde's genius as a talker is that Shaw, Yeats, George Moore and Beerbohm, all famous talkers themselves, agreed that Wilde was the greatest they had known. Max signed a book of his that I had brought with me, complaining as he began to write that it, a wartime edition, had been 'printed on blotting-paper'.

He also paid me the only compliment I can recall having received on my looks; in a letter to Selwyn Jepson he mentioned our visit, and said: 'The young man had a fine head.'

Interesting guests often appeared at the Savile. I met Robert Graves there several times, once carrying an enormous mushroom, a good foot across, wrapped in newspaper. He unwrapped it in one of the public rooms to discuss it with his host, who shared his interest in fungi. There was a Club rule which stated that no business documents might be brought into the public rooms, and this had a wide application, covering works of art and the like that members wished to peruse together, but nobody could be sure whether it covered a mushroom; and anyway, the conversation was scholarly and fascinating, so it was allowed to continue. Graves was large and powerfully built, nervous, touchy and childlike, usually entertaining except for a tendency to read some silly comic verse that he had recently written; I remember one or two vapid limericks. Walking down Bond Street with him one day after lunch, I tried to get him on to the subject of his novels, which I admire, but he dismissed them as hack stuff written for money and would not discuss them. He told me how Wilfred Owen had given him a set of eleven apostle spoons for his wedding ('not one for Judas'). I did not remind him that when editing *Cherwell* I had received a furious letter from him threatening libel for a review by Sidney Keyes we had published which suggested that he and his mistress Laura Riding formed a mutual admiration society.

One of my favourite members of the Savile was Raymond Postgate. Born in 1896, he was an author of considerable variety; his works included one of the earliest books in English about the Russian Revolution, fine biographies of the Irish nationalist Robert Emmet, John Wilkes and his own father-in-law George Lansbury, all doughty fighters for liberty, and several excellent novels, one of which, *Verdict of Twelve*, has often rightly been named as one of the best ten murder mysteries. His father, Professor J. P. Postgate, had been a distinguished classical scholar of such reactionary views that he disinherited Raymond and his sister because of their left-wing sympathies, for which of course he was to blame. Defeated by A. E. Housman for the Professorship of Latin at Cambridge, he had died as the result of a grotesque collision between his bicycle and, of all things, a steam-roller. Life seemed to have departed from his body, but as the ambulance men lifted it, he opened his eyes and said: 'Take me to Addenbrooke's

19 Uppsala, 1948

20 Uppsala, 1949

21 Uppsala, 1950

Hospital. I have a subscription there.' Only then did he give up the ghost.

In 1949 Edward Hulton, the owner and founder of *Picture Post*, started a weekly magazine called *The Leader*, with Stephen Potter as editor. Raymond, a wine and food expert, had long regretted the absence in Britain of any food guide such as the *Club des Sans Clubs*. The only British equivalent was one which paid for itself by advertisements from restaurants which it included, thus, in Raymond's view, compromising its integrity; nor, since it could not afford to pay a staff of inspectors, could its editor and his relations inspect restaurants even once a year. After the war, many ex-servicemen had invested their demobilization gratuities in starting restaurants, but there was no way apart from advertising by which they could become known to potential clients. Raymond hit on the brilliantly simple notion of inviting readers of *The Leader* to send him details of good eating-places in their home area, and to report on those named by others. Stephen liked the idea; so the Good Food Club came into being, and such was the response that when after a few issues *The Leader* closed, the publisher Cassell suggested that Raymond should edit an annual book. Unlike editors of previous British guides, Raymond stipulated in his preface to the first and all subsequent editions that no diner should disclose that he or she was a member of the Good Food Club 'at least until their meal or their stay is over. For if the proprietor knew what they were doing, the tests they make would obviously have no value.' He also laid down five strict rules which differentiated his guide from its British predecessors: no advertisements would be accepted; no free meals or hospitality; no recommendations from innkeepers or those connected with them; no payments for recommendations; and, most importantly, 'no person is authorised to promise or withhold an entry . . . and anyone pretending to do so should be treated by the innkeeper as an impostor'.

The response was extraordinary. It is no exaggeration to say that this initiative of Postgate's transformed the eating scene in Britain. As he wrote in his preface to the 1952 edition: 'A good new restaurant, or an old one which improves its cuisine, need not battle for years in obscurity; it will almost certainly be signalled to the *Guide* by some traveller within the year . . . It is no good the proprietor "playing favourites"; he cannot know which quiet customer is watching him on the Club's behalf.'

I first came across *The Good Food Guide* through Hugh Greene.

We were playing cricket together in 1953 at Great Missenden in Buckinghamshire for the Bushmen, and after the game Hugh suggested that we should dine at the Bell in a nearby village, Aston Clinton, an old inn which had been taken over by an ex-solicitor named Gerard Harris. In its then tiny dining-room we ate wonderfully well and very cheaply, and when I asked Hugh: 'How on earth did you discover this?', he explained about the *Guide*. (Gerard Harris later told me that without it a restaurant such as his, in an obscure village, could never have got off the ground.) I met Postgate at the Savile and soon became one of his inspectors. The job was unpaid; we received £3 towards the expense of each meal. It was not as much fun as it may sound, for by the nature of things one was only required to inspect restaurants about which Raymond had received conflicting reports. Some of these inevitably proved to be poor, and after five bad dinners all one wanted was a plate of cold ham at home. At first I rashly offered to test doubtful Indian and Pakistani restaurants in north-west London. At the first, near King's Cross station, a punch-up developed between the proprietor and a customer who tried to refuse payment for his very drunk companion's curry on the ground that 'She's only toyed with it, she hasn't eaten any, you can sell it to someone else.' The next night, after another curry in Paddington, I got food poisoning, at which Raymond took pity on me and promoted me to doubtful French and Italian restaurants in Chelsea and Kensington.

Unexpectedly, being an inspector for *The Good Food Guide* had a considerable influence on my writing. As well as testing restaurants, I had to write about one-third of the entries, in a close imitation of Raymond's style. He was the perfect model (and editor) for a young writer, demanding maximum concision and clarity, and severe on any hint of pretentiousness or floridity, two faults of which, like most young writers, I was guilty. The *Sunday Times*, reviewing one year's issue, especially praised 'Mr Postgate's inimitable manner of writing', and quoted an entry which had been written by me.

In the early years of the *Guide*, all the office work was done by Raymond, his wife Daisy and me from their home in Hendon. I was always greeted on arrival, however early the hour, by the opening of some special bottle from his cellar. One morning, soon after the present Queen's accession, he said: 'Today I'm going to offer you a Madeira specially bottled for the Queen's coronation.' 'How nice,' I said. 'You don't sound very excited.' I wasn't, for it did not sound particularly enticing, but I said: 'No, I'm sure it's very good.' Raymond said: 'You haven't asked me which Queen.' It was 1837 Madeira, and was remarkable, like a kind of not too sweet butterscotch heavily alcoholized.

Raymond Postgate was an infinitely rewarding man, and to work with him daily was a liberal education. He was, I should think, unique among British authors of his generation in having had one of his books praised by Lenin. Soon after the Russian revolution, H. G. Wells, a close friend of Raymond, visited Lenin, who mentioned approvingly a pamphlet which Raymond had published in 1918 when he was only twenty-two, *The International During the War*. Wells asked Lenin if he would sign a photograph of himself for Raymond, which Lenin did, and this stood proudly framed on Raymond's desk. Unfortunately, Lenin had signed at the bottom of the photograph across his dark jacket – and perhaps the ink in Russia then was of poor quality – so that no inscription was detectable; if you looked hard, you might persuade yourself that something was there. But of course one did not dare to mention this, and no doubt Raymond, whose eyesight was not very sharp, was unaware of the deterioration.

As a distinguished writer on wine, Raymond was naturally a member of the Savile wine committee, and when lunching there he would engage me in long conversations on the subject. I have, sadly, never had much of a palate for wine, so would simply agree with whatever he said, following my usual practice when involved in a discussion about something of which I know little, or in a language which I do not properly understand, of occasionally repeating the last word spoken by the other person with a question mark after it. By this means I have often succeeded in creating an illusion of expertise. At the wedding reception of a friend in France, I found myself cornered by the bride's father who addressed me rapidly in French – which I speak appallingly and understand very imperfectly – about music, of which I know nothing. I followed the principle described. '. . . *à la Conservatoire*.' 'Conservatoire?' '*Oui! . . . Mahler et Saint-Saëns*.' '*Saint-Saëns?*' '*Précisement!*' At length he moved off, leaving me with very little idea of what he had been talking about, but a few minutes later his daughter came up helpless with laughter and said: 'My father says: "Who is that Englishman who speaks such perfect French and knows so much about music?"'

One day at the Savile, the chairman of the wine committee, Bernard Wallis, that old gentleman who had approved Chancellor Thomson's veto against Vilhelm Moberg, said: 'Meyer, a vacancy on the wine committee has occurred. I wonder if you would be willing to fill it?' I said I knew nothing about wine, to which he replied: 'Nonsense. Postgate tells me he has had many conversations with you on the subject, and that you have expressed several excellent opinions.' When I continued to protest, he said: 'You're being too modest. Think it over.' I did, and decided that at worst I could get pleasantly drunk free once a month, and at best I might learn something; and I reckoned that I could probably conceal my ignorance from the others as I had from Raymond; so I agreed. How could my lack of knowledge matter with a team of experts?

In the event, I found that my opinions were decisive. The other members were an Australian who was an expert on cigars, which we also had to decide about, but who seemed to know almost as little about wine as I did and spent much of his time trying to persuade us to buy an Australian champagne which nobody else liked, and a fierce ex-naval officer named Commander Kenderdine, who held as strong views about everything as Raymond but almost invariably differed from him. Wallis always sat on the fence, saying: 'As chairman, I must be neutral.' Thus, with the Australian unwilling to commit himself, mine was frequently the casting vote. At our first meeting, it fell to me to decide whether we would buy a considerable quantity of this claret or that. I was fond of Raymond but frightened of Kenderdine. I tasted both wines, doing everything I had seen the others do, and could not honestly tell any difference between them. Everyone, especially Raymond and Kenderdine, watched me closely. At length I said: 'This seems the better.' Kenderdine smiled, and Raymond looked wrathful. 'But,' I continued, 'will it be in a year's time?' This was regarded as the judgement of Solomon. I forget which we chose – perhaps some of both – but when a year later I returned to live in Sweden, I left with my reputation intact and was succeeded by none other than Ronald Avery, a very considerable expert indeed, who had just joined the Club. For some years afterwards I would be approached as I sat at lunch by old Wallis with the request: 'Meyer, I'd welcome your opinion on a new claret we've been offered.'

When Raymond finally gave up the editorship of *The Good Food Guide* in 1969, he and the Consumers' Association, which by then had adopted it, asked me to be his successor as editor. I was much tempted, but knew that if I agreed I would never write anything else, for it was a full-time job. So I refused, and have never regretted the decision, except occasionally when reading his two successors. But I am sure his shoes would have proved too big for me too.

It was lucky for me that I was not offered this job in 1953, as I probably would have been had Raymond died. My own writing was now very much at a standstill. Some authors write a book every couple of years, some every five years, some no more than five or six books in a lifetime; but it seemed unlikely that I would enter even into this last category. One novel, one rejected play, one unsuccessful radio play and a couple of editorial jobs did not represent much of an achievement at 32, especially when I compared myself to my contemporaries. It looked as though I would indeed end up as a dilettante like my narrator in *The End of the Corridor*. I was empty of ideas, worked half-time on the *Guide*, played hockey or cricket at weekends, and had a number of casual affairs, mostly with foreign girls; even in the London of the fifties, I was discovering, you could lead a varied sexual life if you had the kind of confidence I had lacked at Oxford and gained in Sweden, and this seemed to me to hold more attractions than marriage, though I am sure that had I been doing an honest nine-to-five job I would have wanted a wife to return to in the evenings and children to give me a stake in the future.

Yet, as I now realize, those unproductive and seemingly wasted years were very formative. In the first volume of his autobiography, *Arrow in the Blue*, Arthur Koestler has written: 'In the rectifying mirror of time, the meagre years which seemed to carry me nowhere appear rich with the fullness of experience, whereas the years of purposeful striving were spiritually but a period of marking time.' Temperamentally isolated as I was from my contemporaries in every field of authorship, I needed the kind of company that would advance my intellectual education as Sweden had advanced my sexual education, and had it not been for the Savile I do not know where I would have found it. It is significant that virtually all my new writer and actor friends were of an older generation. For the next quarter of a century I was to remain isolated from the poets, novelists and playwrights of my own age; I did not even fully renew my acquaintance with John Heath-Stubbs until I was nearly sixty. Had Sidney Keyes lived, things might have been different; a circle would have gathered round him.

Koestler himself I met around this time, in the early fifties, though not through the Savile. We had both been close friends of George Orwell, and a mutual acquaintance, Lena Wickman, brought us together soon after George's death. My first impression of Arthur was alarming. The small party included a young man from the Foreign Office who, when George's name was mentioned, made the extraordinary assertion that 'Orwell was a sort of Fascist really'. I have never seen or heard anyone annihilated as that man was. As I was to discover more than once, Arthur when angry became at the same time blazing and ice-cold; years later I heard Michael Foot describe him as the most formidable political debater he had ever encountered. Nor was this a brief demolition job. After Arthur had destroyed the Foreign Office man for ten minutes, Lena suggested that we should go out for dinner to an Italian restaurant. When she attempted to place Arthur at the same end of the table as his victim, Arthur said: 'I shall not eat near that idiot', seated himself at the far end and continued to abuse him across us throughout the meal.

I met Arthur often over the next thirty years. Fortunately, I never incurred his displeasure; being politically naive I always agreed with him, as with Postgate about wine, except once when I rashly said I liked Kingsley Martin, whom Arthur abominated, and received a mercifully short blast.

Arthur loved football, as I do; he claimed to have been a useful outside-left in Hungary, and subsequently a referee. I should like to have seen the player who questioned his decision. He was a fearsome opponent at croquet. Once I lunched with him and his future wife Cynthia at Weald in Kent, where he had bought Vita Sackville-West's old house with its fine gardens. The croquet lawn was set on a kind of plateau with a steep flight of old brick steps leading to the garden below, and Arthur, who took the game very seriously, kept hitting my ball and that of my partner Tony Crosland away down these steps, so that we had a lot of retrieving and climbing to do in the heat. On another occasion I was a fellow-guest with Rebecca West for dinner at his house in Montpelier Square, and it was something to hear those two argue, for she was as formidable a debater as he, and as well informed. Also present was Daphne Hardy, who had translated his novel *Darkness at Noon* into English. Arthur said that as soon as the war ended he had received numerous offers from Germany for the right to publish the book there, but having signed the contract he had been unable to trace his original typescript – he had written the book in German – and never managed to, so that the German edition had to be translated from the English translation, surely the only time that any book, let alone a masterpiece, can have appeared in its original language as a translation. Sadly, he gave up writing novels as early as 1951. I asked him several times whether he would not write another, for even his lesser ones are remarkable, but he always shook his head. It was not, he said, an age for writing novels, though he made an exception for Solzhenitsyn.

He must be the only novelist to have written in three languages: Hungarian, German and English. Like another foreigner who became a master of English prose style, Joseph Conrad, he spoke English to the end of his life with a strong accent which embarrassed him. Someone shrewdly remarked that if Arthur could have been granted two secret wishes, they would have been to be six feet tall (he stood about five feet six) and to speak English with an Oxford accent. Any mistake bothered him. I contributed an anecdote to a book he wrote about coincidences, and when it appeared I had to point out that he should not have referred to my fellow-cricketer (that game again) as my 'cricket partner'. He took the matter very seriously, just as he became disproportionately upset whenever he failed to complete the *Times* crossword.

Soon after my daughter was born in 1968, he and Cynthia came to dinner with us in Hampstead. I had invited the critic George Steiner, an admirer of Arthur, but Arthur was unpardonably rude to him throughout the evening from the moment he arrived; I never found out why. He was notoriously indifferent to children. When I asked if he had ever had any, he replied: 'One bastard in Paris.' (Cynthia, I am sure, would have liked to have children.) But when Maria brought our daughter down, he took a great fancy to her, carried her on his shoulder, and inscribed one of his books: 'To Nora, from Uncle Arthur'. Cynthia, who watched all this with what must have been mixed emotions, afterwards told me that she had never seen him behave like that. Like all their friends, I was amazed when I read that she had shared his suicide. I imagined, as I think everyone did, that she would live for another twenty-five years (she was only fifty-two) as keeper of the flame. None of us realized that she could not envisage life without him.

I saw a good deal of Graham Greene in the late forties and fifties. Once he mentioned that he was writing a film script. He told me the plot and it sounded pretty boring. I wondered who would want to see it. It turned out to be *The Third Man*. Graham's account of it ranks with Orwell's of *Animal Farm* as the most inadequate précis of a work by its author that I have heard or can imagine.

Graham was a great practical joker. Once he heard that Cyril Connolly was giving a party to which he felt he should have been invited, and telephoned Connolly in the middle of it saying in an assumed accent that he was their chimney-sweep and would be coming first thing next morning, so would Mr Connolly please have the dust-covers over all the furniture? The impersonation proved successful, for Connolly, after vainly pleading that the sweep should postpone his visit, obeyed, which must have been a tedious chore in the small hours after the last guest had gone.

Graham also invented a terrible game, usually played around midnight or later. Each of you opened the telephone directory at random, picked a name blindly and rang the number; the winner was whoever kept his or her victim talking the longest. Graham always won. He told me that he had discovered another Graham Greene, a retired solicitor in Golders Green. The first conversation between them went something as follows. 'Are you Graham Greene?' 'My name is Graham Greene, but – ' 'Are you the man who writes these filthy novels?' 'No, I am a retired solicitor.' 'I'm not surprised you're ashamed to confess you're the author of this muck.' 'No, really, I assure you – ' 'If I'd written them at least I'd have the guts to admit it', etc. Graham told me that he had made several such calls using different accents, and that in the end the unfortunate man removed his name and number from the directory. He also kept other people's visiting cards, which he would use for a variety of harmless purposes, such as sending them by a waiter across restaurants to friends who had not spotted him, with cryptic and sometimes obscene invitations written on them. This was the bright side of his temperament. I glimpsed the other side only a few times during these years, but I remember asking Edward Sackville-West, an old friend of his, what he thought Graham would be writing in twenty years, and nodding in agreement as Eddie replied: 'Oh, Graham will have committed suicide by then.' 'The fifties were for me a period of great happiness and great torment,' Graham wrote in *Ways of Escape*. 'Manic depression reached its height in that decade.'

He founded two bogus societies: the John Gordon Society and the Anglo-Texan Society. John Gordon was the editor of the *Sunday Express* and a sanctimonious chastiser of supposed indecencies. Graham had fallen foul of him, I forget how, and conceived the idea of starting this society which both enemies and admirers of Gordon could join. The other founder members included A. J. Ayer, Peter Brook and Christopher Isherwood. He wrote me a vivid account of the inaugural meeting, describing how 'as a result of John Gordon's invitation to violence in his column', the pub had been packed to overflowing with people standing all down the stairs. Gordon had apparently miscalculated and found that his public was against him. 'If it hadn't been for Randolph Churchill overdoing his attacks, all the sympathy would have been against Gordon. However it was all great fun and didn't in fact reach the point of razor-blades or fists.' The Anglo-Texan Society he founded with John Sutro, an old friend from Oxford days, as the result of a conversation in a train. They launched this as a pure joke, but it took off tremendously – Graham told me that the American Ambassador was among the first to respond to their advertisement in *The Times*, followed by several Texan millionaires and business companies as well as numerous individuals from both countries. I believe the Society still flourishes.

Once, at a party in Graham's home in Beaumont Street, Oxford, Enid Starkie, the biographer of Baudelaire and a great talker in the Irish tradition, suddenly asked: 'Which are the three greatest novels?', and everybody had to answer. She named *Madame Bovary*, *Le Rouge et le Noir* and *La Chartreuse de Parme*; mine were *Moby Dick*, *Crime and Punishment* and *Tess of the D'Urbervilles* (and they still would be); and Graham chose *War and Peace*, *Tom Jones* and one out of three late Henry James books, *The Ambassadors*, *The Wings of the Dove* and *The Golden Bowl*, he could not decide which. Then, as later, Graham tended to be, not exactly reticent in company, but content to listen and make the odd observation, to partake rather than dominate.

Suddenly, in November 1953, a flicker of a breeze stirred my doldrums. A director expressed interest in *The Ortolan*. Hugh Greene's ex-wife Helga, who had just started as a literary agent, and had volunteered without much hope to see if she could sell it, telephoned. 'Someone likes your play.' 'Gosh, who?' 'He's a Finnish baron.' This sounded desperately unpromising. I envisaged some monocled old dilettante. But she continued: 'He's a very talented young director. He's just had a success at the Edinburgh Festival with a production of Strindberg's *Miss Julie*.' So the young man came along.

First Steps in the Theatre

Casper Wrede was twenty-four and looked even younger. Having fought in the Finnish Army against the Russians as a schoolboy, he had come to England and had managed to get into the Old Vic School, founded after the war by Michel Saint-Denis, George Devine and Glen Byam Shaw, thanks entirely to his knowledge of artillery. Many more candidates had applied for entry to this prestigious new theatre school than could be accommodated, and what chance had a Finn with no theatrical experience at all? But Glen Byam Shaw was interested in military matters, and in artillery in particular, and on Wrede's mentioning that he had served in the artillery in the winter war, Byam Shaw questioned him closely for half an hour on the subject and then told him that he was accepted. His contemporaries at the school in the early fifties included Joan Plowright, Christopher Morahan, Frank Dunlop, Dilys Hamlett (whom Wrede later married), James Maxwell, Lee Montague and the designers Richard Negri and Malcolm Pride.

In the summer of 1953 Wrede staged Strindberg's *Miss Julie* at the Edinburgh Festival with Dilys Hamlett as Julie and Patrick Dromgoole, later to become a well-known television director, as Jean. This was acclaimed, and as a result OUDS asked him to find a play, if possible a new one, to direct for them at Oxford the following February. *The Ortolan* was to serve this purpose. For the lead he chose Teresa Dunien, a beautiful and gifted Polish girl who had been with him at the Old Vic School. Patrick Dromgoole was one of the men; the other should have been P. J. Kavanagh, the poet, but he had to drop out. The cast included a nineteen-year-old girl called Margaret Smith who was not at the university but lived in Oxford with her parents. When, a year or two later, she became a professional, the actors' union Equity already had a Margaret Smith, and since its rules forbade any two members from using the same name she called herself Maggie, by which we all knew her, and quickly and permanently made her mark.

I owe a triple debt to Wrede. He taught me about playwriting and the theatre in general, he taught me the difference between translating plays and novels, and he turned me from a dilettante into a professional. Incidentally, he also taught me that one of the most important and least publicized roles of a director, where new plays are concerned, is to sit down with the author and persuade him to correct his play's faults, to cut, add and rewrite. This needs great tact, for an author regards his work as, if not exactly sacrosanct, at any rate something that needs to be protected from intrusive hands. I remember there was one long speech of which I was especially proud. Wrede somehow persuaded me that it would be far more effective if the character simply said: 'No'. He directed it beautifully, the young cast – especially Teresa and Maggie – acted it well, and in its small way it was a success. But for a sub-editor on *The Times*, it might have gone further. The local *Times* critic, John Hordern, told me that he had written an enthusiastic final paragraph, but this got subbed for lack of space, so that the review did little more than summarize the plot and praise the production. The *Evening News* thought it 'a considerable triumph', the *Oxford Times* 'tautly written and memorably good'. Harold Hobson gave it a kindly notice in the *Sunday Times*, in which, within the month, I was also praised for my translation of *The Long Ships* and for my hockey goalkeeping for Hampstead; only by a couple of weeks did I miss what would surely have been the unique honour of being commended simultaneously in the literary and sporting pages. Nowadays, such notices would almost certainly have meant a London try-out. But as I have explained, there was no venue for such a minority piece then, and it was never a West End play.

Four undergraduate critics reviewed *The Ortolan* in various magazines, all generously. All were later to make their mark: Montague Haltrecht as a novelist, Peter France as a television presenter, Ned Sherrin as a theatre writer and director. The fourth was a very tall, thin young man named Michael Elliott. He especially, and rightly, drew attention to the production. Elliott was to act as assistant director on two other Wrede productions at Oxford, Marlowe's *Edward II* and the *Hippolytus* of Euripides. Michael Barry, then head of BBC TV drama, subsequently invited both Elliott and Wrede to become trainee TV directors, and they co-directed four plays for him: *Uncle Vanya*, *Twelfth Night*, *The Lady from the Sea* and *The Trojan Women*. This partnership was in due course to have a considerable effect on British theatre.

That summer of 1954 I wrote a black farce, *The May Game*, about a young couple whose married life has become incessant warfare. The title was from Carlyle: 'Not a May-game is this man's life, but a battle and a march.' The curtain was to rise on the husband cowering against a wall while saucepans and crockery rain about his head. When he reminds his wife that this never happened before they married, she suggests that they divorce and live together in sin again; but in those days it was difficult to get a divorce without adultery, which neither wants to commit. On the advice of a neighbour the wife disguises herself as a tart and arranges that a private detective shall find the husband *in flagrante delicto* with this apparent stranger. But they have forgotten that it is their wedding anniversary, and are surprised in the supposed act by her mother and a succession of other visitors including two pairs of workmen – each pair carrying a grand piano – a nun and the Queen's Proctor.

The May Game at first interested no one, and the agent to whom I had moved following a quarrel with Helga Greene disliked it so much that after two West End managements had contemptuously rejected it he refused to handle it further. I then tried to adapt for television two novels which I admired, Hugh de Selincourt's *The Cricket Match* and Marghanita Laski's *The Victorian Chaise-Longue*, and wrote a treatment of the life of Fridtjof Nansen, perhaps the most extraordinary of modern explorers, and of whose later work for stateless persons and refugees an English statesman said: 'No single human being has ever by his own efforts so astoundingly reduced the sum of human suffering in the world.' But each of these was likewise rejected.

All this was profoundly discouraging, and when two friends asked me to be a kind of figurehead to a new organization which they were founding in Stockholm to teach English to foreigners, I agreed. I felt, again, a failure in England. But shortly before I left for Stockholm, in the summer of 1955, something happened. A young man named Michael Codron, recently down from Oxford, who was working for the impresario Jack Hylton, said he would like to offer *The Ortolan*, which he had seen and liked at Oxford, to a director just down from Cambridge, Peter Hall, who had taken over the Arts Theatre in London. Codron did not like *The May Game* any more than anyone else who had read it, but I persuaded him to send it to Hall too, and received a phone call from Hall asking to meet me. Hall said that he was interested that anyone could write two such contrasting plays, that this was the first English example he had read of black farce, and that he would like to stage it. When I queried whether the Arts Theatre was the right venue for a farce of any colour, he explained that he had been invited by two managements to find some new play to direct in the West End, and that *The May Game* would be just the thing. For the leads he intended to approach Dirk Bogarde and Geraldine McEwan.

Off I went to Sweden in high spirits, but on landing in Gothenburg I received a telegram from my brother Peter to say that our father had died of a heart-attack. I wept briefly, for the first time for many years. My early antagonism had changed to a great admiration and fondness. In his last years, illness had moderated his quick temper, and I had come to appreciate his tolerance and wisdom. It must have been frustrating beyond measure for so vital a man to spend seven years virtually confined to a chair (he even had to sleep in it), and to forgo all activity, including sex. But he never allowed this frustration to express itself against my brothers or me. Nor did he ever lean on me to abandon my seemingly failed writing career, as he might not unreasonably have done – I was by now thirty-four – and as Uncle Monty, had I been his son, undoubtedly would have done. He must have felt that I was hardly fulfilling my promise, but if so he never showed it. I am sad that he did not live to see things turn out better for me.

His last years were made more difficult by the attitude of his mistress, Lilian. After my youthful resentment I had come to like her. She was handsome and amusing. Shortly before the war Father bought her a house in Cumberland Terrace, a hundred yards from Lord's Cricket Ground, and on one occasion she gave me a splendid meal of cold salmon and raspberries and cream in the lunch interval. But as a result, I presume, of his illness she became an alcoholic, and would telephone him for, literally, hours on end with dreadful rambling monologues. When I was there I would occasionally pick up the phone in my room to make a call and catch a few ghastly seconds of those slurred and insane accusations and complaints, all the sadder when I remembered how she had been. Sometimes I was with Father when she rang; he simply continued reading his book or newspaper, occasionally clucking in sympathy, or rousing himself to deny something she had said. Once when I asked him why he put up with her, he replied: 'Never forget she is the most miserable person in the world.' She must, of course, have hoped that he would marry her. When I asked him why he had not done so in their early days together, he explained that he could not have endured to be surrounded in middle age by small children which she would have wanted. So she, poor woman, died unmarried and childless. One might suppose that this would have influenced me towards marriage, but I now suspect that it had the opposite effect; that seeing this once happy relationship turn sour and mutually humiliating made me determined that the same thing would never happen to me.

Back in Stockholm after Father's funeral, I told everyone I had a play coming on in the West End. Then one day I opened the *Daily Telegraph* and read that Mr Peter Hall, who had made such a success of the Arts Theatre, was to direct his first play in the West End: *Summertime*, an Italian comedy by Ugo Betti, starring Dirk Bogarde and Geraldine McEwan. In due course an apologetic letter arrived from Hall explaining that he had been offered this and thought it exactly right for those two players, but that he still intended to do *The May Game*. But later that year he was invited to take over the Shakespeare Memorial Theatre at Stratford-upon-Avon, and there was no place in his plans over the next few years for a modern farce.

At or soon after our first meeting, Hall had suggested that I should translate for him a French play, Armand Salacrou's *The Earth is Round*, about Savonarola. I did not tell him how bad my French was, but translated a specimen scene or two with help in Stockholm. Hall liked my effort and sent it to Salacrou's agent in Paris, but she replied that she could not think of entrusting so important a play to an unknown director and translator; so that project was dropped, and *The Earth is Round* remains unperformed in Britain.

But another translation offer was made to me that spring or early summer which was to bear considerable fruit, albeit not for some years. As a result of the good reviews I had had for *The Long Ships*, John Morris asked me over coffee one day at the Savile: 'Can you read Norwegian?' I had never read a word of Norwegian, and was about to say so when I sniffed a hundred pounds hovering in the air, so I replied that it was somewhat similar to Swedish, and Morris said: 'Will you translate Ibsen's *Little Eyolf* for radio?' I got a copy of the play in Norwegian from the library and could hardly understand a word, for while the languages are indeed similar when spoken (though different enough for their films always to be subtitled when shown in the other country), they look very different on the page, rather as though Glasgow Scottish were to be spelt as it is pronounced. So I got a Norwegian friend who was married to an Englishman and spoke English with no trace of an accent to go through the play with me, and produced a version which was done on the radio and, a couple of years later, on stage at the Lyric, Hammersmith, in a short season presented by Michael Codron, his first venture into management (it also included Harold Pinter's first play, *The Birthday Party*, which was so savaged by the critics that it had to be removed after less than a week). Kenneth Tynan gave me a bad review for my translation; later, when I came to learn Norwegian properly, I realized that he was quite right, and when I began to translate all of Ibsen's major plays for a publisher I found that I had to rewrite my version of *Little Eyolf* so completely that barely a line of my original remained. My collaborator, though genuinely bilingual, had continually missed Ibsen's nuances; she could not, as the saying is, read a play, far less sense a sub-text. It taught me the inadequacy of 'crib' translations, still employed by theatres that should know better.

The fact that nobody now seemed interested in *The May Game*, on top of everything else, led me to attempt another novel, about an ageing dramatist, modelled on Eugene O'Neill, who falls in love with a young actress and is destroyed by her. I called it *The Rock of Cashel*, after a line by Yeats, but it ground to a halt after thirty thousand words, and Collins were unenthusiastic about what I showed them. A different publisher might have helped, just as a different theatre agent (David Higham handled only books) would surely have made me write a third stage-play. But I had parted from Helga Greene and was unhappy with my new agent; I had not yet met Peggy Ramsay. Instead I wrote three original television plays in the next twelve months, *Cul-de-Sac* (I do not even remember what that was about), *Two at a Window*, about a mother who falls in love with her daughter's boyfriend, and *The Rocking Chair*, in which the police know that a murder has been committed by one of the victim's three children but cannot prove by which. Although these all interested individual directors, none of them got any further. I also, at Casper Wrede's suggestion, translated another Ibsen, *The Lady from the Sea*, which he was hoping to stage for a new West End impresario, Toby Rowland. But this production, too, failed to materialize. My only small success was to sell an original idea to the Swedish Film Corporation. Entitled *Port of Call*, it covered the adventures of three people who disembark for twenty-four hours from a cruise ship in Stockholm: a famous film star, returning to her native city from America for the first time in ten years and finding herself subtly excluded, a middle-aged sailor seeking the girl he met there briefly twenty years before, and a young sailor who falls in love with a girl who turns out to be the illegitimate daughter of that liaison. Svenskfilmindustri liked this enough to commission a treatment, and at least I got paid for this, though the film was never made.

At the same time, I offered *The May Game* around, and a few glimmers of hope emerged. Terence Rattigan liked it, as he had *The Ortolan*. 'I feel it should certainly have a performance,' he wrote to me, 'and am sending it to Stephen Mitchell [who had presented Rattigan's last two plays] with a recommendation . . . If well directed and played, I feel it must stand a very good chance.' Mitchell 'enjoyed it, but in the final analysis I am not sufficiently enthusiastic to go ahead with a production'. Peter Ashmore, a leading West End director, was keen to stage it, as was an American impresario named Edward Specter who offered to put up half the money, but they could find no West End manager to come in with them. Nobody wanted to touch a black farce. But one good thing came of all this. I was advised to approach a new agent, an ex-actress and ex-opera singer in her late forties named Peggy Ramsay.

In due course I received the first of those eccentrically typed letters circled with illegible handwritten postscripts which were to become part of my life over the next third of a century. Peggy liked *The May Game*. 'I was immensely amused and diverted – full of constant small surprises and funny lines and nice people . . . I can see why managers have not absolutely committed themselves . . . the play leans heavily towards the farce rather than the comedy genre, which always scares them . . . But . . . once the play was on the stage it would be apparent to all managers that it was extremely funny and that audiences would love it.' She took me on. But even she did not manage to sell *The May Game* or *The Ortolan*, though she reckoned that she might have had I been with her from the start. 'My idea of hell is trying to sell plays that have been soiled by other agents.'

Some consolation for all this came in the development of my friendship with Graham Greene. I had seen him fairly often in England without getting really close to him until, in November 1955, he passed through Stockholm on his way to Poland. His Swedish publisher, Ragnar Svanström, gave a dinner for him to which I was invited, and towards the end of the evening Graham

asked if I would join him and the Svanströms as his guest for dinner
the following evening. I explained that I had a date, but he said: 'Bring
the girl,' adding: 'Perhaps you could find one for me.' Immediately
he added: 'No, I was joking', but it seemed a good idea. I pondered,
and thought of Anita Björk.

I had come to know Anita and her husband Stig Dagerman two
years earlier, having met them at a party at Ragnar Svanström's
house in the skerries, and during the summer of 1953 had been a
frequent visitor at their house in Enebyberg, a few miles north of
Stockholm. Stig was the best writer of his generation in Sweden,
and one of the best in Europe, the author of two brilliant plays,
The Man Condemned to Death and *The Shadow of Mart*, and of several
fine novels and short stories. Anita was a beautiful and gifted actress
who had become internationally famous through her performance
in the title role of Alf Sjöberg's film, *Miss Julie*; as a result, she
was offered a Hollywood contract, but the moguls were alarmed
when she arrived with Stig, to whom she was not yet married.
The head of the studio, no paragon himself, begged her to marry
Stig, explaining in a deathless phrase: 'We can't have immorality
in Hollywood.' Anita replied that neither of them wished to marry
and, on being told that under these circumstances the studio could
not employ her, packed her bags and returned with Stig to Sweden.
But a year later, in that summer of 1953, having by then produced
a daughter, they decided they would after all marry. I was a guest
at the wedding feast, at the end of which they pronounced me unfit
to drive home. I protested that I could not occupy the guest-room
on their wedding night, but they overruled me and together made
up my bed before retiring into the bridal chamber. The three of us
had many splendid evenings that summer. We would talk about
literature and the theatre until the sun rose around two o'clock.
Then Anita would go to bed, and Stig and I would abandon these
subjects for our greater love, football, which we would discuss for
another hour or two before sleep finally overcame us.

But about eighteen months later Stig was found dead in his garage
with the car engine running. None of us was sure whether he had
intended to kill himself. He was a manic depressive, and had several
times attempted suicide, but always, except on this occasion, ended
by turning off the engine and walking out into the night air. His death
had occurred twelve months before Graham's visit to Stockholm. I
had seen Anita once or twice since. She was lonely and depressed, and
I thought it might cheer her to come out if she could be persuaded.

Ragnar and I phoned her and she agreed. When we told Graham, he became embarrassed and said: 'I didn't mean it seriously. I hate blind dates, they're always a disappointment.' He recalled that he had met her and Stig at the Stockholm premiere of his play, *The Living Room*, the opening performance of which had to be delayed because Graham and the director of the Dramatic Theatre got stuck in a lift. He seemed to remember Stig more vividly than he did Anita, and mentioned that he had particularly liked him, but said nothing about her.

The six of us dined pleasantly next evening, 12 November 1955, at Djurgårdsbrunnsvärdshus, a lovely old restaurant set in the great park of Djurgården. Around 11 p.m. the Svanströms retired and my girlfriend and I invited Graham and Anita back to my one-room flat on Valhallavägen. As we went into the kitchen to make coffee, I turned to say something and noticed the way Graham and Anita were looking at each other as they talked on the sofa. 'Do you think there's something starting between those two?' I said, and she replied: 'I was wondering.' Nothing happened that evening, but when I returned to London for Christmas Anita flew with me, and on the day of her arrival an affair began between her and Graham which was to last, with considerable intensity on both sides, for nearly four years.

Graham has not had many affairs, as he once pointed out to me, contrasting what he proudly regarded as his restraint in this field with my own somewhat frivolous attitude. As far as I can recall, he has had only four in all the years I have known him, none of them casual.

He came often to Sweden during those four years. I would meet him at Bromma airport and drive him to the house at Enebyberg which I knew so well. But that house held memories for Anita, and soon she moved to Saltsjö-Duvnäs on the other, southern side of Stockholm. Since Anita was usually acting in the evenings and sometimes filming in the day too, I saw much more of Graham in these years than ever before, and it was now that I first became intimate with him in the sense that he spoke about himself as he had not done previously with me. We would wander round Stockholm, the atmosphere of which he had caught uncannily in *England Made Me* twenty years before on the strength of a two weeks' visit. We dined and went to cinemas (seldom, if ever, to theatres, since he could not understand more than a few words of Swedish), then came back to my new flat on Döbelnsgatan with its two balconies high above the city and drank and talked until it was time for him to collect Anita at the stage-door of Dramaten as, half a century earlier, August Strindberg had waited for his third wife, the actress Harriet Bosse, thirty years his junior. There were only twenty years between Graham and Anita. I wish now that I had kept a diary instead of just an engagement book, but I have always shrunk from it, as from carrying a camera; I think it was Thomas Hardy who said that he once tried taking a notebook round in his pocket but gave it up because he found it paralysed his powers of observation.

I remember asking Graham how he could be a Roman Catholic, since the dogmas of that religion seemed in so many respects contrary to his temperament, especially as regards extramarital sex.

He said: 'When you were a schoolboy, did you go through a religious phase?'

'Yes.'

'Did you believe that the flames of Hell were beneath the floor-boards waiting to swallow you up?'

'Yes.'

'Did you like that feeling?'

'Of course not.'

'Did you get out of feeling like that?'

'Yes.'

'Some of us never get out of it.' A pause, then: 'I wouldn't recommend anyone to be a Catholic unless they have to be.' On another occasion, he said: 'Never forget how lucky you are in two respects. You like people unless you've a reason to dislike them, and you're happy unless you've a reason to be unhappy. I'm the opposite.'

His Catholicism made it impossible for him to divorce and remarry, but he tried earnestly to persuade Anita to come and live with him in either England or France. She was fluent in both English and French, and could, at thirty-two, have continued her film career, and perhaps her theatre career too, in either country. But unlike so many Swedes, especially those in her profession, she was unwilling to emigrate. In addition to her daughter by Stig, then three, she had a young son by a previous marriage, and she said she wanted to bring them up in Sweden as Swedes. Moreover, she felt deeply rooted there herself; following the success of the *Miss Julie* film, she had had several opportunities to pursue an international career apart from the Hollywood fiasco, but had refused them. Perhaps the Hollywood experience had made her unwilling to submit herself to the whims of foreign producers. I am sure she was as much in love with Graham as he with her. He considered emigrating to Sweden, but he found the long, dark winters oppressive, and felt he was too old at fifty to learn a new and completely strange language. (He is not a facile linguist, although later he managed to build sufficiently on his school French to get by when he went to live in Antibes. Despite the amount of time that he spent in various South American countries, he never acquired more than a rudimentary smattering of Spanish.) He also disliked the long evenings alone when Anita was at the theatre; apart from the Svanströms and myself, he had no friends in Sweden. Had she devoted herself mainly to films, as she would have done in England or France, they would have had the evenings together.

'Unendingly grateful for the way you rally round,' Graham wrote on a Christmas card to me at the end of 1956. I performed occasional errands for him, such as sending Anita roses on her first nights with notes attached which he posted to me. His inscriptions to me in various books refer to my role in launching the affair. 'To Michael, to whom I am grateful for a reason.' 'In memory of an evening in Nov. 1955 when I was so angry with you' (for arranging the blind date, before things turned out as they did). 'Remembering many drinks and many problems in Stockholm.'*

One evening early in 1957 Graham and I dined at a restaurant called Tre Remmare, the Three Goblets, in the old town of Stockholm. I told him how my writing had come to a standstill, and he at once said: 'Go away for three months.' 'Sicily?' I hazarded vaguely, and he said: 'No, further away, the Far East. You don't know how many of those countries will be open for travel in five years. Burma's gone already.' We came back to my flat, I took out my school atlas, by now ludicrously out of date with many of those Asian countries still in Empire red, and euphorically (we had drunk a good deal) he planned my route, naming various people to whom he would give me introductions – his old MI6 friend Trevor Wilson, who had been expelled from Hanoi by the French and was now in Malaya; a Chinese Oxford contemporary in Hong Kong, Harold Lee; and two people, a politician and a prince, in Bangkok. 'You must smoke opium in Bangkok,' he said. 'It's legal there.' The prince, if not the

---

* On one occasion he told me that some time in 1956 he spent an evening with Somerset Maugham, who for once threw off his shyness and reminisced fascinatingly about writers and others whom he had known in the 1890s. Graham sat entranced, drinking steadily, and next morning had a fearful hangover and could not remember a word that Maugham had said.

politician, would show me where and how to do it. We must have had some idea of linking up, for I see that on 15 March that year he wrote to me saying that he would not be going to China so that we could not meet there as planned: 'I have got more and more fed up with the choice of travelling companions and I think more fun might be got in Algeria.' So I was never with him in Asia, except at a few airports *en route* to the South Seas two years later, and this is another of my great regrets.

Next morning, Graham's grandiose scheme for me seemed impossible. Unlike him, I have always disliked travel; I do not enjoy holidays, and even the prospect of a night away from home makes me fretful. I dismissed the project. But Graham nagged at me for months, sending advice on what places I should visit: Malacca ('very beautiful') rather than Kuala Lumpur ('an official capital with hideous buildings'), and warning me to avoid Jakarta ('I believe it is one of the most disagreeable spots in all the Far East' – though in the event I rather enjoyed it), and Rangoon ('you may find yourself sharing a dirty bedroom with several other people'). I don't know why he so pressed me to go. Perhaps he sensed that I needed to escape and knew I would not do it without being pushed.

So that autumn I apprehensively booked my many-legged round-trip ticket. Graham offered to give me a send-off evening in Paris. As we entered a restaurant for dinner, we bumped into Arthur Koestler coming out. Graham cried: 'Hullo, Arthur!' Arthur, about eight inches shorter, looked up at him and said: 'How can you look me in the face?' 'What do you mean?' 'If you want to pretend you don't know, O.K.,' said Arthur in his most withering voice (and no one could be more withering), and, after saluting me amiably, walked out into the night. Graham could not think what Arthur was referring to. 'I've always been very fond of him,' he said, and it bothered him throughout the meal and recurred at intervals to puzzle him throughout the evening. The only possible reason he could think of was that he had expressed unwillingness to sign some corporate letter which Arthur had organized on I forget what subject. Arthur was an unforgiving person (as, to a lesser extent, was Graham), and when fifteen years later I mentioned Graham's name in Montpelier Square, Arthur waved his hand and said: 'There are some people one doesn't talk about.'

After dinner, Graham and I visited the Crazy Horse strip club, where he was clearly well known. Much to my disappointment, he suggested in the interval that we should forgo the second half of the show and move on to a brothel where, he said, they could arrange a better exhibition. We paid to see two girls put on an unconvincing lesbian performance; I thought they had been more attractive and inventive at the Crazy Horse. We must have drunk a lot, for next morning I woke with a hangover which lasted right through the long flight to Colombo.

11

An Innocent in the Far East

My projected three months' trip stretched itself to seven and a half months. I visited Ceylon, Singapore, Malaya, Java, Bali, Sarawak, Vietnam (then between its wars), Thailand, Cambodia, Hong Kong, Macao, Japan, China, India and Nepal. It was the most uncomfortable, lonely and educative period of my life. How often I cursed Graham as I plodded through the Sarawak jungle, was grilled for hours by commissars in Chinese police stations, robbed in Colombo and caught in anti-European demonstrations in Jakarta; how grateful I am that he made me do it all. His introductions proved sometimes useful, sometimes not. The Thai prince did indeed take me to an opium den, as I shall describe, but his compatriot politician turned out to be a predatory homosexual; he drove me to Chiangmai in the north to attend a ceremonial visit by the King, but took offence when I told him I would be staying in a house there loaned to me by the opium-smoking prince instead of in the hotel with him, and revenged himself by refusing to vouch for me as a bona fide journalist (I was writing a series of articles for a Swedish newspaper), so that I had to get into the royal celebrations by subterfuge. A few years later I was alarmed to read that he had become a cabinet minister, but he did not hold that office for long. In Macao a Chinese who, Graham assured me, owned a club 'where you will be entertained free of charge with opium and massage' was away, but his son showed me round the town and seemed unperturbed when I expressed a fear that we might fall foul of the local gangsters; later I learned that his father was the Al Capone of Macao.

Some notes from a Far East diary

Ceylon. The rats gnawing the hard skin on the feet of sleepers in the streets of Colombo. The leper with elephantiasis in one foot helping the fishermen to land their catch of five-foot sharks, a merry fellow on good terms with everyone who evidently regards himself as no outcast. The boy who exhibits to us a screaming child of three, revealed, when he strips off his loincloth, as a hermaphrodite with both male and female sexual organs imperfectly developed. A crocodile asleep by the side of a lake, its great jaws wickedly open; a long-tailed mongoose gliding beautifully across the path – one has only to see a mongoose run twenty yards to understand how it can outspeed a cobra in the strike. Splendid peacocks gaze at us from the trees, crying like whipped children; a stork asleep in a tree, white as ermine; and all the time the invisible cicadas sing their hissing song like a railway engine slowly releasing its steam. A notice at the entrance to a game reserve: ALWAYS GIVE ELEPHANTS RIGHT OF WAY.

I wanted to walk in the grass by the river but was told it was full of leeches. Some months ago a man fell from a tree in the jungle and injured his spine. He tried to crawl home, which he could normally have done in an hour, but the leeches got him first. When his body was discovered near the jungle's edge there was not a drop of blood in him. A human body contains ten pints of blood and the leeches had taken it all.

An Englishman tells me how, driving through a village a few months previously, he noticed a small commotion and a man with a *catty* – a villainous long-handled knife somewhere between a sickle and a machete – tried, with the usual Sinhalese courtesy, to thumb a lift. The Englishman was about to oblige him when he noticed that the man was bleeding from several wounds, so decided to drive on. A quarter of a mile along the road he came across another man with a *catty* who was bleeding even more than the first man and was running at a good pace. It transpired that there had been a fight between the two, and the first had worsted the second but had been the slower of the two at running, so that when his adversary fled he had been unable to catch him up and finish the job. He had begged a lift in order to do this, surely the only recorded instance of a man trying to thumb a lift to complete a murder.

Walking alone through the village of Negumbo at noon,

I hear a powerful voice behind me roar: 'Do I see a Britisher without a hat?'

I turn and behold an elderly gentleman wearing a topee and a concerned expression advancing towards me. He is very dark-skinned.

'My God,' he says. 'Are you a Britisher?'

I admit to this.

'Then where is your hat?' he cries. 'I can't see a Britisher without a hat.'

I don't see why a Britisher should stand in more need of a hat than other people, and say I am happy without one, but the old gentleman will have none of this.

'I will buy you a hat,' he says, seizing me by the arm.

'No, really, I never wear a hat.'

'You think I am trying to sell you one?' he says accusingly.

'Not at all,' I reply unconvincingly, for that is exactly what I had thought.

He tightens his grip on my arm and introduces himself as Mr Powell of Darjeeling, a retired schoolmaster. 'I am not Sinhalese, though I live here,' he explains. 'I am Indian, and you are British, and therefore I am going to buy you a hat.'

I do not see the logic of this, but Mr Powell is not to be gainsaid. He leads me by the arm into a clothes shop, where the proprietor, another old gentleman, greets him as a friend, albeit with respect. Mr Powell commands him to bring out his hats. But I have a large head, size eight, and none can be found to fit me.

'We will try elsewhere,' says Mr Powell, and we proceed to another shop. The tailor, who is called Mr Fernando, has become infected with Mr Powell's enthusiasm, and follows with two of his assistants, business being somewhat slack. Here, too, we draw a blank.

By now it has become a point of honour for Negumbo that I should not leave the village without a hat. From shop to shop we go, and as we leave each shop the proprietor and one or two of his assistants join our party, so that soon we number over a dozen. Every few minutes, Mr Powell repeats his tremendous cry, like an evangelist's slogan: 'I can't see a Britisher without a hat.' I feel very ashamed and un-British without one. But the Sinhalese have small heads, and although I try on all imaginable sorts and shapes –

topees, panamas, trilbies, even pork-pies – nothing can be
found to fit me. I do not know how long we might
have gone on searching if, by good chance, we had not
passed a board saying: LICENSED ARRACK TAVERN.
This suggests to Mr Powell's intelligence an honourable
way out of the impasse.

'If I cannot buy you a hat,' he says, 'I can at least buy
you a drink.'

This suggestion is greeted with grunts of approval from
everyone in our party, including myself, and we repair
into the tavern. *Arrack*, a sticky yellow liquor distilled from
coconuts, is poured in large measures, and an equal quantity
of ginger beer is added. Mr Powell toasts the British, and
the hat is forgotten.

We talk about many things, on all of which Mr Powell
holds strong opinions. The British, he gives me to
understand, have done nothing wrong. Any troubles there
may have been, anywhere and at any time, have always had
some other root. I try to argue, but Mr Powell points out
that among the subjects he taught as a schoolmaster had been
history. 'I am eighty-nine,' he says, 'and I have forgotten
some things, but not as much as I remember.' He paints a
powerful picture of British infallibility as the *arrack* flows.

At last it is time for me to go. We all shake hands, and
I promise Mr Powell that I will write to him. But he shakes
his head and two huge tears roll down his cheeks.

'We shall not meet again,' he says. 'I shall not see another
winter.'

'Indeed you will, and we shall meet again.'

'No,' he says, 'I shall not see another winter.'

'You've been saying that for twenty years,' says Mr
Fernando unfeelingly.

'This time it is true. Do me a favour,' he begs me.

'Anything. What?'

'Take a photograph of me.'

So there, standing outside the *arrack* tavern, I take a
photograph of him and his friend Mr Fernando, whereupon,
dabbing his eyes but seeming somewhat comforted, he goes
his way. But he has not walked more than a few yards before
he turns and shouts: 'Get a hat! I can't see a Britisher
without a hat!'

I fly to Kuantan, halfway up the east coast of Malaya, and
spend three days motoring north towards the Thai border
with Graham's friend Trevor Wilson, the State Information
Officer of Pahang. He was one of the first three Englishmen
to enter Paris after the 1944 liberation, and was British
Consul in Hanoi during the French war in Vietnam. At the
bar of a rest-house I meet an Englishman who Trevor
tells me is said to know more about the jungle than any other
white man.

This man says the dangers of the jungle are much
exaggerated. All animals, snakes and crawling insects are
terrified of man and, since they can hear or smell him
a long way off, lose no time in getting out of his path. The
main exceptions are beasts that are too old or too lazy
to avoid you; a python may be asleep on a branch, cannot be
bothered to move, finds you, a good prospective meal,
standing below and drops his coils; or an old tiger who,
because of his slowness, has not dined well for a day
or two, may feel inclined to take a chance and lie in
wait for you. But such things, he says, happen rarely; usually
even the tigers slink away in good time, and the worst
things are mosquitoes and the risk of being scratched by
broken bamboo, which is highly poisonous. The upas tree
also brings out nasty flesh ulcers if you brush against it, but
this is fairly uncommon. The most hostile of the jungle
beasts is not the tiger or the cobra but the wild ox, which
can toss a man thirty feet into the air with its horns.
But if an animal such as a tiger realizes that you are hunting
him it is a different matter, for then he will turn and
fight.

Trevor says that you can escape mosquitoes for the night
if you sleep in a river more than a hundred yards wide, since
mosquitoes cannot fly more than fifty yards without rest; but
that bathing in these rivers is rendered dangerous by a fish
rather like a pike which fastens very sharp teeth on anything
remotely resembling a worm. Human toes come into this
category and, of course, penises.

A Chinese restaurateur in Penang asks me if it is really true
that Europeans regard their wives as more important than
their mothers. Such a viewpoint, he assures me, would be
unthinkable in a Chinese. 'If I go home and my wife and my

mother have quarrelled, I do not ask who is right. I know
my mother is right.'

Most visitors to Bali never get beyond Denpasar, the capital,
a dull little town geared to tourism. No wonder I met so
many people in Singapore and Jakarta who had visited Bali
and come away disappointed. Luckily a Swedish
photographer has advised me to stay in a remote village
called Ubud in the centre of the island.* He gives me
an introduction to the *tjokorde*, or village chief, and I stay for
ten days in a hut adjoining his house, ten of the most
extraordinary days I have ever spent.

Balinese village life, seemingly as free as the air but in
fact hemmed in by a thousand taboos, flows around me.
Everywhere I turn I come up against a taboo. If I try
to pat a child's head the mother will snatch the child away in
alarm, for that is taboo. Whenever I cross a threshold,
even that of my hut, I must be careful not to step on any leaf
or petal that might be lying there as an offering to the gods
or evil spirits. If some unusually trusting mother allows me
to hold her baby for a few seconds, I must be sure not to let
any part of its body, even a toe, touch the ground, otherwise
the evil spirits might mistake it for an animal and then
it would become like an animal. No baby is allowed to touch
the ground until it is three months old. And everywhere
there is an offering; I see them on every threshold and
ledge.

Each morning I rise soon after six as it grows light,
drink some coffee on my little verandah and go for my
daily walk through the ricefields. Workers wearing huge
conical hats walk with eight-foot hoes on their shoulders;
women pass in single file, bare-breasted and with bowls or
baskets on their heads. The government in Jakarta has passed
a law forbidding Indonesian women to go bare-breasted,
but nobody in Bali obeys this law except in the towns. Dogs
rush out and howl at me, hating the smell of a white
man.

The ricefields are unlike those in Ceylon and Malaya. The

* Sadly, Ubud has now become a tourist attraction. In 1957, I was the only stranger
there.

Balinese cut the hills into steps and let water trickle gently
down from terrace to terrace; since rice takes six months
to ripen they keep fields in differing stages of ripeness so that
there are always some ready to be reaped. Thus in these great
amphitheatres some terraces are dressed with ripe rice waving
like corn, others with only the tiny fresh shoots pricking
the surface of the water, and everywhere the glistening
cascades tumble down from field to field. Along the terraces
at different heights, like something staged, move the men
in their great conical hats, hoeing and probing, or rolling the
underwater beds of flooded fields ready for sowing, with
rollers drawn by yoked buffalo. Tiny structures like roofed
dovecotes stand here and there, altars to the goddess of
the harvest, each containing small green trays of banana leaf
with a few grains of rice or flower petals. Frighteningly
realistic scarecrows dangle from poles like hanged men.

The *tjokorde* tells me of any ceremony about to be
performed in Ubud or any neighbouring village. Not a
day passes without my witnessing some rite – a tooth-filing,
a cock-fight, a cremation, a corpse-washing. I see a young
couple having their teeth filed on the morning of their
wedding. The Balinese, being Hindus, believe in
reincarnation, and if your teeth are pointed when you die
you may be reincarnated as a pig or a dog, so it is most
important that they should be made flat. The operation is
performed by a man with a big rough iron file such as one
might use for sharpening a crowbar. The boy and the girl,
one after the other, lie with their heads on the man's lap and
he files away vigorously, making a frightful sound. I wonder
how the patients can bear it, especially when the file gets on
to the eye-teeth, but they never utter a whimper, not even
the girl, only sitting up every half minute to spit out the
filings into a cloth. This cloth will be kept very carefully, for
if an enemy were to get hold of the filings and cast a spell
on them, the spell would also fall on the body from which
they came.

At dusk, soon after six, my houseboy brings me my
dinner on the stone porch of my little hut. Then, around
eight, a clanging and thumping announces that the village
orchestra has begun its nightly practice. Music is as much a
part of Balinese village life as religion. Around a raised,

roofed platform squat thirty men with gongs, drums, a
kind of xylophone with iron keys and bamboo pipes, and
kettle-shaped brass bells which they hit with iron batons. The
drummers hold their slender drums across their laps like
concertinas, beating opposite ends. Behind the great gongs sit
three small girls aged eight or nine, gossiping in whispers,
apparently indifferent to the music.

The faces of the players are quite expressionless in the
glare of the hanging lamp as their wooden hammers and iron
batons rise and fall. After about ten minutes one of the
girls suddenly stops her whispering and walks up on to the
dais. She is wearing a tight brown sarong from her hips
to her ankles, and the upper half of her body is covered by a
close-fitting blue coat with long sleeves. She poises herself
with feet apart and knees and arms bent, like some strange
spider, and begins to dance.

She dances with short, jerky movements like a puppet,
switching her head from side to side and, independently, her
eyes also, as though some terror lurked just behind her
line of vision. Her tiny, bare feet stamp the floor. Her hands
are bent back as though by some unseen force. Each of
her fingers moves with the same disturbing independence as
her eyes. She looks tall under the lamp above the squatting
orchestra, although she is only eight. The eyes of the players
are raised to her from their glistening faces as though she
were a priestess and they her acolytes.

For ten minutes she dances violently thus, while her two
companions still gossip behind the gongs, never throwing
her a glance. Then, abruptly, she stops and shuffles flat-
footed back to the other girls, no longer a priestess but a
tiny, gauche child. The last crashing note of the music
hangs and dies as she walks, and the silence that follows
seems almost deafening until one's ear attunes itself to the
croaking of lizard and bullfrog in the windless equatorial
night.

One morning the *tjokorde* tells me that an old woman has
died and that her corpse will be ceremoniously washed this
afternoon. When anyone dies in Bali, three things happen to
the body. It is publicly washed; then it is buried; then, weeks
or months later, what remains of it is dug up and cremated.

Around three o'clock, several sharp taps on a drum

announce that the corpse-washing is about to begin. A rough
bier of bamboo, like something between a stretcher and
a four-poster bed, has been placed near the hut in which the
dead woman lies on her own broad bed. Everyone who is
not working in the fields has come to see her corpse washed,
three hundred people crammed into the tiny compound,
to say nothing of numerous dogs, chickens and pigs which
scuttle between their feet. Overhead, the equatorial sun is
hidden behind thick grey cloud.

As I arrive, the nearest male relatives of the deceased,
a dozen lusty fellows, pick up the corpse from its bed and
carry it to the bier, at the head of which a little gnarled priest
stands. There they strip her of all her clothes, leaving only
a tiny black square of cloth over her private parts, one
man holding it in place throughout the ceremony. She is an
old woman with only three or four teeth, discoloured by
betel-chewing, protruding from her upper jaw. Mercifully,
she had been married and so had had her teeth filed flat,
otherwise we would have had to see them being filed in her
dead mouth. Her belly is swollen, her breasts withered,
and the soles of her feet are as hard as shoe-leather with sixty
years of tramping the baked earth. Two coins, each with
a hole in its centre, lie over her eyes, lending them a
gruesome, staring aspect.

Now the washing begins. The priest, shrivelled as a
walnut, fills half a coconut shell with holy water and
sprinkles it lightly over her body. The relatives rub it all
over her breasts, belly and limbs with the palms of their
hands. The mouth sags open, the holed coins stare at the
clouds. Then the priest shakes an unsavoury-looking salve,
like lightly scrambled egg, over her, and this too the relatives
rub all over her skin, with revolting effect, rolling her
from side to side to ensure that not a square inch remains
unanointed. Next, he takes a fresh egg and cracks it gently so
that the inside is just able to ooze out. This is rubbed
all over the top of the yellow salve as a symbol of rebirth.
Then, still half full of meat, it is dropped on to the ground,
where a dog eagerly gobbles it up.

Everyone, including the washers, is laughing, talking,
eating and spitting. If a person has led a good life, he
or she will be reincarnated in the form of some superior

147

being, so that a death is a cause for rejoicing, and this disagreeable ceremony is conducted in an atmosphere of irreverent hilarity.

Now the priest puts broken splinters of glass over the coins on her eyes, that these may be bright and sharp in her next life, and shakes iron filings into her mouth, covering her few discoloured teeth with them, that her new teeth may be as strong as iron. He shakes more of these filings over her arms, rubs coconut oil into her matted black hair, and combs it. One of the elder relatives walks up the hill behind the compound and comes back with a perfect banana leaf, six feet long. A corpse is always covered with a banana leaf before being shrouded, but it must be a perfect one and this is not easy to come by, as banana leaves tend to shrivel round the edges. But he has found a fine one and they cut a foot off its length so that it fits her and lay it over her naked, salve-smeared, egg-smeared, filings-covered body. Round body and leaf they bind a white cloth, then a coconut mat, then a mat of bamboo sticks, and carry it back to the bed from which they took it an hour ago.

Everyone except me has brought an offering, and now these are heaped round the shrouded body on the broad bed on which she has lain nightly for more than half a century. There are hundreds of them, rice cakes moulded into elaborate shapes, and small ridged trays of banana leaf containing grains of rice and flower petals. The bed is not big enough to hold them all and two other beds have to be carried from the huts where her children and grandchildren live. The priest lights a joss-stick and blesses the offerings one by one, chanting tonelessly. He is in no hurry and this takes a full half-hour, during which time everyone else lights cigarettes, chats, and chews and spits betel.

At last he is finished, and twelve men carry the bier with its corpse to the graveyard, up a steep and narrow path so slippery with the night's rain that I can hardly scale it in my shoes (but their prehensile feet grip their way as securely as birdclaws), and across a stream by a bridge consisting of two thin bamboos tied together with banyan roots. How they got bier and corpse across amazes me still. At the graveyard two gravediggers are waiting with spades, an old man and a boy, like the two in *Hamlet*. They have dug a shallow grave no

22 Graham Greene

23 Raymond Postgate

24 Arthur Koestler

25 Casper Wrede

26 Maggie Smith in *The Ortolan*, Oxford, 1954

more than three feet deep, and into this the shrouded and
basketed corpse is laid. Everyone wants to help put her there;
at one time I count six people in the grave as well as the
corpse. At last she is laid out to their satisfaction and the
gravediggers are allowed to shovel the earth over her.

But not completely. For in Bali there is a good day and a
bad day for everything, and the priest has declared this to be
a bad day for burial. But since it would obviously be foolish
to keep the corpse above ground in this climate, the Balinese,
ever practical, have evolved the sensible solution of holding
a bamboo tube over the corpse's face and piling the earth
all around her. Thus, technically, the body remains unburied.
When a good day for burial comes, all that is required is
for someone to pull out the bamboo tube and kick earth into
the hole.

There she will lie until, months later, when the flesh has
gone and only the bones remain, her skeleton will be dug
up, cremated, crushed to powder, and scattered over the sea.

Thailand is the one country in south-east Asia where opium-
smoking is legal,* and Bangkok contains no less than 360
licensed dens, plus goodness knows how many unlicensed
ones. So when Graham's friend the prince suggests that
we repair for a few pipes after dinner, along I go.

The den occupies a four-storey house and has a capacity of
300 lamps, one for each smoker. Dreadfully thin people
lie around on the ground floor; opium wastes away the
flesh. The proprietor kicks these figures contemptuously aside
and leads us up to the first floor where things are more
respectable. We strip to our underclothes, lie down on
bamboo mats and are served with excellent tea and expertly
massaged by stern-faced middle-aged women. In the next
compartment, separated from us by only a wire netting,
five youths are quietly playing cards.

The prince buys a small tin of opium for a few shillings; it
looks like black Vaseline. I extract a small blob on the
end of a metal pin, and hold it against a vertical banana leaf
above a small open lamp, rotating it slowly. Within a minute
it attains the consistency of chewed chewing-gum. I press it

* No longer now.

149

into a little hole near the bottom of the pipe, a long graceful
instrument like a thick clarinet, and then take one long
inhalation lasting perhaps ten seconds. That is all; a pipe lasts
no longer. The blob of opium is now a charred coal.
It tastes like very mild pipe tobacco, with a slight herbal
flavour. Taking things easily, I smoke four pipes over two
hours; they leave an effect of pleasant light-headedness but no
particular stimulation, and make me garrulous, though as
everyone else has become garrulous too, nobody listens.

During my third pipe two armed policemen stride into the
den. I tremble; but they are not interested in us. They arrest
the five card-players for gambling in a public place, which
the opium den, being licensed, officially is. The remaining
295 of us continue smoking, within the law.

When I go to bed at four I drowse half-awake for an hour
as though pillowed on cloud before being roused to pay an
early visit to the river market. I feel as though I had slept for
twenty-four hours, and have no reaction except that I cannot
focus my eyes on the newspaper at breakfast. By the time
I return a few hours later, even this inconvenience is gone. It
struck me as rather nicer than gin, both in its taste and its
after-effects.

The comforts of Hong Kong, the fleshpots of the East. But
after a few days I find myself longing for the confusion and
discomfort of Indonesia, with its ricefields and gorges and the
continual feeling of something unexpected about to happen,
whether it is an attempt on the President's life or simply a
forbidden cock-fight, a movement in the grass that might be
a snake or a woman lying half-naked and asleep by the side
of the road.

The journalists here tell me that it is impossible to get into
China. They have all tried and been refused visas. Then one
of them asks if my passport describes me as a journalist or
simply as a writer. 'A writer,' I say, and he says I may stand
a chance, since the Chinese regard journalists as cunning and
inquisitive and writers as gullible. I apply and get a visa.
Before I leave Hong Kong I am recruited as a British spy.

The *Daily Telegraph* correspondent asks me over a drink
if I would be willing to note a few things at Chinese airports.
I agree vaguely, and forget about it. A Mr Hooper telephones

and asks if he can come and see me; when he arrives I cannot
make head or tail of what he is talking about, and say so.
He says: 'You're the right man for us.' My supposed pretence
of not knowing who he was is a big point in my favour;
it shows that I have my wits about me. He says I am to
note the types of Chinese aircraft at the various airports I
shall pass through, since some of my travel in China will
be done by air. I protest that I cannot tell one motor car
from another, let alone aircraft. He says he will teach me,
and under the show of meeting daily for chess he explains
diagrams of various aircraft and then tests me to see if I have
remembered which is which. I fail all the tests dismally; it
is the Oxford radar course all over again. But they have no
one else, so he wishes me luck and I promise I will do my
best. But when I look down on my first Chinese airfield as
we come in to land and try to focus on the aircraft standing
there it makes me feel sick; I can only do it from higher up,
whence I cannot tell one aircraft from the next even if I could
remember which is which. Mr Hooper is very disappointed
when I return. 'We were rather relying on you.' I would
probably have been spotted making notes and ended up in a
Chinese jail.

A performance in Peking of Ibsen's *A Doll's House*, in
Chinese but directed by a Norwegian. The audience is greatly
excited by the plot, for marriage is traditionally regarded
as sacred here. In an interval I see an old couple talking
animatedly, and ask my guide if he can eavesdrop and
tell me what they are saying. He returns. 'They have been
married for thirty-five years, and the woman is saying to the
man: "This is exactly how you have treated me all the
years we have been married".'

The zoo in Chengtu where the prize exhibit is a blackbird
which has been taught to say in Mandarin: 'Long live Mao
Tse-Tung.' The keeper tries to get him to perform, but
he remains obstinately silent. I suggest that he has become a
Rightist, but nobody thinks this funny.

The greyness and dullness of Peking, apart from its six
or seven showpieces such as the Forbidden City. The twelve
whites who ask me to join them in a restaurant and turn
out to be western communists, some under sentence of death
for treason should they return home. Most plainly hate the

countries of their birth, but one, Alan Winnington,* speaks
with nostalgia of the London he will never see again, asking
about journalists he knows and Fleet Street pubs and cricket.

In Sarawak my host, Tim Dix, takes me up the river to visit
some Dyak headhunters. Unlike most primitive peoples, they
live not in individual huts but in communal buildings called
'longhouses', anything from forty to a hundred yards long. It
is a long journey to get there, though only seventy miles
on the map. First, we go upriver for three hours in a motor
launch. The Rejang is as broad as the Thames at Westminster
and lined with impenetrable jungle. I see no beast or bird
apart from a snake which swims across just ahead of us, its
head raised above the water. I ask about crocodiles, and am
told that although they are quite common even experts find it
difficult to distinguish them from the driftwood which floats
about the river and lies along its banks. They wait until they
see something edible – a human or a monkey – near the
water's edge, then float past it pretending to be a log, flip it
into the water with their tails and hold it beneath the surface
till it drowns. When a crocodile has eaten enough to satisfy
its immediate needs, such as a leg, it will store the rest in
a kind of underwater larder until it gets hungry again; it likes
its meat high.

Eventually we turn into a smaller river and change into
a boat of shallower draught. We proceed in this for another
two hours, admiring the numerous varieties of orchid which
hang from the trees; they are almost as common as weeds in
Sarawak. But as the river is low we have to stop a good way
from the longhouse and go the rest of the way on foot
– only about a mile, but the nastiest mile I have ever walked.
The path is a series of steep climbs and descents and is
greasy with recent rain, no problem for the natives who walk
barefoot, but I, having been advised by Tim to wear tennis
shoes, spend much of the time on my seat or stomach.
Then we come to a river. It is in fact the river we have just
left, winding across our path, and the only bridge is a
narrow tree-trunk no wider than a telegraph pole, greasy
with mud and with no handrail but a slack rusty wire at knee

* Brother of the film critic and caricaturist Richard Winnington.

height. It has been only roughly trimmed of its branches
and is covered with spiky protrusions which preclude sitting
astride it.

I have always had a peculiar horror of walking along
narrow surfaces over any kind of drop, however small,
and the water thirty feet below seems uncommonly full of
driftwood. It probably is just driftwood, but the odds against
one of those logs being a crocodile aren't long enough
to be comforting.

Our guides scamper across in their bare feet, and Tim,
who just missed his rugger Blue at Oxford, says: 'Well,
let's go.'

'Not in a thousand years. We'll have to go round.'

'There's no way round.'

'Look, Tim, I'm sorry, but I can't and won't go across
that thing. I'd rather turn back.'

'We can't go back because it'll be dark in two hours, and
we can't navigate the river after dark or the driftwood will
rip the bottom out of the boat. We can't sleep in the boat or
we'll get murdered by mosquitoes. We've come six hours
to see these headhunters and it'd be silly to stop now.'

All this is true, and I realize that I have got into a situation
from which there is no retreat and I will have to go across
that tree trunk, crocodiles or no crocodiles.

One of the native boys, something of a psychologist, runs
across the tree trunk from the far bank and holds out a thin
bamboo pole for me to clutch. From a practical point of view
it is utterly useless, but in two senses it gives me something
to hold on to. I grasp it with one hand, and the rusty wire
by my knee with the other, and edge my way across, not
daring to look down. Somehow I manage it.

'Never again, Tim, not for all the money in the world.'
(It hadn't yet occurred to me that I would be coming back
the next day.)

'There's another one half a mile on.'

There is, and I have to face the whole business again.

At last we reach the longhouse, where the chief receives
us warmly and gives us nuts and fruit. I change into a
clean shirt and we sit down to wait until the younger
men and women come back from the fields. A long broad
corridor runs down the centre of the longhouse and acts as

153

a kind of common-room. Off it at intervals doors lead
into private apartments; each family has its own. The walls
are decorated with photographs and advertisements from
British and American magazines; Lana Turner is there and a
fine reproduction of Trooping the Colour. Thirty or forty
fighting-cocks are tethered down both sides of the corridor,
great savage brutes almost the size of turkeys, plus the usual
assortment of mangy, ill-tempered dogs which one finds
all over Asia and which are a much greater menace than the
snakes and spiders.

The chief feeds us in his living-room on rice and a lean
and muscular cock, then we and all the other families move
into the corridor and the evening's entertainment begins.

Tiny coconut-oil lamps are lit all along the corridor.
These finger-nails of flame have the most beautiful effect,
particularly on the line of human heads that dangle from the
centre of the roof, shrivelled and smoke-blackened. 'Old
enemies,' the chief explains with a laugh, which we echo
rather half-heartedly.

The longhouse orchestra strikes up, a dozen or so splendid
young girls naked to the waist and armed with a formidable
assortment of cymbals, gongs and drums. They crack away
deafeningly at these while our tumblers are filled and refilled
with *arrack*, and one by one the chiefs rise, wearing long
feathered headdresses and carrying swords and shields, and
perform a slow and stately dance. I sit drinking my *arrack*,
having forgotten tomorrow's walk back over the bridges, at
peace with the world.

After about six dances, the music stops. I applaud with
the rest, and wait for the next to begin, but nobody seems to
be moving and I notice that for some reason they are all
looking at me. A ludicrous possibility occurs to me but I
dismiss it. Then our interpreter, a young native policeman,
says: 'Now you must do the dance of thanks.'

'Ah. I'm afraid I don't dance. Please explain to them
and say how much I have enjoyed their hospitality and their
dances and everything.'

'I'm sorry, I can't tell them that.'

'Why on earth not?'

'You are the guest of honour, and you must do the dance
of thanks.'

'Why not Tim?'

'Because he has been here before.'

'Look. The only dances I know are fox-trot and waltz.
I can't dance them solo. And if I could, I couldn't do them to
this music.'

'Well,' says the policeman patiently. 'You'll have to do
something.'

I look around. They sit there smiling, a good two hundred
of them, in the shadows under the long row of skulls, with
the fighting cocks lining the walls behind them. Once again,
as at the two rivers, I realize that there is no retreat and
no way round. It is like one of those dreams in which one is
waiting in the wings to go on as King Lear without knowing
a single line of the part.

I stand up in my muddy khaki shorts and filthy tennis
shoes. An excited murmur of anticipation arises from the
two hundred headhunters and their wives and children. The
orchestra strikes up its hideous din. As I move forward
the chief offers me his sword and shield. I take them, and
advance into the open space to the accompaniment of Dyak
music and without the foggiest idea of how I am going
to get through the next five minutes.

Well, whether it is the *arrack* or the music or what,
I find myself fighting an imaginary opponent twice my size,
a Goliath. At first he overpowers me and forces me back
to the edge of the ring and to my knees, from which
position I defend myself desperately against a rain of gigantic
blows. Somehow I fight my way up to my feet and back
into the centre of the ring. Then his strength tells again and
I am driven back, the orchestra banging away like mad
all the while. Inch by inch I regain the centre of the floor. By
this time I have had enough, and drive my sword into
his huge chest and fell him. As he topples, I ease my sword
out of his flesh and set my foot on his head. The orchestra,
which has evidently been following me closely, utters a
final crash of triumph.

There is tremendous applause. The chief asks something;
the interpreter explains: 'He wishes to know whether this
is an English or a Swedish dance.' I say Swedish; there seems
less likelihood of this being queried by future visitors. I
am toasted in *arrack* by this headhunter and that, and drink

155

goodness knows how many tumblers more. At last they
decide to call it a night and retire. I am left on the hard floor
of the corridor with a coconut mat about a millimetre
thick, a thin cushion and a blanket.

They extinguish the lamps, and I am lying there in the
dark trying to get used to the floor when suddenly I spot a
single, beady eye staring at me a foot and a half from
my head. After a moment it is joined by another eye next to
it. I wonder what it can be – too small for a dog or a
pig, too big for a chicken. I strike a match, and see that one
of those enormous fighting cocks has wandered to the limits
of its tether, a frayed string, and is looking down at me
with a disagreeably predatory expression. It occurs to me that
somewhere, years ago, possibly in my nursery, I have read or
heard something about birds pecking out the eyes of sleeping
humans. Probably an old wives' tale, I assure myself, but
as my match goes out there stands this great brute with its
monstrous beak and claws and that frayed string round
its leg, and I do not like the way it is looking at me.

I pull the short blanket over my head, but this exposes my
feet, which within three minutes are both covered with
mosquito bites. I curl up in the blanket with my feet and face
and everything inside, a hideously uncomfortable position
to be in on a wooden floor one degree from the Equator.
The heat, the hardness of the slats beneath the thin mat,
the irritation in my feet and the proximity of the fighting
cock are almost unbearable. By two o'clock, however, thanks
largely to the *arrack*, I am beginning to drift into some
kind of uneasy unconsciousness when it begins to rain.
The longhouse has recently been fitted with a corrugated iron
roof, of which the chief is very proud because it withstands
falling coconuts. Imagine the sound of tropical rain on a
hundred yards of that. It is past three when I finally manage
to doze off, and sharp at four every fighting cock in the
longhouse crows. Under the raised floor the chickens begin
to squawk and the pigs to squeal. There is not much chance
of anyone oversleeping in a longhouse. I cannot face the
plate of entrails which is offered me for breakfast, recall that I
have a bar of chocolate in my pocket, put my hand in
and find that it has melted. I now remember that I have got
to cross those two bridges again.

But here at least I am lucky. The rain in the night has swollen the rivers, and our guides are able to paddle the boat almost up to the ground where the longhouse stands. I get in and we start back on the long journey to Sibu. The earth is already beginning to steam from the heat of the newly uprisen sun. It is Christmas Eve.★

I have said that these months in the Far East were the most educative period of my life. Living in Sweden had taught me to look at Britain from the outside. The Far East taught me to do so towards Europe. Asians, I learned, regard Europe rather as we do the Middle East, as a small section of the globe full of little countries which cause trouble out of all proportion to the space which they occupy. The year before I went to the East, Russia had invaded Hungary, but this made little impression in Asia, because few Asians knew exactly where Hungary was. But when, a year after my return to Europe, China occupied Tibet, the effect was dramatically different. As I wandered round that vast continent, it seemed to me, from the conversations I had, that virtually every Asian country except Japan would go Communist within five years. Everywhere I went in 1957 and 1958, the young spoke of the new China as the young in Europe must have spoken of the French Revolution 160 years earlier. But China's occupation of Tibet changed that. This was imperialism, and every Asian knew it. In 1959 the Chinese did not bother about world opinion because to them, as to the ancient Greeks and Romans, all other peoples were barbarians, and they did not mind what these people felt about them any more than the Greeks and Romans minded what their barbarians felt. Thirty years later, things have changed. The Chinese now mind what the outside world thinks. But in 1959 they did not, and thereby missed an opportunity that may not occur for them again. Asia then was ripe for Communism.

I also for the first time understood, as no one who has not visited the Third World can, the true meaning of poverty. Nowhere in Europe does poverty exist as it does in the Third World, and no amount of reading about it can compare with seeing it. It is the same with totalitarianism. I was lucky that I did not go into China as an invited guest but saw it from a worm's-eye view. I was dragged into police stations, grilled and threatened, psychologically (never, thank

★ A year later Tim Dix told me that when he next visited the longhouse, the chief asked him: 'And how is the dancer from Sweden?'

heaven, physically) intimidated, spied upon. But when afterwards, in Singapore, I denounced the state of things in China, then still somewhat idealized in the West, someone asked: 'If you were a poor Asian, would you rather your children grew up in China, where they would have no freedom of thought but would be well fed and clothed and would have every chance of living to seventy, or in Calcutta, where they could think freely but would probably not live to be ten?' It is a question I have never been able to answer.

12

A Window Pane

I had no clear idea what to do when I returned to Europe in 1958. I was now thirty-seven and had achieved very little, especially when I compared myself with my Oxford contemporaries who had survived the war. Iris Murdoch, Philip Larkin, John Heath-Stubbs, Kingsley Amis, John Mortimer, Francis King, Kenneth Tynan, Michael Flanders and Donald Swann had all made their mark. I was far from sure whether I should continue as a writer, but what else could I do? I didn't want to return to teaching. I was financially independent but didn't want to be a drone. I decided to go on living in Stockholm, where I felt less of a failure. But before I left London that summer, Casper Wrede mentioned that he was going to direct Ibsen's *The Lady from the Sea* on television that autumn, together with Michael Elliott, and asked me to come and go through with him the translation which I had, as I thought, completed two years earlier. I imagined that this might take an evening; in the event it filled three of the most traumatic and educative weeks of my life.

Casper knew Norwegian as well as he knew Swedish, Finnish and English, in the last of which he was sufficiently expert occasionally and legitimately to correct mine. He sat with Ibsen's original text on his knee while I read out my version. Line by line he destroyed what I had written. 'You've used twelve words where Ibsen used seven.' 'Yes, but – ' 'You're translating it as though it was dialogue in a novel. Play dialogue is much tighter' (a fact which Rattigan had impressed on me with regard to *The Ortolan*, but which I had forgotten). 'You've put the key word in the wrong place . . . This line should be evasive, you've translated it too directly . . . You've put in an image that isn't there, Ibsen's spareness is better . . . This line would get a laugh in the Norwegian, yours won't . . . Ibsen repeats a word that appeared three lines earlier, you've missed that.'

By the time we had finished, barely a line of my original version remained.

When I was a schoolboy I used to play rackets, a game that needs exceptionally tightly strung rackets. Our professional, a splendid old gentleman named Walter Hawes who had been a famous champion, used to string rackets as he talked, and I remember how after each line of gut had been pulled through its two holes as tightly as one would imagine possible, he would loop the loose end of the gut round the stump of an old handle and twist it until the gut in the racket became so taut that it seemed about to snap. That is what stage dialogue has to be like; it is to novel dialogue as the gut in a new racket is to the gut in an old one which has been lying next to a radiator all winter. This is the first principle of play translation, and I have dwelt on it because it remains surprisingly unappreciated. I don't suppose I would have learned it if I had not had the good fortune to work with a director who was also bilingual in the languages involved.

I never saw that *Lady from the Sea*; I had to go back to Sweden before it was shown, on 24 August 1958. It was performed live, as most television plays were then, and no recording was made. The great Norwegian actor Claes Gill played Dr Wangel, and I especially regret that I missed his performance. He was one of the finest of European actors, and also one of the best Norwegian poets of his time, a remarkable maverick who took up acting in his middle thirties after a vagabond youth (he once advised me that the best place to sleep out of doors in winter was on a ship in the docks if you could slip aboard, because you could curl up round the funnel and so keep warm). He told Casper that he found it exciting to play Ibsen in English, since Norwegian has changed as much in the century since Ibsen wrote as English has changed in two hundred years, so that Ibsen in the original, modern though his language was for its time, sounds to present-day Norwegian ears as Sheridan would to us had he written tragedies. Thirty years later an equally great Norwegian actor, Espen Skjønberg, said exactly the same to me after playing Brendel in *Rosmersholm* and Old Ekdal in *The Wild Duck* in English at the Royal Exchange Theatre in Manchester. I made it a rule never to use any word that would not have been current English at the time the play in question was written; apart from the intrinsic vulgarity of anachronisms, any attempt to update dialogue will date within a decade.

Laurence Olivier was planning to do *John Gabriel Borkman* on TV that autumn. He saw *The Lady from the Sea* with his wife, Vivien

Leigh, who told him that he should get Casper to direct him. Neither Olivier nor Casper liked the version they had, so one midnight in Stockholm I was woken by a telephone call from Casper asking if I could translate *Borkman* in a month. My Norwegian, though still shaky, had been much improved by the work I had done with Casper on *The Lady from the Sea*. I went through the same process with him on *Borkman*, and by the time we had finished I knew the language pretty well.

The news that Olivier was to appear on television caused a sensation. Unlikely as it must seem now, television then was still regarded with suspicion by leading actors and writers, much as the cinema had been in its early days. Six years earlier I had been one of a group of thirty or so established or supposedly promising novelists, playwrights and poets whom the BBC had invited for a weekend to try to persuade us to turn our hands to this upstart medium. Olivier's decision was a great turning-point for television in Britain. At a stroke, it made it respectable.

Borkman had a powerful cast, with Irene Worth and Pamela Brown as the elderly twin sisters, and it should have been even stronger, for a little known twenty-two-year-old named Albert Finney had been engaged to play the son, but was released because a film offer was made to him. Casper directed it beautifully, but Olivier, fine in his first two acts, inexplicably shrank from the great final scene on the mountain, which humbler actors than he often manage to bring off. He was so displeased with his performance that he refused to allow the recording to be sold to America, which was bad luck for the rest of us. He was, as always, very professional to work with, punctual to the dot and agreeable to all; but he had made up his mind how he was going to play the part, and when Casper tried to get more out of him for the last act, Olivier told him: 'This is the performance you're going to get.' It was especially sad, for I have never seen the earlier and more difficult acts better done. Olivier's inability to portray any kind of close relationship was no handicap, because that is one of Borkman's limitations too. Irene and Pamela were both superb, as was old George Relph as Foldal. Relph had begun his stage career in 1905, the year Irving died; he told me that in those days the theatres were so full of smoke and noise from the audience that actors had to wave their arms when they spoke so that the spectators would know which of them was talking. Vivien Leigh, who was playing in Giraudoux's *Duel of Angels* at the Apollo, turned up at the studio after the performance. She said she had watched most of it on a set in her dressing-room. When I said: 'Surely you can't have managed to see much', she replied that she had cut a lot of her speeches, which must have been difficult for her fellow-actors as well as bad luck for her audience. That evening I found her enchanting. When the black mood was on her, she was famously impossible.

Casper, together with a civilized impresario named James Lawrie, now booked the old Lyric Opera House at Hammersmith for a five-month season to start the following January. He assembled a strong group, led by Patrick Wymark and Patrick McGoohan, named it the 59 Theatre Company, and commissioned me to translate Strindberg's *Creditors* and Ibsen's *Brand*. *Brand* was to be directed by Michael Elliott, which rather worried me, as he had never done anything on the professional stage and seemed a very shy and withdrawn person. It had never been professionally performed in Britain apart from a solitary Sunday-night performance in 1912, and when I read it my doubts increased. Ibsen had written it as early as 1865 to be read, not acted, and in intricately rhymed verse; the first performance of it in 1885, I discovered, had lasted for six and a half hours. I had five weeks in which to translate it, cutting as I went. I returned to Sweden that December of 1958 full of foreboding.

Stockholm in winter is not the most cheerful of cities, and my depression deepened as I started to translate. What on earth could I do with this powerful but seemingly intractable text? I knew I could not turn it into rhymed verse, since rhyme in English is death to any stage dialogue except comedy, and anyway I had never been much of a poet. I began to put it into prose, and the result was dreadful. It might, I reckoned, be all right for the lighter passages later, such as the scenes with the Mayor and the Provost, but for the high drama of Act One, and especially for the long reflective monologues, it was hopeless. The whole project seemed lunatic, and what could the shy young man in London who had never done anything in the professional theatre before make of this unwieldy old play?

At times of misery, I eat the way other people drink, so I went to the then best restaurant in Stockholm, the Theatre Grill, taking my awful typescript with me. As I stared over the food at my dead prose, I wondered if I might turn it into blank verse, and began to tinker with it to that end, but the result was turgid. The problem seemed insoluble, and I cursed Casper for having saddled me with it. Casting around for a lifeline, I thought of T. S. Eliot's *The Family Reunion*, one of my favourite plays, and the form he had used of a free verse often bordering on prose which could move between comedy and high tragedy without incongruity; the audience, said Eliot, should not be conscious that they were listening to poetry. That seemed a possible solution, and by the time the coffee had arrived I had convinced myself that it was the only method that might work.

I duly translated an act a week, finishing each draft on Friday night, revising over the weekend and posting it to Michael Elliott on Monday morning. In January I came to England to work with him on the script. Line by line we went through it, he with my translation on his knee while I read Ibsen's text to him, translating literally. Jolly singing accompanied this process from the next room, where George Hall, our musical director for the season, daily rehearsed a charming couple called the Terry Sisters for some very different play. Eventually Michael and I hammered out a text that we thought might work.

Meanwhile, the season opened with a spirited production by Casper of Büchner's *Danton's Death*. Patrick Wymark was a splendid Danton, and the actor whom Michael had chosen for Brand, Patrick McGoohan, played St Just. He seemed an ideal Brand; but he was not the easiest person to get on with, and he decided, for one reason or another, that he would not play the part. We asked two or three other actors, including John Neville and Ian Bannen, to take it over, but they all said no, and we were in despair. Then by good luck McGoohan came to Michael's flat one day, found him busy and our draft on the table, leafed through it and declared that he would do it after all.

Casper followed *Danton's Death* with a fine production of *Creditors*, as good a Strindberg production as I have seen in this country, with a marvellous performance by Mai Zetterling as the man-eating woman novelist whose former husband returns incognito to destroy her new marriage. I cannot imagine that this role has ever been better played. Sadly, although she was only thirty-three, it was to be her last appearance on any stage, apart from a few unhappy previews of *Hedda Gabler* the following year in New York. Like so many of her generation in Sweden, she gave up acting, in her case to become a film director. She is good at that, but the theatre lost a major actress.

Creditors was acclaimed, but it shared a double bill with Thomas Otway's version of Molière's *The Cheats of Scapin*, in which the leading actor (now dead) camped it up outrageously and got the bird from an outraged gallery. Our houses were not good for either this or *Danton*; a week of fog was followed by several weeks of snow, and although Hammersmith was no further from most people's homes than the West End, there was little local support and no casual trade, for the theatre was tucked away behind a market and difficult to find even if you were looking for it.

In such unpropitious circumstances, *Brand* started rehearsal in March. Three weeks were all we could afford to prepare this complex play, and McGoohan was delayed filming in Canada, so he had only two and a half weeks. Dilys Hamlett was Agnes, Patrick Wymark the Mayor and among the crowd were three youngsters who were to make their mark as writers, Ronald Harwood, Paul Bailey and P. J. Kavanagh.

I had gone back to Stockholm after the opening of *Creditors*, and returned to London only in time for *Brand*'s dress-rehearsal. The voyage across the North Sea, never pleasant in winter, was the worst I have known. I crouched over the basin in my cabin praying that the ship might hit some forgotten mine, so that my misery might cease. I also vowed that, if this did not happen, I would never travel on the North Sea again, a vow that I kept even though it meant doing without my car in Sweden. So, that evening of 7 April 1959, I turned up at the Lyric Opera House, one of the prettiest, if also one of the most run-down and draughtiest, theatres in London.

How can I begin to convey the doomed quality of that unforgettably appalling evening – or rather, night, for the succession of disasters had by no means concluded at midnight? *Brand* is set mostly out of doors, and Richard Negri had designed magnificent sets, but the effect of these depended considerably on a complex lighting scheme. Our lighting designer was a young stage-manager who had never lit a play before this season, Richard Pilbrow; he was soon to establish himself as the leading lighting designer in London. But that evening, everything that could go wrong did. Actors spoke from the dark while spotlights illuminated empty corners of the stage. Our equally complex and ambitious sound scheme, with its storms at sea and final avalanche, fared little better. Worst of all, McGoohan, not surprisingly after only two and a half weeks, did not know his lines or his moves (and Brand is on stage virtually throughout the play). Around midnight – the performance was scheduled to take two and a half hours, including two intervals – we started the last act. This takes place on the top of a mountain, and Negri had designed long plywood fingers to which some kind of muslin was glued, giving an eerie effect of icicles. The glue on these had melted, and the muslin hung limply down like stockings on a line. That somehow seemed to epitomize the evening. When at last it was over, around 1.30 a.m., Michael, Casper and I went off to the only place where one could get a meal at that time then, the Cromwell Road Air Terminal. There, under harsh neon strips, we ate under-fried eggs with chips, all slimy; the other tables were mainly occupied by ladies of the streets. I remember nothing of the conversation, only my certainty that the show, on which we had built such hopes, was beyond salvation.

Next day, at lunch at the Savile, I met two drama critics who said: 'Looking forward to your play tonight.' I wanted to beg them not to come. When I arrived at the theatre that evening and went to the gents, another two critics positioned themselves on either side of me at the urinals and said: 'Looking forward to this.'

Michael had spent the whole day trying to iron out the technical problems, and had had no time for a second dress-rehearsal. He went into McGoohan's dressing-room before curtain-up and, since McGoohan was an explosive and unpredictable actor, asked him to hold back and not release emotionally too early.

The curtain rose, and technically at least things went well. The lighting and sound were right, and McGoohan, though occasionally in his nervousness he repeated a word or a phrase, found his positions and knew his lines. But he was holding back to such an extent that the play did not catch fire. By the second interval Michael was convinced that the evening was a failure, and walked outside until the bell to avoid hearing audience comments.

Then came the fifth act. Ibsen was a master of the final act, but he never wrote a greater one than in *Brand*. When the villagers who have followed Brand up the mountain turn on him and stone him, McGoohan suddenly unleashed all his terrifying power, and from then until the final moments, when the gipsy Gerd fires her rifle at the supposed hawk and brings down the avalanche on them, the audience was gripped as seldom happens in a theatre. Michael had devised a marvellously simple yet effective method of suggesting the avalanche. The rifle-shot evoked a distant boom, the pale sun behind the gauze began slowly to contract and distend like a human heart, the darkness and the roar intensified until, following Brand's cry: 'If not by Will, how shall Man be redeemed?', there was sudden silence, the invisible ghost of Agnes replied: 'He is the God of Love', the avalanche descended with redoubled force and the curtain descended with it. The audience rose and cheered; never have I heard a reception to equal that.

When the actors had changed, we went to the pub to celebrate.

McGoohan was brooding and gloomy. 'It didn't work,' he kept saying. A girl student in a long striped scarf came round asking the actors for autographs. She asked Michael for his, then Negri, then me, the first time anyone had done that. 'I'm only the translator,' I said modestly, to which she replied: 'Oh, sorry, I thought you were an actor,' and passed on.

Next day the reviews were unanimous and enthusiastic. Audiences crowded in; we took £201 one evening that week, which seemed enormous with the prices we were charging. For a month we played almost to capacity (the theatre held 800), making up the losses we had incurred on *Danton's Death* and *Creditors*. Even the weather had relented. We decided to run *Brand* for an extra month, but our bad luck returned. May brought a heat-wave. Nobody wanted to spend those sweltering evenings in a theatre, least of all to see Ibsen at Hammersmith. In that month we lost all our profits and more. We had to close. We had, it seemed, failed.

Yet how often since have I met actors, directors and ordinary theatre-goers who have said to me: 'That 59 season was the most exciting I ever saw.' It made several reputations: Casper, Michael, Pilbrow, Negri and of course McGoohan. In a smaller way, it made me. Offers poured in for McGoohan: to play a secret agent named James Bond in a film series that was being planned; to act the part finally played by Alan Bates in *Zorba the Greek*; to be Iago to Paul Robeson's Othello at Stratford. To all these, and many others, he said no. One reason, as regards the film parts, was that he would not act any part in which he had to kiss any actress who was not his wife (and she, looking after him and their small sons, had little time for acting). In all the years since *Brand*, I believe McGoohan has never again appeared on the stage, except in a semi-professional *Master Builder* in Los Angeles.

Several years later, I received a telephone call from McGoohan at Elstree, where he was making a television series. He said he was going to make a film of *Brand* and asked if I would come and talk about it. Seated behind a desk, for he was the executive producer as well as the star of the series, he outlined his plans. I asked, 'Who's going to direct it?' He took up a defensive posture. 'I am. You're wondering why I haven't asked Michael Elliott?' 'Well, yes.' McGoohan said: 'Michael has a feeling of guilt towards me. He got good reviews for his production, and I'm glad. He's a nice fellow. But he knows that I directed that production.' I did not know what to say. McGoohan was the kind of actor who only took direction if you persuaded him that he had thought of the idea first, so that Michael had continually had to say: 'Pat, I wonder if we shouldn't go back to that idea you had of turning upstage on that line.' As a result, McGoohan had become convinced that all these improvements had in fact been his. He took me into the studio restaurant for lunch, and when I asked what he would recommend, he said: 'I'm having a salmon steak, but they have to be ordered in advance. The lamb stew's usually quite good.' I thought he might have ordered two salmon steaks, but justice was done, for when his arrived it was fried to a frazzle, and my stew was reasonably eatable. The film never got made.

A quarter of a century later Michael, who had by then founded and run for a decade with spectacular success the Royal Exchange Theatre in Manchester, adapted *Moby Dick* for the stage and asked McGoohan to play Captain Ahab, a part for which he was wonderfully suited, for though he could not act relationships he was splendid at loners. McGoohan agreed, but then saw a television film of *Jamaica Inn* in which he had appeared, and telephoned Michael to say that he felt he could no longer act. All efforts by Michael to persuade him failed. So Ahab was played, magnificently as it turned out, by Brian Cox, and McGoohan remained retired from the stage.

Translating plays suddenly became a way of life for me. An editor at Jonathan Cape who had seen *Borkman* suggested that I should tackle all of Ibsen's major plays, but before the contract was signed he heard that the Oxford University Press had commissioned a don at Newcastle University to do the same, and decided that there was not room for both projects. I first learned of this in Stockholm through seeing in *The Times*, which had recently run an interview with me on the subject, a small headline: PUBLISHERS DROP TRANSLATION. Who's this poor fellow? I wondered and, reading on, found it was me. No other publisher seemed interested. The Newcastle don asked if I would care to share the work with him, but I wanted to do the lot, and felt that he as editor might hold different ideas about translation to mine, as indeed proved to be the case when his versions appeared. That summer, on my way to another Collins cricket match, I mentioned my problem to a lady to whom I was giving a lift. She said she worked in Doubleday's London office and asked me to send her a specimen translation. I didn't at first bother, for she was such a modest person that I assumed her position to be somewhat minor; but she wrote to me, and phoned me, until, more out of politeness than hope, I sent her *Brand*. She turned out to be head of the Doubleday London office, Barbara Noble; Anne Freedgood in the New York office recommended acceptance of the scheme, and Rupert Hart-Davis, thanks largely to Mai Zetterling's husband David Hughes who worked for him, took it up in London on condition that I also agreed to write a biography of Ibsen. So cricket led to the publication of my Ibsen translations and biography as it had to that of my novel.

Translating seemed an answer to my lack of creative drive. It also suited me temperamentally, like keeping the score at cricket matches, something I still occasionally enjoy now that I am too old to play. People sometimes ask me if I have never wanted to direct. Three times I directed a play, at drama schools in the seventies, but although I quite enjoyed it, I did not really relish being at the helm. I like being on the sidelines. I like the sessions with the director before rehearsals start; I like the questions the actors ask about their lines, their eagerness to hear me read out what the Norwegian (or in Strindberg's case the Swedish) literally mean, the confidence and insight it gives them to feel in direct touch with the original, the often valid suggestions they make for improvement. Casper told me how, when he had been assistant director on a famous Ibsen production in the fifties, the actors had simply rewritten the lines ('You say such-and-such, I'll say such-and-such'). How close to Ibsen's original intention can that have come?

Ideally, I would never publish a translation before it has been through the testing-fire of rehearsal and performance, though in practice this has not always been possible. I always like to be at rehearsals for at least the first week, so that the actors can raise any problems concerning their lines. Sometimes they merely want to make a line easier to say when it should not be easy for the character to say it at that particular moment, and then one has to explain this to them. Fortunately, stupid actors seldom seem to get cast in Ibsen or Strindberg plays, and intelligent ones often make suggestions which are improvements. Enid Lorimer, a fine Australian actress then aged around eighty, told me, when she was rehearsing Brand's mother at Hammersmith in 1959, that I had made one speech impossible for her to speak. I looked at it, and it seemed all right. But then she spoke it and I saw what she meant. I had filled it with sibilants, and she had false teeth and sounded like a steam train entering a tunnel. Most actresses who play that part, I realized, or at any rate many, are likely to have false teeth; so I altered it accordingly. A few months earlier, when Olivier was rehearsing *Borkman*, he asked if I could lengthen a certain line which he had to deliver walking towards the window, so that he could turn at the window on the final word. I checked with the Norwegian, and found that I had in fact written a shorter line than Ibsen, so that the actor was unconsciously asking that I should get closer to the original. Incidentally, when a theatre has scripts made which omit Ibsen's stage directions so that the director can plot his own moves, it is amazing how often one finds the actors or the director unconsciously reverting to the moves that Ibsen suggests. I have seen innumerable examples of this.

One of the most difficult problems that face a play translator is rendering the sub-text: the meaning behind the meaning, what lies between the lines. Ibsen was a supreme master of sub-text. If I ask you a question concerning which you have no inhibitions, such as the weather or football or your feelings about a film or a dress, you reply directly. But if I question you on a subject about which you feel guilt or inhibition – your relationship with your sexual partner, or with your parents, or religion or whatever it may be – then you reply not directly but evasively and in a circumlocutory manner. Almost all of Ibsen's main characters are, like Ibsen himself, deeply inhibited people, and at the crises in his plays they are brought to bay with what they fear and have been running away from. Then they talk evasively, saying one thing but meaning another; but to an intelligent reader, director or actor, the meaning behind the meaning is clear, and the translator must word his sentences in such a way that the sub-text is equally apparent in English. These scenes are especially rewarding for actors, since they have to speak one set of words but act another. William Archer, Ibsen's Victorian champion and a fine translator of narrative prose, nevertheless missed nuance after nuance in his versions of the plays; and later adaptors, whose main aim was to produce dialogue as 'easy to speak' as possible, made all those complex Norwegians chat away as cheerfully as characters in a soap opera. This combination of evasiveness and clarity is, I think, the most difficult of all the problems that face an interpreter of his plays.

I have referred to the tautness of stage dialogue; but sometimes a dramatist deliberately relaxes this tautness, just as certain tennis-players will choose a less tightly strung racket for certain conditions, to impart more spin to their strokes. Thus Ibsen, in particular, some-times introduces a deceptive apparency of yield into his dialogue, which is like the yield of barbed wire; at first it seems to give, but then its sharpness becomes disturbingly apparent. The translator must vary his tautness as the dramatist does. Likewise, he must follow the dramatist's changes of tempo. Ibsen was adept at varying the tempo of his dialogue; it is as clear in his texts as though he had written *andante* or *allegro*.

Strindberg presents two difficulties of a different nature to a translator. One is the jagged directness of much of his dialogue (though elsewhere he can be woolly and vague, especially when writing in verse – my heart always sinks when I turn a page and see that he is about to break into verse, for I know the cloudy obscurities and platitudes that I must expect). But in plays such as *The Father, Miss Julie, Creditors* and *The Dance of Death*, the characters speak with a terrifying nakedness of emotion from which many a translator has shrunk. Strindberg's dialogue in such cases is like broken glass, and one must not file down the edges.

The other great problem with Strindberg is the apparent inconsequentiality of some of his dialogue. He knew that people, especially in moments of high emotion, do not think or speak consecutively, A,B,C,D,E; they think A,Z,B,Q,H. Another hazard with Strindberg is that one must resist a tendency to sanify his dialogue. Almost all of his characters are, at the time we see them, in a highly charged state like the characters of Dostoevsky or D. H. Lawrence, a frenzy not far removed from insanity. Insanity is something that all of us recoil from, and I have often noted in myself a shrinking from this aspect of his work. To omit that, or tone it down, would be like reproducing the paintings of Van Gogh or Edvard Munch (two artists with whom Strindberg had much in common) as though they were the work of Claude or Corot.

Naturally, the different ways in which different characters speak must be carefully watched, and this is particularly important in matters of social class. A translator has failed badly if he makes all the characters sound alike. Another and perhaps more difficult problem is that of lifting the language. Any major dramatist possesses this gift; his characters suddenly rise to eloquence, perhaps to poetry, even if it be the poetry of prose. One of the most difficult passages in Ibsen is that in the final act of *John Gabriel Borkman*, containing the marvellous visionary speeches which Borkman delivers as he looks down from the mountain. Unless one can lift the language here to something approaching the original, the actor can do little with it; it becomes, as Laurence Olivier once said of a certain Ibsen translation in which he appeared, 'like straw in the mouth'.

I have become used, though not resigned, to my translations being plagiarized. This is usually the fault of the actors rather than of the adaptor-translator. Unhappy with this or that line, they look up my version, simply because it is the most readily available, and, ignorant of the law of copyright, ask the director if they can use my words without saying where they come from. There was a *Lady from the Sea* in the West End where this happened, a *Wild Duck* where a scrutiny of the prompt copy showed forty-two speeches erased and my own lines substituted, a *Peer Gynt* on television when I suddenly woke up to hear my own rhymed couplets coming from the screen, a *Father* which contained more speeches of mine than I could immediately count. Luckily, few productions of Ibsen or Strindberg in this country do not contain at least one actor or actress whom I know personally or have taught at drama school, and on the last occasion cited above both the leading man and the leading lady told me that the director-adaptor had explained how he had consulted all the available versions and taken what he thought the best lines from each. He suggested, however, that they should consult other versions and use whatever lines they preferred, correctly assuming that I and other translators would not want the expense and general hassle of a lawsuit with the probability that he would not be in a position to pay damages or costs if he lost. I wrote an open letter to *Private Eye* publicly accusing him of plagiarism and challenging him to sue me for libel. He didn't, and has not plagiarized me since. It is surprising how often one hears of such breaches. A young American composer once told me that a university in California had staged my translation of *A Dream Play* with his music, that they had not paid him and he betted they had not paid me, which proved to be right. A friend recognized lines of mine in a *Wild Duck* performed at a Massachusetts College, and they were forced to pay up too. But actors are the main source of information, since their evidence can hardly be challenged.

When my translations first appeared, they were sometimes referred to as 'modernized'. They are no more modern than the original dialogue. For years most British readers without a knowledge of Norwegian assumed that Ibsen wrote like William Archer. He did not. Ibsen wrote a sharp, modern dialogue in advance of his time, closer in its economy and wit to the language of Shaw than of Pinero, but Archer, apart from missing much of Ibsen's waspish humour, translated him back in time into the heavy verbiage of *The Second Mrs Tanqueray*, exactly the kind of language from which Ibsen was trying to free the theatre. The same was true of Strindberg's early translators. But the most difficult thing, if the translator is a creative writer himself, is to keep himself out of it, to resist leaving his thumbprint. Gogol once observed that the ideal translation should be like a new window pane. One should not be aware that it exists.

13

A Long Game of Scrabble

When I returned from the Far East in the summer of 1958, Graham Greene suggested that I should accompany him to Cuba, then still under the Batista dictatorship. He needed to go there to plan the filmscript of *Our Man in Havana*. But I had had enough travel for a while, and refused, a decision that I have often regretted. 'I enjoyed the louche atmosphere of Batista's city,' he was to confess in *Ways of Escape*, '. . . the brothel life, the roulette in every hotel . . . the Shanghai Theatre where for one dollar 25 cents one could see a nude cabaret of extreme obscenity with the bluest of blue films in the intervals.'

Things were not going so well between him and Anita. I see from my engagement book that I met him in Stockholm at the end of August, and it must have been then that he wrote in my copy of his play *The Potting Shed*, published that year: 'On what could be a sad occasion – the last *smörgåsbord*.' On 24 October he wrote from London:

> Just got back three hours ago from Havana . . . I'm very
> tired and a bit depressed. I find after all these weeks that I'm
> just as much in love with Anita as ever – can't get her out of
> my system. Give me news of her. I wish to God that she'd
> live half her time here – then I could stand half in Sweden,
> but I'm afraid the affair's gone flat for her. Well, I'll have
> to console myself with the South Seas.

This last was a reference to a plan he had begun to hatch for him and me to go together to Tahiti.

Tahiti figures in several of his dedications to me from that time: 'In the hope that it will produce Tahiti, this damp squib' (*Our Man in Havana*); 'After 3 schnapps, and in hope of Tahiti' (*The Living Room*). I remember the *Living Room* lunch well, for it almost landed me in jail. We ate at Stallmästaregården on the northern outskirts of Stockholm, and each of our three schnapps measured six centilitres, so that when I drove him back I had almost a fifth of a litre of the stuff inside me. I still then had my first car, a green Sunbeam Talbot which fell to pieces later that year, and after I had dropped him my engine stalled on a busy roundabout in front of the Royal Theatre. Two policemen approached. The laws on drunken driving are very strict in Sweden, and the length of time spent by an offender in prison corresponds to the amount of alcohol in his or her blood. When I cautiously explained my mechanical problem to them (in English, for I hoped that any slight slurring might thus be less obvious), they ordered me to telephone a garage. Reluctant to leave the car and try to walk to a kiosk, I said: 'How can I leave the car in the middle of the roundabout?' They accepted the logic of this, and together pushed my car, with me at the wheel, to the side of the road, then mercifully strode off while I pretended to be looking up a telephone number. There cannot be many a motorist who has had two Swedish policemen push his car while he steered with a third of a pint of aquavit inside him.

On 15 November, Graham wrote me another depressed letter about Anita.

> She doesn't even acknowledge . . . the play [*The Complaisant Lover*, which he had recently completed]. A strange girl. I won't ring up in case a stranger is now installed, and I don't feel I can write again. I write very warmly and was quite prepared to work out an arrangement, but I can't *pester* the girl. If you see or write to her, you can indicate that she's still, unfortunately, in the blood stream and I'm quite unable to look for a successor. If only she'd take a week's holiday in London, but I expect she's found a satisfactory successor. Anyway she's one of the nicest people I've ever met, and my only regret is losing her.

A short while later (the letter is uncharacteristically undated), he wrote to tell me that Anita had finally broken things off. 'No more actresses and no more Swedes . . . Don't worry about the South Seas. It may not be possible for me, as I have to fit in leper colonies in the Belgian Congo before rehearsals of the new play. Script finished today [of *Our Man in Havana* film]. I dread the finish as now there's nothing to do but brood. Why can't one fall out of love as easily as one falls into it?' On the back of the envelope he wrote: 'Petulant tone due to painful liver.'

Graham's play, *The Complaisant Lover*, directed by John Gielgud with a cast headed by Ralph Richardson and Paul Scofield, opened at the Royal Court Theatre in Liverpool on 11 June 1959 for a short tour before coming to London. That happened to be my thirty-eighth birthday, and Graham invited me to travel up with him for the first night, promising me as an additional present a bottle of Cheval Blanc 1950 (a wine mentioned in the play) to accompany our lunch on the train. As we waited on the platform at Euston station, Graham clutching the precious bottle, John Gielgud and the formidable impresario Binkie Beaumont, who was presenting the play, appeared. 'Oh dear,' said Graham. 'We don't want them to join us. This bottle won't do for four.' I had never met Beaumont or, except momentarily, Gielgud, and would happily have forgone my share of the wine in exchange for three hours of their company. But Graham, after introducing me to them, said: 'I'm afraid we can't join you for lunch. It's Michael's birthday and I've promised him this wine and there isn't enough for four.' Beaumont and Gielgud both gave me a look. So Graham and I drank the wine, an incongruous accompaniment to one of British Rail's nastier lunches ('choosing to forget', as he had written a quarter of a century earlier in *Stamboul Train*, 'that a train reduces all wine to a common mediocrity'), watched by Beaumont and Gielgud, both considerable connoisseurs, from another table, and arrived in Liverpool slightly tight, having also consumed a good deal of whisky.

It was a strange evening. At the theatre, Graham and I sat next to an imperious American lady named Mrs Irene Selznick, who had bought the Broadway rights. She was not only the wife of the producer David O. Selznick but the daughter of Louis B. Mayer, two of the wealthiest men in Hollywood, and was in a bad temper because, she asserted, Binkie Beaumont had not met her at the airport. Beaumont himself and Gielgud had prudently seated themselves elsewhere. As we took our places, Sir Malcolm Sargent greeted Graham effusively from the row behind us. Graham shook his hand without enthusiasm, turned to me and said quite loudly: 'Dreadful man. Flash Harry. I can't stand him.' After the final curtain, he asked me if I would take Mrs Selznick back to the Adelphi Hotel where we were staying and look after her while he went round with Gielgud and Beaumont to see the actors, presumably wishing to exclude her from the discussion that was about to take place. This did not please Mrs Selznick, whose humour was worsened when Sargent, having accompanied her and me to the exit, then made his excuses on the ground that he had to go backstage to greet his friends in the cast. Mrs Selznick was furious. 'That,' she informed me, 'is what we call the brush.' I tried to assure her that nothing could have been further from Sir Malcolm's mind, but she commanded: 'Take me back to the hotel. I need a drink.'

The prospect of entertaining Mrs Selznick for what might well be the best part of an hour in the bar of the notoriously expensive Adelphi Hotel worried me. Apart from all else, I had not much money left, having felt bound to pay for our numerous whiskies on the train in gratitude for the Cheval Blanc, and Mrs Selznick looked in need of consolation. But worse was to come. After rapidly downing a couple of drinks, she said: 'I am ravenous. Thanks to your Mr Beaumont I have had no lunch. Let's eat.' Having been on the receiving end of several looks from Mr Beaumont earlier that day, I suggested that we ought perhaps to wait for our host, but Mrs Selznick rose and strode into the dining-room, where the first sight to meet our eyes was Sir Malcolm Sargent seated alone at a table with a bottle of champagne in an ice bucket. 'That man!' cried Mrs Selznick. 'I refuse to eat in the same room as him.' I explained that I did not think the management could well ask him to leave, especially since he was almost certainly staying in the hotel, and pointed out a table for eight, fortunately at the far end of the room, which looked as though it might be for our party and proved to be so. She seated herself, perused the menu, and was about to order when, not a moment too soon, Binkie Beaumont arrived, with Graham, Gielgud, Ralph Richardson and his wife Mu, and Paul Scofield.

It was daunting company for an unknown author to find himself in. I had met Richardson once or twice at the Savile Club but did not know him, he plainly could not remember having met me, and I knew none of the others except Graham apart from my unfortunate encounter with Beaumont and Gielgud. It was by now approaching midnight and the kitchen was about to close. Everyone forwent starters and quickly chose a main dish except Richardson who, professing himself ignorant of French, in which the menu was printed, demanded a full explanation of various dishes, posing many a supplementary question ('Wild mushrooms? You actually send chaps out into the fields of Liverpool to gather them? Do they have to go at night?', etc.) Eventually he decided he did not like anything described and asked if he could have scrambled eggs and sausages, which were not on the menu but which they agreed to provide.

Richardson then talked enthusiastically about cars and aeroplanes, which none of the rest of us knew anything about. 'Oh, Johnny, did you read in the paper about that fellow Campbell? Isn't it wonderful?' 'Campbell, Campbell. Ralph, I can't recall an actor of that name.' 'No, no, no, Donald Campbell.' Gielgud and the rest of us looked blank. 'Ah, come on, Johnny, you know. The fellow who's just beaten the world's speed record.' 'Oh, Ralph,' said Gielgud. 'I do so admire you. You know about the most extraordinary things, machines of all kinds and animals and everything. I don't understand anything in the newspaper except the theatre page, I turn straight to that and that's all I can understand.'

After dinner, we went into the lounge for coffee. Lady Richardson retired; then Richardson said: 'I must take Ambrose [or some such name] for a walk. Without fresh air he can't sleep.' Whether Ambrose was a child or, as seemed more probable, a dog, none of us knew. Ralph then went upstairs and reappeared in a hat, alone as before, saying: 'Here we are. I'll just take him round the block.' It was like the play *Harvey*, in which the chief character supposes himself to be accompanied everywhere by a rabbit which no one else can see. Someone was brave enough to ask: 'Where is Ambrose?' 'Haven't you met him?' said Ralph, and drew from an inside pocket a tiny hamster, which he then carried out into the night. *The Complaisant Lover* proved a triumph, and rightly so, on Broadway as well as in London; Mrs Selznick's ordeal had been worth while. None of us could have foreseen that it would be Graham's last success in the theatre. He inscribed the copy he gave me: 'In memory of Liverpool'.

I did not think we would ever get to the South Seas; Graham always seemed committed to dashing off somewhere else. 'I can see now,' he was to write later, 'that my travels, as much as the act of writing, were ways of escape', and he quoted Auden: 'Man needs escape as he needs food and deep sleep.' But that autumn of 1959 he began to make plans for our journey, and on 20 December we set off from Heathrow. We travelled first class; I think my ticket, right round the globe, cost around £650. Graham had apologized for not being able to leave earlier, saying in his defence: 'We don't need to waste time in Singapore and Bangkok and such places' – rather a blasé observation, I thought, for I would have loved to revisit them in his company, and also to see a little of Australia, where I had never been. But no; we had to be in Tahiti by Christmas. The only place *en route* where I managed to persuade him to leave the airport was Sydney, where we had a couple of hours to spare, ate a fine lobster lunch at the Rex Hotel in King's Cross, and took a taxi ride round the city, admiring the wooden trams and the Victorian wrought-iron balconies. We drove past the cricket ground, at which Graham stared glumly, expressing his relief that there was no match being played which I might have bullied him into watching for a few overs. I am still embarrassed when Australians ask me if I have been to their country and I have to reply: 'For three hours.' (We had also had an hour at Darwin airport, watching the sun rise.)

Graham had an idea that we might recoup much of the difference between our fares and that for tourist class by our consumption of free drinks, and from the time we left Heathrow he kept a note of all we had, calculating what each drink would have cost had we had to pay for it. But although we availed ourselves of every offer, the resultant sum mounted so slowly that he stopped keeping a record after we left Jakarta. The first night we spent out of the plane was at Fiji, where we admired the landscape as we drove into the capital, Suva ('Tahiti'll have to be good to be more beautiful than this,' he remarked), but spent a dull evening. A young American in the hotel, recognizing Graham and evidently unaware of his tastes, took us for a gay couple and attempted to strike up an intimacy, explaining that he was a friend of Terence Rattigan, a writer whose work Graham particularly disliked; nor did he much like Rattigan as a man. (Graham once said to me that he thought talking to Rattigan was like walking on very slippery parquet flooring. I thought this an unfair judgement, since Rattigan had been kind and helpful to me in my early days, although he knew I was not of his persuasion.) We then enjoyed the unusual luxury of three Christmas Eves and two Christmas Days.

To get to Tahiti from Fiji, we had to take a New Zealand Airways flying-boat to Samoa and spend a night there, a prospect that pleased Graham, since he was a remote relation and an admirer of Robert Louis Stevenson, who had spent his last years there. This involved crossing the International Date Line and so going back a day. On Christmas Eve we departed from Fiji and crossed into 23 December, but then the pilot learned that the sea was too rough for us to land at Satapuala, so we turned and, in due course, found ourselves back in Fiji for our second Christmas Eve. Next morning a huge chambermaid woke us with cries of 'Merry Christmas!' Off we went again in the seaplane, entered our third Christmas Eve, and in due course landed successfully at Satapuala. *En route*, we had been given a particularly disgusting meal, the worst Christmas lunch that either of us had ever eaten, though it was not to retain that distinction for long.

We had been advised in Fiji that the best hotel in Samoa was the White Horse Inn. Graham and I both liked the sound of this, but the New Zealand cabin attendant told us that we should not stay there but at Aggie Grey's. This recommendation was confirmed by the pilot when he came round to chat with the passengers. Aggie Grey, he explained, was one of the great characters of the South Seas. Now aged, she had known Somerset Maugham and many great writers of an even older vintage, though unfortunately, not being much of a reader, he could not remember their names. We told him we had already wired for rooms at the White Horse Inn, but he said he could telegraph a message to Samoa cancelling the reservation and booking us in at Aggie's if she had any vacancies, which was, however, doubtful since her hotel was so famous and consequently in great demand. But luck, it seemed, was with us. Aggie could fit us in.

Our hearts did not exactly rise when the taxi deposited us at Aggie Grey's, still less when we entered. We had been told by the pilot that Aggie was an eccentric and that her hotel was not like other hotels, but it looked run-down and sordid to a degree. There was no air-conditioning, or if there was it was not working, and no mosquito nets over the beds, which were hard and lumpy. When we went down for a drink before dinner, the only lounge was furnished with a miscellany of ancient chairs, many of them with broken springs showing through the upholstery. These lined the four walls, so that we and the other guests sat staring at each other across the intervening space as though awaiting a performance of something in the round. One large and comparatively comfortable-looking chair was vacant. This, it was explained to us, was Aggie's.

After an impressive delay, Aggie entered, a rather tall old lady, or do I remember her as tall because she was so daunting? A kind of agreed hush fell over the guests; it was as though we were in the presence of royalty, and, as with royalty, we nodded assent to whatever she said and asked no questions. We had a nasty dinner, and a bad night on the uncomfortable beds, devoured by mosquitoes. If this was the best hotel in Samoa, we wondered, what could the White Horse Inn be like? Next morning we were woken, for the second successive day, with cries of: 'Merry Christmas!' It was pelting with rain, and there was nothing to do but read until lunch, which Aggie had hinted the previous evening would be something special. Graham said: 'At least it can't be as bad as New Zealand Airways.'

In due course, and with ceremony, the feast began. The starter was a tinned-crab cocktail, tasting mainly of tin with an undertone of rust, swathed in an evil bottled mayonnaise. This was followed by an indeterminate, dark-fleshed and sinewy bird. Graham said: 'Do you think we'll get anything to drink?' I said I feared not, since otherwise we would surely have been offered something with the crab, but now the waitresses reappeared with bottles and began to fill glasses, beginning at the far end of the table where Aggie sat. The liquid they were pouring was plum-coloured, like the linoleum at Earleywood, and the labels seemed to have only a single word on them. 'Can you read that?' Graham asked (it was a long table). I said: 'I think it says Armagnac.' 'Don't be silly, Armagnac isn't that colour.' 'I know, but that's what it says.' Graham's expression as it was poured into his glass was something to behold. It tasted like syrup of figs, a laxative much prescribed in his and my childhood, when all medicines were nasty to discourage malingering. Then the pudding arrived. This was a sickly white, like spotted dick, undercooked and suety. Graham and I agreed that we could not remember a nastier meal, even at school or during the war (though New Zealand Airways must have surpassed themselves next day, for in a little paperback volume of Gauguin's paintings which he bought me as a New Year's gift, Graham wrote: '. . . in memory of a terrible Christmas at Aggie Grey's and a worse Christmas meal Samoa-Papeete'). In the afternoon we braved the rain and visited Stevenson's house, with its grate for the open fire which he needed even in that climate, but it was too muddy to climb the hill to his grave.

Next morning we had a five-hour delay at the airport, waiting for the waves to subside sufficiently for the seaplane to take off, but at last we left and, after a brief stopover in the Cook Islands, arrived in Tahiti, Graham's promised land. Neither of us liked Papeete, the capital, a squalid and dreary little town like the nastiest section of the Marseilles waterfront plonked down in the tropics. We stayed at first in a smart-looking hotel which turned out to be infested with rats. But fortunately we made the acquaintance of a splendid Swede, Bengt Danielsson, and his attractive French wife Marie Thérèse. Danielsson, a bald and bearded giant in his late thirties, had been a member of Thor Heyerdahl's Kon-Tiki expedition, the only

27 Helen Mirren in *The Ortolan*, Manchester, 1966

28 With Dyak headhunter women in Sarawak, 1957

29 With Graham Greene in Fiji, 1960

30 Photograph of me
by Graham Greene in Tahiti, 1960

31 My father in old age

Swede among those Norwegians; a professional anthropologist, he had settled in Tahiti and knew it and the other South Sea Islands better than any native, being fluent in several of the local languages as well as in half a dozen European tongues. He found us a bungalow on the shore ten miles outside Papeete which Marlon Brando had occupied during the filming of *Mutiny on the Bounty* a few years previously, and a cook and a maid to look after us. As we drove out to inspect it, Graham said: 'I hope it's more than a mile from the nearest Catholic church.' 'Why?' 'If it's further than a mile we are excused from attending.' He didn't drive a car, though he had done so in Africa during the war. I said: 'I can drive you to within a mile and you can walk the rest.' To his relief, it was more than a mile, and although I several times repeated my offer he never availed himself of it.

We both found Tahiti disappointing – not particularly beautiful, even outside the capital, and much less attractive than Fiji – and stuffed with French *fonctionnaires* and rich French and American drop-outs. The native girls were mostly ugly – as I suppose we might have expected if we had studied Gauguin's paintings more closely – lived in equally ugly huts of planks and corrugated iron, and rode around on motor cycles. They also had very bad teeth, the result, Danielsson told us, of living largely on tinned food brought in by American ships. Graham wondered how they could have earned the reputation of being beautiful, and decided it must have been because until the coming of steam the island lay six weeks' sail from the nearest mainland, so that after that much celibacy even the Tahitian girls must have seemed desirable. We were invited to a series of dull parties, all with the same guests and the same servants (the guests brought theirs along to help), and the same uninteresting food. The Danielssons were our only refuge. But perhaps the dullness helped Graham, for the block which he had encountered on his new novel, *A Burnt-out Case*, now dissolved, and it made good progress.

He kept to a strict routine. He rose each morning at 6.45 and, after breakfast, sat down at the window-seat at one end of the verandah with a wad of paper on his knees, large double sheets of lined foolscap. 'I have a passion for writing on clean, single-lined foolscap,' says Bendrix, the protagonist of *The End of the Affair*. 'A smear, a tea-mark on a page, makes it unusable' and, like Bendrix, Graham made a mark every hundred words to 'help calculate the weight I have given to a scene' (as he was to confess in a broadcast on his eightieth birthday). A decade after Tahiti, when he began *Travels with my Aunt*, he changed to plain paper because he felt 'imprisoned' by the lines. He wrote in longhand with a fine pen in a very small, almost illegible script, for two hours each day; no more, no less. In those two hours he would write seven to nine hundred words, the equivalent of two to three printed pages. (In *Ways of Escape* he refers to his 'usual stint of 500 words' per day on *The Power and the Glory*, but that was in the afternoons after writing 2000 words each morning on *The Confidential Agent*; and a complaint he had made to me earlier that year from Jamaica that he could manage 'only 500 words per day' confirms that he expected a larger daily output at this time.) At 9 a.m. he would stop. This was when I got up, and as I walked along the verandah to the shower room he would look up and say, somewhat complacently I felt: 'Nine hundred words this morning', or, even worse, 'Finished my work for the day' – a depressing remark with which to be greeted when I hadn't yet begun and the thermometer was climbing towards ninety. He said he liked to stop writing when it was going well rather than continue until he dried, because that made it easier to start next day. Then he spent the rest of the morning reading – mostly history, with an occasional novel or thriller, such as Rex Stout – while I struggled at my end of the verandah trying to translate Strindberg's *The Ghost Sonata* (and, later, Ibsen's *The Wild Duck*), incongruous texts in the sweltering heat with the Pacific twenty feet away. Last thing at night, Graham always read through what he had written during the morning so that it would be fresh in his mind when he started again next day. He said he liked to let the unconscious work on it while he was asleep.

During our month on Tahiti, he wrote about a quarter of *A Burnt-out Case*. He seldom spoke about it, and I didn't question him; he once told me that talking about a book he was working on dissipated the excitement of private communication between pen and paper. In any case, I have always found that when he did say anything about a work in progress or just completed, he usually gave a largely false idea of what the book, or play, was about (as with *The Third Man*). But that is true of most good authors of my acquaintance; bad ones are often better at summarizing their books than writing them.

One afternoon when we were driving around the island in a fearfully battered little Citroën we had hired – the windows wouldn't open, a great disadvantage in the tropics, and just before we left the brakes broke, luckily in someone's gravel drive and not on a curve by the cliffs – he told me that *A Burnt-out Case* was the most pessimistic novel he had ever written and that he feared it was gloomy and would bore people, a prognostication which proved quite incorrect. He also told me that he was finding it much more difficult to write novels now than twenty years ago, but there is no internal evidence of this any more than in his subsequent novels, though the extra difficulty continued. But this again is a common characteristic among authors; as they grow older, they know more about the technique of writing but become more exacting, tougher in their demands on themselves, less willing to throw a new handful of characters on the fire, as someone said of Dickens, or to digress into comedy or descriptive narrative that is not integral to the plot.

Once he got stuck on a point of plot. We were swimming, or rather floating on the surface, watching through glass masks the tiny multi-coloured tropical fish moving in and out of the equally multi-coloured masses of coral that lay on the sea-bed in huge rough lumps that cut your leg open if you grazed against them, and when we stopped for breath, he said: 'Why should a man who is absolutely dead inside, with no desire for religion or beauty or women or anything, travel several hundred miles down a river to see a girl he doesn't particularly want to see?' There had to be this meeting between them – it leads up to the crisis of the book – and it had to be in the town, not in the leper hospital where the man was living. Why should he go there? 'To see a doctor?', I suggested. No, there were doctors in the hospital where he was. It was a problem, and we stood there in the blue water with our masks pushed up on to our foreheads like motor-cyclists' goggles trying to think of a motive. I suggested that he might have toothache and have to visit a dentist, but Graham said he had had too many dentists in his novels and plays – a dentist had been the chief character in *The Complaisant Lover*, there had been another in *The Power and the Glory* – everywhere he went, he said, he met dentists (his travel book, *The Lawless Roads*, is full of them, and even on Tahiti our first guide before we met the Danielssons had been one), and he didn't want to introduce another into *A Burnt-out Case*, least of all as motivation for the main crisis. In the end he solved it very naturally; the trip downriver seems such an integral part of the plot that it seems impossible that it could ever have presented any problem of motivation.

We played Scrabble regularly. Graham had brought a board with him, and we had begun while waiting for take-off at Heathrow. We had played on the aircraft, in the airports at Singapore, Bangkok, Jakarta and Darwin, on Fiji and at Aggie Grey's. To my surprise, he was not very good at it. He dislikes crosswords and perhaps the two go together. He even, dare I say it, occasionally mis-spelt a word ('awry' was one, though I cannot remember how he thought it should be). We had made the mistake of not bringing an English dictionary with us and, Tahiti being French, there was none on the island, or anyway none that we managed to find. Occasionally Graham would come up with some improbable word, usually containing a Z or a Q, the highest-scoring letters in Scrabble, claiming that it was an Elizabethan obscenity ('zeb') or the like and swearing that he would prove it from his fifteen-volume *Oxford English Dictionary* when he returned to Albany. Even with such devious strategies, he hardly ever managed to win.

Sometimes these games led to angry exchanges. It was always oppressively hot and humid in the middle of the day, and we had little to do except read and swim. One afternoon he claimed 'quoign', which he said was a building term, though he was not sure precisely what. It would have been an important coup for Graham had I allowed it, for it placed the Q on a treble space, worth thirty points. When I queried it, Graham triumphantly quoted what he claimed to be a line from *Macbeth*. 'Yon castle's quoign doth Duncan's spirit haunt' or something of the sort, and when I said this didn't sound like a Shakespeare line to me, he retorted: 'I know I am right, because when I was at school I learned the whole of *Macbeth* by heart.' 'Really?' I asked, and he said: 'Yes, from the first line, "So fair and foul a day I have not seen" to the last, "Whom we invite to see us crowned at Scone".' I said: 'That doesn't impress me. The first line of *Macbeth* is "When shall we three meet again?"' 'No, that's the second scene. The play begins with Macbeth and Banquo walking across the blasted heath.' 'No, the witches.' Our argument became so heated that we resolved to drive off at once to find a Shakespeare, but that proved as elusive as an English dictionary. None of the French in our neighbourhood possessed one. Eventually we made the longer journey to the Danielssons, who had one indeed, but only an American paperback unpromisingly entitled *Everything Shakespeare Ever Wrote*, with modernized spelling. We looked up *Macbeth*, and I was proved right about the opening scene, which annoyed Graham; then he tracked down his line, which was not by any means as he had quoted it but did contain the word in the sense of which he had spoken, but spelt 'coin'. This, he said, was clearly a modernization. Eventually we agreed to hold the score for that game (we were playing Aggregate Scrabble, the winner being he who had scored most points, not won most games, when we got back to London), and the matter was held in abeyance until we reached San Francisco several weeks later.

He told me proudly that he had given up sugar in tea and coffee so as to lose weight, and produced a little tin of tablets which he shook into these beverages instead. However, in the middle of each morning he would drink a large Planter's Punch, the rum in which must have been the equivalent of many lumps of sugar.

Graham was content on Tahiti because his novel was going well. I was restless. The proofs of my first four Ibsen translations would be due from Doubleday and Hart-Davis sometime in the late winter or early spring, I didn't know when, and I fretted at the thought that I might return late for them and so give my rival in Newcastle the chance to publish ahead of me. Moreover, now that I had finished both *The Ghost Sonata* and *The Wild Duck* I found myself with no more work to do on Tahiti. Sometime that January I asked Graham if he would mind my leaving in two or three weeks, and this led to one of the very few rows we ever had; his book was going well and he wanted to stay. He said, in effect: 'Yes, go, I'll be happier alone.' But this mood of his did not last, and at the end of January we left Tahiti together.

On one of our last nights, we managed to find someone who could provide us with opium. He was a French doctor, small and wizened, looking remarkably like the Graham Sutherland portrait of Somerset Maugham. We went to his house with the Danielssons, neither of whom had smoked opium before. The doctor greeted us in a long flowered robe. Somewhat to my satisfaction, Graham drew either too slowly or too fast on his first pipe, so that it went out prematurely, while I managed mine in a single deep inhalation. '*Bien, monsieur, bien,*' said the doctor, '*Vous avez la disposition*' – the only time I have ever been praised for anything in French, except by the bride's father for my knowledge of music as described earlier. Sadly, I remember nothing else of that evening, as is often the way with opium. It was the second and last time I smoked it, an agreeable experience which left no hangover, but one which I have never had any particular desire to repeat.

We spent a couple of hours on the island of Borabora between changing planes, and wished we could have had longer there. After another night in Fiji we flew on to San Francisco. It was my first visit to the States, and Graham's first to San Francisco. He liked it greatly, as I did; this, he said, was a city he wouldn't mind living in. We arrived in the evening, and the first thing we did next morning was to find a second-hand bookshop to check up on 'quoign'. It turned out to have a Q, which pleased him, but not a G, and this was important because it meant that the Q would not have been on the treble space. Graham refused to accept this and insisted that the matter be held in further abeyance until he could check in his larger dictionary in London (which, however, gave no authority for the G).

He had various acquaintances in San Francisco, who invited us to a series of expensive restaurants where the menus read dazzlingly and the food arrived looking wonderful but tasting of nothing at all. After three or four such meals, we wondered if we had lost our sense of taste in the South Seas; but one lunchtime, needing a quick bite before going to a vineyard run by monks, we joined a queue at a self-service eating-house in Union Square called Lefty O'Dool's (after a baseball star), where we ate, for practically nothing, the best meal we had had since our lobsters in Sydney. Unfortunately, we had to return hospitality to all the people who had entertained us, and could not very well ask them to queue with us at Lefty O'Dool's, so we had to give them expensive and tasteless meals like the ones they had given us. But on the two or three other occasions on which we found ourselves alone, we made a bee-line for Lefty's. I wonder if it still exists?

We spent six happy days in San Francisco. Then Graham's daughter Lucy, who was living in Canada, arrived in a two-ton Chevrolet truck to drive us eastwards. We crossed the Sierra Nevada mountains and the spectacular Nevada landscape until we saw a hideous plastic arch straddling the highway, bearing the message: WELCOME TO RENO. THE GREATEST LITTLE CITY IN THE WORLD. Here we were to spend the night. We reconnoitred the city. Three out of every four establishments seemed to be gambling-booths; the fourth was usually a chemist's. We decided to spend what remained of the afternoon on the fruit-machines, and were puzzled by a large notice which read: NO INDIVIDUAL IS PERMITTED TO OPERATE MORE THAN TWO MACHINES SIMULTANEOUSLY. 'Surely you mean one?' Graham asked of a gigantic attendant, who replied: 'No, two's O.K.' We looked around and saw a number of people doing just that, working one machine right-handed and the other left-handed. The attendant, surprised at our naivety, explained that many people lacked the patience to wait for the wheels to come to rest and so operated two machines in tandem. The place was unbearably hot, and Graham noticed that several of the customers were wearing gloves. The attendant again pitied our ignorance: 'After three or four hours, your hands begin to bleed.' We enjoyed amazing luck, for I won a jackpot and Graham two. Our hotel, naturally, contained a casino, and as we passed through it on our way to an early bed (we had to rise at 6 a.m. to make Salt Lake City before dark), the scene resembled something from a Hollywood western, with handsome blondes dispensing the chips to men clutching rolls of dollar bills. Eight hours later, when we left, the scene was the same, except that the men's faces were covered with stubble, the rolls were smaller and the blondes haggard. Next morning, in Salt Lake City, we parted, Graham driving on with Lucy to Canada and I flying to New York.

Such was our round-the-world trip. Looking back on it, what astonishes me is how seldom we quarrelled, considering the pressure on two people of being together for two months, especially two natural loners in unfamiliar surroundings and, for most of the time, in tropical heat. Perhaps the fact that we were loners helped; neither of us demanded attention or conversation. If I have dwelt on the lighter moments, it is not because we had no serious conversations, simply that when two people have known each other for years one conversation tends to be rather like another. No doubt we held many discussions about literature, a few on politics and none or almost none on religion. I remember asking about Evelyn Waugh, whom, alas, I never met, and Graham saying: 'I'm very fond of him. He can be difficult.' 'In what way?' A pause, then: 'He quarrels with waiters.' Can anyone ever have been so completely summed up in four words? I also remember being disappointed by Graham's lack of enthusiasm for Hardy's novels. We discussed the merits of any female who crossed our path. Graham invented a new method of grading them, according to how many ships they would launch compared with Helen of Troy. 'Four hundred?' 'Twenty barges?', and other such sexist judgements. Another game was to pretend, when one saw a girl who looked attractive from the back, that one had committed oneself to an attempted seduction; then one looked at her from the front and decided whether or not one was glad that the commitment was only imaginary. I may add that Graham had no affairs, and attempted none, during our holiday, but this may have been because no one attractive and available presented herself. He spoke often and sadly of Anita, but also occasionally of Yvonne, a French lady whom he had met shortly before in the Congo and who in due course was to take Anita's place.

That summer of 1960 an extraordinary row blew up in Sweden over *The Complaisant Lover*. In the last act, the husband goes out to the garage; the others wonder why he is so long there, and suddenly fear he may have gassed himself. Several Swedish writers who had been friends of Anita's husband Stig Dagerman were quick to point out that that was how he had died, and suggested that Graham had drawn the parallel deliberately, to wound either Anita or Stig's memory or both. In Sweden there was a good deal of envy of Graham for his having been Anita's lover. He wrote begging me to assure her that 'nothing was further from my mind than to hurt her over the garage scene. After all, garage deaths are very common and there was no other form of playing with suicide that the husband could do. Anybody can sit in a car and imagine such a thing but you can't put cyanide in your mouth or a revolver in your ear without becoming melodramatic.' Unlikely as it must seem to anyone who does not know Stockholm and the petty jealousies that exist in literary circles there (Strindberg, who suffered much from it, called envy 'the Swedish vice'), it was rumoured, I think falsely, that this antagonism was partly responsible for Graham failing to receive the Nobel Prize – not that this bothers him, for the ridiculousness of most of the awards has devalued the prize except in terms of money, which he does not need. He seems likely to join the distinguished list of writers whom the Swedish Academy has deemed unworthy of the prize since it was inaugurated in 1901, a roll-call that includes Tolstoy, Ibsen, Zola, Chekhov, Gorki, Strindberg, Hardy, Rilke, Henry James, Conrad, Frost, Proust, Joyce and Virginia Woolf.

14

Two Kinds of Director

My first four Ibsen translations appeared that May of 1960, simultaneously with those of my Newcastle rival, James McFarlane. At a cordial meeting the previous summer, arranged by the Norwegian cultural attaché, McFarlane had expressed the opinion that our projects should not clash overmuch, since he felt that his were for students, mine for the theatre, and so it turned out. Other theatres, as well as television and radio stations, commissioned me to do further translations; and by the end of 1963 I had translated twelve Ibsen plays and eight by Strindberg, and had had thirty-six professional productions put on in the major English-speaking countries. I had been fortunate in my early collaborations with Wrede and Elliott, but there followed two others which showed me the other side of the coin.

An American beef millionaire named David Ross, who owned his own theatre on Fourth Street, Manhattan, and had ambitions as a director, contacted me in London to say that he wanted to stage *Hedda Gabler* and to ask me to do a new translation. (He had recently had a success with a Chekhov play starring Franchot Tone.) 'As I see *Hedda*,' he informed me at our first meeting, 'this is fundamentally a play about a guy who wants to lay a broad.' I suggested Mai Zetterling for the title role, and he signed her up. After a couple of weeks of rehearsal I received a distraught letter from Mai asking if I could fly over and give her some help. I arrived in time for the first run-through and was appalled at what I saw. The supporting cast were amateurish and self-indulgent, and the play scarcely seemed to have been directed at all. Mai was completely lost and was giving no sort of a performance. Ross asked me to dine with him and tell him my impressions. I delivered a flood of criticisms, all of which he scribbled down on a pad without querying one of them.

When we returned to the theatre for another run, Ross announced to the cast: 'Before we start I'd like to give you a few notes.' They looked astounded. Notes were evidently not routine procedure in a David Ross production. He began to read out my long list. To the Mrs Elvsted, who had been intolerably slow, he ventured: 'Lori, don't take this as a criticism, I'm not in any way criticizing you, you're fantastic, they're going to love you, but honey, could you maybe get just a little more pace on it, especially between sentences?' 'David,' she said, 'I've got to have time to make my transitions.' 'O.K., O.K.,' said Ross, and went on to the next point. As note followed note, the cast's eyes swivelled towards me.

At length they began the re-run, but after a few minutes Mai pleaded a headache and they broke for the evening. Next morning, Ross came to collect me at my hotel. 'What'll you say?' he cried. 'What'll you think?' 'What's the matter, David?' I asked. 'The cast say that if you come to any more rehearsals, they'll walk out.' 'What about Mai? I wouldn't be here if she hadn't asked me to come.' 'She's as upset as the rest.' So I had to absent myself until the first public preview a week later, which proved as horrendous as I had feared. I saw no point in waiting for the press night and flew home next day, asking my publisher, Anne Freedgood, to send me the reviews.

Ten days later a large envelope from New York arrived at my London flat. I had no desire to read whatever butcheries the critics had written, so ran my bath and glanced at the paper, then opened the envelope to be confronted by rave headlines. At first I thought they must be reviews of some other production, for they carried photographs of an actress of whom I had never heard, Anne Meacham. But the rest of the cast was the same terrible bunch that I had seen. Mai, as she tells in her autobiography, felt unable to continue and withdrew after the Saturday preview (her doctor, she says, told her that her decision saved her from having a nervous breakdown). At 2 a.m. that night, Ross phoned Anne Meacham, who had played Hedda in some out-of-town production, and asked if she would be willing to open in the part on Wednesday. After some persuasion she agreed, rehearsed for four days, and played it – melodramatically, I am told, but *Hedda* had not been seen in New York for years, so that to most of the critics it was a new play, and the effect must have been like that of an unsubtle performance of *Hamlet* on an audience that had no idea of what was coming next. The rest of the cast, in panic, at least talked fast, as panic-stricken people do, and the production ran for over three hundred and fifty consecutive performances, which remains a record for any Ibsen play anywhere, ever. Anne Meacham won an award for the best performance by an actress off-Broadway, the terrible Tesman for best supporting actor, and David Ross was named best director of the year.

Ross turned up three years later in London to tell me that he had signed Donald Wolfit to play Borkman in the West End and that he wanted to use my translation. It was the only time I have refused permission for a translation of mine to be used. I have worked with other bad directors, and some more disagreeable, but David Ross's productions had the effect, even when successful, that one could hardly bear even to meet again anyone connected with them. He died a few years later. He was not an unamiable man, but knew less about directing than anyone I have known. He had a passion for Dover sole, and when he had eaten what seemed to be all its flesh he would pick up the backbone in both hands and finish it off like a corn on the cob.

In 1962 I was involved in another dire production, under much grander auspices. The Royal Shakespeare Company wanted a one-act play to accompany a new short piece by Harold Pinter, *The Collection*, and Peter Hall who was in charge and was directing the Pinter asked me to translate Strindberg's *Playing with Fire*. This is a black comedy about six people on holiday, five of whom are on heat for someone not their rightful partner, and a good cast had been assembled, led by Michael Hordern, Sheila Allen and Kenneth Haigh. The director was a jolly, fat man (fat men, I have since decided, should never direct Strindberg). The husband and wife in the play, like most Strindberg couples, hate each other when they are not actually fucking (his characters can hardly be said to make love, or even to sleep together), but at the first run which I was invited to attend, the wife and husband showed every sign of mutual affection. I whispered to the director: 'They shouldn't do that, they hate each other.' 'No, no, they've been making love all night.' I said: 'They haven't been making love, they've been fucking.' He said: 'What's the difference?' At that I gave up; anyone who doesn't know that difference should not direct Strindberg. I took two young actresses from the Royal Theatre of Stockholm to the premiere, and dared not look at them as the audience greeted the play with ribald incomprehension. But in those days, British audiences had not yet caught up with Strindberg.

On the whole, however, I was wonderfully fortunate with my directors and with the productions with which I was associated. That same summer of 1962, *Brand* was twice powerfully staged, by Val

May at Bristol, with the young Paul Eddington splendid in the title role, and by a Cambridge undergraduate named Trevor Nunn on the Edinburgh Fringe with a cast that included John Cleese as First Villager and Tim Brooke-Taylor as the Sexton. One of the pleasures of looking through old programmes is the discovery of subsequently famous names in tiny, sometimes even non-speaking roles. A *Master Builder* at Stoke-on-Trent around this time included in the crowd for the final scene two boys on vacation from Manchester Grammar School, Robert Powell and Ben Kingsley; an undergraduate *When We Dead Awaken* at Cambridge was directed by Jeffrey Tate, and a *Miss Julie* at Stoke-on-Trent by the very young Alan Ayckbourn; a *Hedda* at Leicester had Anthony Hopkins as Judge Brack, and a student production from the drama school LAMDA of *Playing with Fire* which toured the West Country was led by Stacy Keach.

In 1962, Michael Elliott was appointed artistic director of the Old Vic, the youngest, at thirty-one, that that theatre had ever had, and in September he opened his season with a memorable *Peer Gynt*, surely the finest production of that play yet seen in Britain – certainly, in my view, better than Guthrie's of 1944, which was visually exciting without getting to the heart of the play (Guthrie himself later told me that he did not rate it particularly highly). Not only was Michael's production in the best sense spectacular, a joy to look at and listen to; it was, as Ibsen intended, disturbing (during our pre-production discussions Michael described it as being about the kind of legged things that crawl out when you lift a stone). Richard Negri designed it superbly, as he had *Brand* at Hammersmith; Leo McKern was splendid as Peer, as was Dilys Hamlett as Solveig, and Wilfrid Lawson an unforgettable Button Moulder, the last role he was ever to play on stage. Lawson's memory was by now shaky, and he tended to improvise the lines, so that McKern had to remember his own lines and say them regardless of what came out of the Button Moulder's mouth. This did not always make strict sense, but the audience was spellbound, assuming occasional incomprehensibilities to be the result of either Ibsen being obscure or bad translation. On at least one occasion, Lawson announced that he was a 'Mutton Boulder' (whether accidentally or out of mischief none of us could be sure), and one night he collapsed on stage just before his final exit and lay there crooning happily to himself. McKern and Dilys Hamlett entered for their great final scene to find the stage, instead of being bathed in brilliant light, completely dark except for two spotlights searching neurotically for them, while two stage-hands removed the Button Moulder. Nobody laughed; Lawson's power and dignity were such as to still any hilarity at his misfortunes or misdemeanours.

Lawson was a strange, unhappy, fascinating man. His performance in Strindberg's *The Father* in 1953 will never be equalled; for his final entrance on the opening night, he punched his fist methodically through the locked and barred door, so that all one saw was a bloodstained hand with splinters of wood sticking out of it groping for the key in the lock, and as the Nurse put him into the straitjacket pretending that it was a child's pyjamas he crooned happily like a baby while, as with a baby, long strings of saliva dropped from his mouth. I never saw him give anything but a magnificent performance on stage, drunk or sober. His successes were mainly in modern roles, for he appeared in very few classical plays outside Shaw. His Antony in 1934 was criticized as being badly spoken, but Michael MacOwan, one of the best directors of that decade, told me that he thought it in advance of its time and in accordance with subsequent taste for its deliberate anti-romanticism. In that 1962 Old Vic season he nearly played Othello. Mogens Wieth, a great Danish actor who spoke English with no trace of an accent, had been persuaded to attempt the role in London after having had a triumph with it in Denmark. Wieth, however, had been very ill and his doctor had forbidden him to travel, but, at a pre-production party at the Old Vic, he told me that he was determined to do it, even if it killed him. He died of a heart attack the following day, aged only forty-three. Michael and Casper (who was to direct *Othello*), thought hard about asking Lawson to stand in, and Lawson himself dropped a hint that they might consider him, but they decided that the risk of him mangling familiar speeches and perhaps forgetting whole sections of the play was too great, and gave it to an actor who was both too young and insufficiently powerful. I do not know which I regret the more, not having seen Wieth or not having seen Lawson play the role, especially since Leo McKern proved a tremendous Iago.

Michael had exciting plans for a second season at the Vic, with a company to be led by Patrick McGoohan and Albert Finney; one of his projects was a *Henry IV* with McGoohan as Hotspur and Finney as Prince Hal. But as his first season ended, the board of the National Theatre, which had played a couple of pilot seasons at Chichester, decided to open in London with the Old Vic as their base. Olivier as director of the National was keen that Michael should be his number two, and repeatedly begged him to accept the post, but Michael refused. He felt that Olivier, then fifty-five, would probably continue for ten or twenty years and, though he liked and admired Olivier, he did not want to be anyone's number two for that long.

During the next few years Michael received many offers: to run Chichester, to succeed George Devine at the Royal Court, to be head of television drama on BBC 2. He refused them all, and much besides, to the despair of his friends, the more so since he never had any money to speak of. His reasons were logical. Chichester wanted a more commercial approach than his to please its largely south-coast public, and the Royal Court audiences would expect him to find new dramatists comparable to those whom it had discovered under Devine, such as Osborne, Wesker, Arden and Storey. If no such talents emerged, he would either have to present inferior modern plays or be criticized for falling back on classics (as Devine had often been compelled to, but people had forgotten that). Michael wanted a new theatre where he could do as he wanted, if possible a new structure so that he could have a say in its design. Such an opportunity seemed increasingly unlikely, and as he approached forty his talent seemed to be going to waste.

Then in 1969 the Arts Council told him that they were being criticized for supporting too much theatre in London and too little in the provinces, and asked if he would run a new theatre which they had in mind to create in Manchester, where there was a catchment of eight million people living within fifty miles, including Liverpool, Leeds and Sheffield. Thus, with Casper Wrede and other colleagues from the 59 Theatre Company, Michael established a successor, the 69 Theatre Company. While searching for a suitable site, they opened with a couple of seasons at the little University Theatre in Devas Street, but apart from holding only 350 people it lay some way out. Sites in the city centre were extremely expensive and almost impossible to come by. Then Peter Henriques, a local stockbroker who was chairman of the 69 Theatre board, said: 'I have an idea which you may think mad', and took Michael to the old Cotton Exchange, a handsome Victorian building which had been empty for some years because the cotton trade had died and no one could think of a new use for it, but could not be pulled down because it was listed as being of architectural importance.

Richard Negri designed a circular theatre with three tiers to stand in the great hall, with space for 720 spectators, none of them more than thirty feet from the stage. This, the Royal Exchange Theatre, opened in 1976, and Michael, together with Casper Wrede, Braham Murray and James Maxwell, ran it until his death, making it the most distinguished and acclaimed theatre outside London, some would say superior to any in London including the National. Such was Michael's reputation, and the personal esteem in which he was held, that many of the country's leading actors gladly came up to work for him at a fraction of the salary they could have commanded in the West End. Various attempts were made to seduce him to London; but, apart from bringing some of his best Manchester productions to the Round House in Chalk Farm, which alone in the capital had facilities for presenting theatre in the round, he refused them all, save only an invitation to stage Handel's opera *Samson* at Covent Garden, a project he was working on when he died. He had also agreed to direct this in New York and Chicago, as well as his own adaptation of *Moby Dick* in New York; at last he would have earned some money (his salary in Manchester was tiny compared with those of the heads of the big London companies).

I have been lucky enough to work with many fine directors, and I hope none of them will feel offended if I say that Michael Elliott was the best. He combined technical mastery with a brilliant visual sense, the ability to penetrate to the heart of the most resistant text, and the gift of extracting the best from everyone he worked with. Whether you were an actor, a writer or a stage hand, you knew that he would get the best out of you, and that none of you would rest until he had done so. Yet all this was done with gentleness and courtesy; he made you feel a partner, not a pawn, and that in a small way you were helping to make theatrical history.

His name is perhaps especially associated with his Ibsen productions, and he had much in common with Ibsen; both possessed a rare combination of austerity, sensuality, poetry, strength of will and integrity. His productions of *Brand*, *Peer Gynt*, *Little Eyolf*, *Ghosts* (on TV), *When We Dead Awaken* and *The Lady from the Sea* will hardly be equalled; visual images from them, the memory of chained and tormented spirits seeking salvation, remain after ten and even twenty-five years. But equally fine were his *Miss Julie* (with Albert Finney and Maggie Smith), *The Family Reunion*, *Crime and Punishment* (with Leo McKern and Tom Courtenay), Sophocles's *Philoctetes* and, shortly before he died, *Moby Dick* – these last four, together with *When We Dead Awaken* and *The Lady from the Sea*, all produced in Manchester. His genius was for tragedy; but his *As You Like It* at Stratford in 1961 with the young Vanessa Redgrave was as unforgettable as his *Brand*. If he had a fault as a director, it was that his intense truthfulness made him unwilling to paper the cracks in a flawed play, and this was perhaps why he directed comparatively little contemporary drama, though when a new play did take his fancy, such as Ronald Harwood's *The Dresser*, he did it superbly. The theme of that play, the relationship between a dresser and a tyrannical actor-manager, must have been close to his heart, for he too regarded himself as the servant of a series of demanding masters: the great dramatists.

To work with Michael Elliott was to embark on a voyage of discovery, as that driving imagination gradually illuminated unexplored landscape. If you translate a play from the original, with no crib or intermediary between you and it, you come very close to the author, and this is especially so if, as in my case, you have done this with all his major plays. I reckoned that I knew Ibsen's plays better than anyone except Ibsen himself, but Michael got deeper to the heart of them than I did, and the talk to the cast with which he prefaced the opening rehearsal, always a model of clarity that would have been comprehensible to a child, was as much a revelation to me as to the actors who had simply read the play once. My only regret was that his advice to them during the actual rehearsals was always given so quietly and privately that I, sitting on the perimeter of the rehearsal space, was seldom able to hear it.

One of his greatest virtues was his ability to persuade a performer to come round to his own point of view and amend his or her performance accordingly. At the public dress-rehearsal of *As You Like It* in 1961, Vanessa Redgrave, then twenty-three and undertaking her first major role, gave a quite different interpretation from that which had previously been agreed. It was applauded, but altered the whole balance of the play and made things difficult for the rest of the cast. Michael had an awkward decision to make, for to try to persuade her to revert to her original interpretation for the premiere could easily have broken her confidence. But although he disliked confrontations, Michael never shrank from them. Vanessa was understandably upset, but did as he asked – you could not disobey him – and her performance on that press night, which I attended, was a triumph, as was the whole evening; it remains the finest production of a classical comedy that I have seen. Michael and Vanessa had similar disagreements regarding *The Lady from the Sea* seventeen years later, but again, with marvellous tact allied to that unshakeable will, he persuaded her, with equally memorable results. I had seen her act this role four years earlier in New York in a production directed by Tony Richardson; her performance then was impressive, but nothing like as subtle as the one Michael got from her.

He was a master of the spectacular, and many of his visual effects were unforgettable: the storm at sea and the avalanche in *Brand*; the troll scene in *Peer Gynt*; the Furies in *The Family Reunion*, huge figures which suddenly materialized around the perimeter of the stage; the change in *When We Dead Awaken* from the middle to the top of the mountain, effected by the opening of sleeves suspended above the stage which covered the slopes with a light layer of snow; Ellida's first entry, barefoot through water, in *The Lady from the Sea*; the sinking of the harpooners' boats in *Moby Dick*, when the whole surface of the Royal Exchange stage swelled hugely upwards to become the whale, overturning the boats and toppling the sailors into the water. But he used this mastery sparingly, to serve, never to distract from, the play. Ernest Newman, the great opera critic, wrote of an early and extravagant production by the young Peter Brook of I forget which masterpiece that it was as though a small boy had clambered up on to Michelangelo's statue of David and scrawled his own name all over it in large letters of blue chalk. You could never say that of any of Elliott's work. Like a great pianist or conductor, he regarded himself as an interpreter; what mattered most was to present, as clearly and evocatively as possible, the dramatist's intention.

Michael's father, Canon W. H. Elliott, had been a famous preacher, whose eloquence drew large congregations at his church in Chester Square. He must have been a daunting figure; when Michael's sister Joan, who lived in Singapore and had not seen *Brand*, asked him what the play was about – its theme is the danger of narrow-minded fanaticism – Michael replied: 'Father.'

In several ways, Michael Elliott reminded me of George Orwell. Both were unusually tall, thin almost to the point of emaciation, plagued by ill-health and cut off in their prime (Orwell at forty-six, Elliott at fifty-two); both combined vision and a shining integrity with much warmth and humour lurking behind a veil of austerity. Both drove themselves hard and shunned pity; both, once they had dropped their natural reserve, were enormous fun to be with. Neither suffered fools gladly; both regarded lack of integrity as the unforgivable sin.

For the last eight years of his life, Michael was on a kidney machine, which in his case meant that he really slept only every second night. Few of his friends were allowed to know this; self-pity was one of the things he despised most. Although I was closer to him than most people, I never fully appreciated until after his death how greatly he suffered physically: how after six hours on his machine he would sometimes break into tears, something I could never have imagined him doing, and say that he could not stand the regular and repeated pain any longer. He had three kidney-transplant operations but, although the rate of success for these is generally high, none worked for him. In the spring of 1984 he was staying with me in London when a telephone call came at two in the morning to say that a matching kidney had reached the hospital in Manchester and that he would have to be there in six hours. He took a taxi up the motorway, full of hope, but this, his second operation, failed as the first had done. Within a few weeks he underwent a third operation. This time the new kidney worked, but by ill luck his own remaining kidney became infected, he had to undergo a further eight-hour operation to remove it, and the accumulative strain proved too much for even his will to live. Manchester Cathedral was filled for his funeral service, and no parting words could have been more appropriate than Bunyan's hymn which we sang with that long coffin before us: 'Who would true valour see, Let him come hither. Here's one will constant be, Come wind, come weather.'

15

Actors Old and New

In 1963 Casper Wrede wanted to stage *The Father*, but we could not think of any actor with sufficient power. Cricket, yet again, came to the rescue. I went that summer to see England play the West Indies at Lord's, and found myself seated next to Trevor Howard, whom I had not previously met. We got on well and watched together for the full five days. It was one of the great Test matches, the balance swinging now this way, now the other, and at one particular crisis I glanced at Trevor, saw his agonized profile and thought: 'That is Strindberg's Captain.' By the end of the final day we had become friends, rather as though we had gone through Passchendaele together. I telephoned Casper and suggested Trevor for the part; Casper phoned Trevor. Trevor had seen Wilfrid Lawson's great performance in the play ten years previously and was tempted, but hedged. Among other things, he said: 'How do we get a decent translation?' Casper mentioned my name. 'Never heard of him.' 'You watched the Test match with him.' 'God,' said Trevor. 'That chap? He never said he was a translator.' (How could I have said during those palpitating hours: 'You may be interested to know that I translate Ibsen and Strindberg'?) Trevor continued: 'Oh, he'll be all right,' and the project got under way. He had difficulty with his lines until the end of our opening week in Brighton – it was some years since he had appeared on the stage – but was splendid as soon as we got into the West End. I found him a wonderfully warm and rewarding man, unspoiled by fame.

I regret that Trevor appeared so seldom in the theatre once films had claimed him, for he was a magnificent stage actor in either tragedy or comedy. He was the best Lopakhin in *The Cherry Orchard* that I have seen, the best Captain Plume in *The Recruiting Officer*, and the best Petruchio. He also told marvellous stories about the great

Hollywood stars. In one I remember, he had accompanied one of the very biggest of them to Tokyo to publicize the Japanese opening of a film in which they had appeared together. On their first evening, they were taken to a geisha house, where skilled geishas danced and sang for them. Trevor said it was slightly dull though very pleasant, but the superstar became bored and turned round and sat astride his chair with his back to the girls. At length he took from his pocket a roll of banknotes which the film company had given him on his arrival as pocket-money; whether it was a hundred or a thousand pounds worth, Trevor didn't know, but it was more than any of the girls would earn in a week. He wondered, as no doubt the girls did, what obscenity the star would ask them to perform in return for this. But what he did was more obscene than any of them could have imagined: he took out his cigarette-lighter and quietly burned the lot.

I still had my flat in Stockholm at this time; I did not know how long this sequence of theatre, television and radio productions would continue, and although London was no longer the city of failure for me, as I had come to regard it, I did not know whether it might not become so again. I still regarded Sweden as my base and myself as a foreign exile, though I had acquired a tiny flat in Paddington. At first, I used the latter only for brief visits; then, as my translations came to be staged more and more, the balance changed, and in time the apartment on Döbelnsgatan became a place which I visited for six weeks in the spring and six in August and September. I used to reckon that I did more work in those three months than in my nine months in London; it helped to have the North Sea between me and my contemporaries, beside whom I still felt small.

In Stockholm in 1963 I met W. H. Auden for the first time. He had come there to give a public reading of his poems, which he did rather indifferently, affecting an American pronunciation of certain vowels which matched ill with his otherwise English accent; nor was I taken with his contemptuous dismissal of questions afterwards, as though most of them were not worth his attention. I wondered if this was perhaps an American custom, having heard Saul Bellow accord the same treatment to an invited audience, which included several figures not less distinguished than himself, at the American Embassy in London. But at the dinner which followed Auden's reading, seated next to him, I found him agreeable and amusing. Doubleday had got him to write an introduction to my translation of *Brand* when they had published it in 1960, and although it was one of his shallower efforts it had helped to launch the series. He had also agreed to co-operate on a translation of the poems of Dag Hammarskjöld, who had been killed in an air-crash, and invited me to lunch with him the next day to discuss some points regarding it. Our lunch lasted for over three hours, but I found him rather disappointing on anything but a light level; all the answers came quickly and glibly, as one might have expected from someone like Beverley Nichols. He made one interesting remark, however. I asked if he had known anyone whom he had admired as a writer but disliked as a human being, and he at once named Yeats and Brecht. Yeats he had found unwilling to allow any merit to any other living poet – although his own stature was by then unquestioned – and inclined (as Sassoon had told me) to drone away boringly on the occult; and he had found Brecht hypocritical in his profession of Communist ideals while living in an eight-room apartment surrounded by servants with an Austrian passport and a Swiss bank account. (Eva Tisell, his agent for the West, and an old friend of Brecht from his Hollywood days, told me that although he wore the traditional Communist jacket he always had these made at the most expensive tailor in West Berlin.) Auden added that Brecht treated women worse than anyone he, Auden, had known. He then said it was odd that I should have asked him that particular question because he had once asked Eliot the same thing. Eliot had been silent for a while, and had then admitted that there had been three writers whom he had admired but greatly disliked: Ezra Pound, Wyndham Lewis and James Joyce, although, as Auden commented, few people had done more than Eliot to advance the reputation of all three. When I expressed surprise that Eliot had disliked Joyce, Auden said that although he himself had never met Joyce, everyone he knew who had had disliked him. Cyril Cusack later confirmed this, saying that nobody in Ireland seemed to remember Joyce affectionately. When I asked why, Cusack replied: 'He used people.'

I could have met Brecht, for in 1956 Eva Tisell, who visited him annually in East Berlin, suggested that I should accompany her there that summer. But I explained that I liked to play and watch cricket in the summer, and asked if we could postpone it, and Brecht died later that year. Three years later I spent a day with his widow, the actress Helene Weigel. She was visiting Stockholm with the Berliner Ensemble and wanted to revisit the house on Lidingö, outside Stockholm, where she and Brecht had lived in 1938–40. Eva asked if I could drive them there. We walked round the house; then Helene mentioned that a working-class couple named Andersson who lived nearby had agreed to keep some of their possessions when the Brechts fled to America after Hitler's invasion of Denmark and Norway. She wondered if they were still alive. We rang their bell, and the door was opened by a young woman who turned out to be the Anderssons' daughter. She said her father was dead and her mother alive, but paralysed; she then asked if Helene would be willing to say a word to her, since she had been much excited when her daughter had shown her the announcement in the paper that Frau Weigel was coming to Stockholm. When we entered the bedroom, the old woman tried to raise herself in bed, made inarticulate noises and began to weep. The daughter said: 'She is weeping for joy', and Helene sat on the bed and talked to her, holding her hand, although the two had no language in common. That day I found her a warm and easy person.

Helene once told me why Brecht (she always referred to him by his surname only) had made the daughter in *Mother Courage* dumb. Apparently they were very poor when they lived in Sweden, and it occurred to him that although Helene could speak little Swedish, she could act a dumb girl. For the mother, she said, Brecht had in mind the Swedish actress Naima Wifstrand; but Hitler intervened, and by the time *Mother Courage* received its premiere Naima Wifstrand and Helene Weigel were both too old to play the roles which Brecht had written for them, although the mother was to prove Helene's greatest triumph.

About ten years later I met Helene again, when the Berliner Ensemble visited London. The National Theatre gave a party for them and invited me in the mistaken supposition that I could speak German. She stood surrounded by her actors, and I reminded her of our visit to the Anderssons. When I got to the part where she had comforted the old woman, she said: 'It is not true. You are making this up', and when I began to give details, she again denied it angrily. I can only suppose that she did not want the tender side of her nature to be revealed to her company. Her demeanour that evening suggested nothing so much as a *Gauleiter*. Similarly, in Stockholm she had talked intelligently and sympathetically about Ibsen and Strindberg, but when at a public discussion in London the day after the party I asked why the Berliner Ensemble never staged these playwrights, she dismissed them with a scornful laugh as unworthy even of comment. The official Ensemble line was that Ibsen and Strindberg were bourgeois playwrights. I wished that I had been left with the memory of her on the old woman's bed at Lidingö. But she was a tremendous actress.

My first volume of Strindberg translations appeared in 1964, and the Swedish Academy awarded me their Gold Medal, something they hand out every ten or fifteen years. I was the first Englishman to receive it (the second was Laurence Olivier), and was invited to receive it at the Academy's annual public meeting in December. It was a fine windless winter evening, the snow falling in thick flakes, and I thought I would walk the half hour to the Old Town where the Academy has its house so as to spin out the luxury of going to get a medal. Unused to wearing tails and a boiled shirt, however, I had not realized that a stiff collar takes on the temperature of the air around it. Mine was somewhat tight, and after ten minutes my neck felt as though gripped by a band of icy iron. I began to feel dizzy, and only just made it to the hall, which fortunately turned out to be so hot that the collar quickly melted. A few more minutes, and I would either have collapsed in the snow or arrived seemingly drunk, which would have been especially embarrassing since the Swedish royal family was present.

Two of the Academicians read tedious half-hour papers, our awards were announced, and I and my fellow recipients, the actress Inga Tidblad and a huge and splendid old man aged nearly ninety named Sigurd Curman, who had been the city archivist, retired with the 'Immortals', most of whose predecessors have been forgotten by posterity, for an excellent dinner. The president for the evening was Ragnar Josephson, a professor of art history who had for some years run the Royal Dramatic Theatre. He was said to have done that well, but on this evening at least he was unbearably pompous, and under his guidance the post-prandial discussion drifted off into the woolliest kind of abstract consideration of the nature of modern art. I could see old Curman getting restless beside me, and suddenly he said: 'I read in the newspaper recently that some young people led a cow into the Museum of Modern Art, the cow shat on the floor, and the young people said that this was an artistic "happening". I wish to ask the Academy: "Is it art when a cow shits on the floor?"' Other Academicians held forth on the subject, none of them confronting the issue. Curman said: 'For the third time, I ask: "Is it art when a cow shits on the floor?"' None of the Immortals had the courage to say no.

Around 2 a.m., Josephson suggested that it was time to go to bed. Curman was flabbergasted. A bond of cynicism had sprung

up between us during the evening, and he turned to me. 'Are they
going to bed already?' he asked loudly. 'It's hardly gone two.' He was
clearly used to the kind of all-night celebrations which Strindberg,
less than thirty years his senior, enjoyed and described, ending with
an oyster breakfast. It was still snowing outside, but since I could
now unfasten my stiff collar I decided to walk home, and on one of
Stockholm's many bridges I opened my leather case to have another
look at my medal. The heavy golden disc fell out and rolled towards
the edge of the bridge, where by great good luck it stopped in a
lump of snow. Another inch, and what would I have done? Gone
to a police station and said: 'I have dropped a medal on to the ice?'

That same month I finished translating the sixteenth and, as far as
I was concerned, last of Ibsen's major plays. (Though one, *Emperor
and Galilean*, was to wait twenty-four years for publication. Casper
Wrede and Michael Elliott, who planned to stage it together, asked
me not to have it printed lest this might give others the idea that
it was stageable. Several times this big project, demanding a large
cast and needing to be spread over two evenings, seemed about
to materialize, most nearly at the Edinburgh Festival in the early
eighties, but the size of it always deterred managements, and when
Michael died in 1984 I finally decided to publish it before I followed
him.) I now had to embark on the Ibsen biography which Rupert
Hart-Davis had commissioned. I had no real idea how to go about
it, but Rupert gave me two excellent pieces of advice: 'Make your
first sentence "Henrik Ibsen was born on . . . at . . .", to save the
reader searching back through the opening chapter to remind himself
how old Ibsen was in any future year, and buy a fat exercise book with
enough pages for you to devote an opening to each year of Ibsen's
life, so that you can note each event in its chronological position.'
This proved invaluable, for it meant that one's attention was drawn
to unexpected juxtapositions of personal and public events. I had
no theory about the writing of biography when I began, though
I developed a few. I think a biographer should state the facts and
comment only sparingly, leaving the reader to draw his or her
own conclusions. I also think it is important to vary one's focus,
moving away periodically from close-up to a long-distance shot
which shows what else is happening in the subject's country, or
in his or her field elsewhere in the world. And I do not think that
a biography should end with the subject's death; when the subject
is a writer, especially, there needs to be an epilogue to tell how
his influence and reputation waxed or waned after his death, and

what happened to at least the main supporting characters in the story.

Ibsen and, in due course, Strindberg presented very different problems. Ibsen I could identify with; I know and understand that kind of loner. Many of my favourite writers belong to that category: Hardy, Wordsworth, Carlyle, De Quincey, Herman Melville, Orwell and Greene. The main difficulty in writing a life of Ibsen lay in concealing from the reader that, outwardly, nothing very much happened to him after he had fathered an illegitimate child at the age of eighteen. His inward life was of course fascinating, but it is difficult to write simply about a man's inward life for 800 pages. This meant that one had to try to paint a vivid picture of the different environments in which Ibsen lived, the small town where he was born, the larger but still small Norwegian cities in which he worked as a theatre director, and the very different worlds of Rome in the 1860s and Dresden and Munich in the last decades of the nineteenth century. In addition, one had, of course, to portray the changing world of the European theatre. But mainly one had to analyse his development as a dramatist and how, writing in a language which hardly any foreigner knew, and coming from a country which had never previously produced any writer who had been heard of outside Scandinavia, he contrived to change the entire course of drama throughout the western world.

After the final volume of my Ibsen biography appeared in 1971, I received several requests to write a life of Strindberg, but I shrank from it for seven years, for three reasons. Firstly, Strindberg's collected works fill seventy-five volumes. He wrote more rubbish than any other great writer, even Wordsworth, including sixty plays (over half of which are never performed even in Sweden), novels, short stories, and theses on every imaginable subject, including philosophy, politics, religion and, most dauntingly, various branches of science, including alchemy. The prospect of wading through all this, to say nothing of the extensive literature that has been written about him in various languages, seemed too much to contemplate. Secondly, Strindberg did not differentiate between truth and reality as we understand them, so that one cannot believe a word he writes about himself or anyone unless it is otherwise confirmed, even on such simple details as when he wrote his plays. Thirdly, and perhaps most importantly, a list of the characteristics which I most dislike in human beings would be headed by racism, hysteria, self-pity, malice and vengefulness, and Strindberg possessed all these in full measure.

Until his last years, when he mellowed generally, he was a violent and sustained anti-Semite. But these qualities are precisely what repel many readers (and theatre-goers, though his racism is not apparent in his plays), and too many of the books that praise him have been written by people apparently blind to his failings both as a human being and as a writer, in the old Victorian tradition of hagiography which is said to date from Dean Stanley's life of Thomas Arnold. In the end I felt it was time that someone who recognized both his genius and the qualities in him that inspired affection and love – even from those to whom he behaved most monstrously – tried to paint him, warts and all.

Each of these biographies took me precisely the same time to complete: five and a quarter years. Although they are both very long, over eight hundred and six hundred pages respectively, they should have taken less time. I am a miserably undisciplined worker; for two or three weeks at a stretch I seem unable to face the typewriter or even open a book; then self-disgust takes over, and I grind away again. In theory I sit at my desk for three hours each morning; when a project approaches its end, I sometimes also manage a couple of hours in the early evening. But often the morning passes without my even beginning to work. Yet every good writer whom I have known hates the actual process of writing; Orwell did, so does Greene. I know one or two bad ones who enjoy it, but the only good writer I have heard of who did is P. G. Wodehouse. For some reason it is different with painters, who all seem to approach their canvas as eagerly as though it was a desirable mistress. I handed in my Ibsen biography seven years behind schedule, the Strindberg three years. But I know that I will always finish whatever job I have in hand; in that sense at least I have a reliable track record.

In 1965 Michael Elliott staged *Miss Julie* for the National Theatre at Chichester, which found me working with Maggie Smith for the first time since she had appeared as an amateur in *The Ortolan* eleven years earlier. She had made her mark outside Oxford as a comedienne in a revue on the Fringe at the Edinburgh Festival, but quickly established herself as a considerable straight actress. Her leading man, Albert Finney, then twenty-nine, had recently alarmed his agent by insisting on accepting a percentage of the profits in his film of *Tom Jones* instead of a fee, and was proved right, for it netted him £1 million. Unlike some of his contemporaries who became international film stars, Finney remained, like Trevor Howard, blessedly unspoiled, indulging himself only, or almost only, in buying a Rolls and a racehorse. Actors are regarded by insurance companies as a high driving risk, and Albert's brokers insisted that he employ a chauffeur, which embarrassed him, as did the fact that when the car was driven down to the house he had taken for the summer near Chichester it proved too long for the garage and had to have a plastic envelope wrapped over the back end, which stuck out. Thus most mornings Maggie collected him in a battered Hillman Minx. During one of the rehearsals he received the news that the University of Sussex had made him an Honorary Doctor of Letters. When he telephoned his father, a bookmaker in Salford, with the news, his father's only comment was: 'Doctor of Letters? You haven't written us a bloody postcard in three months!' The horse won a race that summer, and Albert said that leading it in afterwards was a greater thrill than anything he had experienced in a theatre.

The great actors of the previous generation – Olivier, Richardson, Gielgud and Redgrave – all came from the south of England, except Robert Donat who was from Manchester. But the ones who came to prominence in the 1960s were almost all from the North or Midlands – Albert Finney and David Warner from Manchester, Tom Courtenay and Kenneth Haigh from Yorkshire, Alan Bates from Derbyshire, Nicol Williamson from Scotland – or from Ireland, like Peter O'Toole, or Wales, like Anthony Hopkins. Beatrix Lehmann, who had joined RADA as a student in the same year as John Gielgud, told me that all the men of her year looked elegant and spoke elegant Oxford English except one, who was fat and ugly and had a broad Yorkshire accent. None of them could at first imagine how he had got in or what parts except comic character roles he would be able to play. It was Charles Laughton. None of the Gielgud generation except for Donat could sustain any provincial accent for more than a few minutes except as a caricature. Things have changed a good deal since then.

In 1966, *The Ortolan* was revived by the touring Century Theatre, based in Keswick, in a good production by Braham Murray, the Maggie Smith role being played by a nineteen-year-old actress making her professional stage debut, Helen Mirren; and the following year Peter Dews directed a *Peer Gynt* at Birmingham with three as yet unknown actors who were soon to become famous: Brian Cox as Peer, Anna Calder Marshall as Solveig and Michael Gambon as the Button Moulder. Cox, at twenty-one, was a remarkable Peer, the best, with Leo McKern, that I have seen. The country lad of the first three acts came naturally to him, but he was equally convincing

as the middle-aged wit of Act Four and the patriarch of Act Five.
I have never seen a young actor able to act old age so naturally.
Later that season I took Michael Elliott up to see him play Iago
to Gambon's Othello, and this was the beginning of a fruitful
partnership between Cox and Elliott, culminating eighteen years
later in Cox's magnificent Captain Ahab in Elliott's last theatre
production, *Moby Dick*. A natural Ibsen actor, Cox has already, in
addition to his Peer, been a superb Brand, Gregers Werle in *The
Wild Duck*, Ejlert Loevborg in *Hedda Gabler* and Ulfhejm in *When
We Dead Awaken*. I hope I shall live to see his Dr Wangel in *The
Lady from the Sea*, Solness in *The Master Builder* and, especially, his
Borkman.

One of my regrets is that I never worked with Edith Evans. The
only Ibsen role she ever played, apart from the tiny part of the Nurse
in a film of *A Doll's House*, was Rebecca West in a modern dress
production of *Rosmersholm* in 1926, in which she is said to have
been very fine. Why did she never play Mrs Alving in *Ghosts*, or
Ella in *Borkman*? And what an Aase she would have been in *Peer
Gynt*. Lewis Casson once remarked: 'Edith's got PQ. Sybil hasn't
PQ.' Nobody knew what PQ meant. At last someone asked, and
Lewis replied: 'Peasant quality.' One would have expected Sybil
Thorndike to have had it and Edith Evans not, but the reverse was
indeed the case, as I saw Edith prove as the Welsh housekeeper in
The Late Christopher Bean and the gipsy woman in *The Old Ladies*,
and also in an unforgettable reading of Hardy's monologue 'A
Trampwoman's Tragedy'.

I came to know Sybil in 1968 when, in her eighty-sixth year, she
played the Nurse marvellously in a television production of *The
Father*. The director had to ask her not to put on an old walk; she
said: 'You mean my usual walk, like this?', striding vigorously across
the floor, which was exactly what he did want. At one rehearsal
she whispered to me: 'I'm playing truant tomorrow.' 'Sybil, why?'
'They're building a new theatre at Leatherhead which they're naming
after Russell [her brother] and me, and they want me to knock down
a wall of the old building.' 'Knock down a wall?' 'They're giving me
a battering-ram.' Two days later there appeared in the newspapers a
photograph of Sybil in an extraordinary hat wielding the ram, which
was suspended in a cradle. I never admired her in high tragedy – I
found her Medea and Jocasta both hammy – and wondered how
she could have been so admired as St Joan until I heard her, in her
eighties, read passages from the play on radio. Then I understood.

Sybil, apart from being the most generous person I have known, possessed a unique, in my experience, quality of saintliness, and this quality, divorced in her from any suggestion of priggishness or false piety, made the character totally credible.

Her husband Lewis Casson came to the TV recording of *The Father*. He was then ninety-three and full of vitality. As a youth he had attended several of the earliest Ibsen performances in London in the 1890s, and told me that William Archer and the American actress Elizabeth Robins, who organized most of these, lent a puritanical air to the proceedings which he thought had hampered the British view of Ibsen ever since. He still had a remarkable memory and corrected me on a point of detail concerning a production by Granville Barker of *The Wild Duck* in which he had appeared in 1905. I checked, and he was right. When my daughter was born that autumn Sybil and Lewis sent us a card of congratulation, and I reflected that if, which is quite possible, Lewis's parents had received a similar card at his birth it would have been from someone born in 1782, seven years before the French Revolution.

1968 was a big year for me, for apart from *The Father* and the birth of my daughter, of which more anon, Michael Elliott directed two superb Ibsen productions, *Ghosts* for television and *When We Dead Awaken* at the Edinburgh Festival. Celia Johnson, Donald Wolfit and Tom Courtenay headed the cast of *Ghosts*. It was the last performance Wolfit gave before his death, and the only time I worked with him, though I had known him for some time. He had mellowed considerably since being knighted. The time was past when, as Leo McKern, a great admirer of his, has told, Wolfit genuinely believed that nobody in the audience could be interested except when he was speaking (in *Tamburlaine*, he once walked off the stage in the middle of a long speech which Leo was addressing to him, and returned only on Leo's last line). He still, however, possessed little sense of the ridiculous. At the first rehearsal of *Ghosts* I was chatting to Celia when Wolfit swept in. He greeted me warmly, and I said: 'You know Celia, of course.' She said: 'No, we've never met,' and he, taking her hand in both of his, said: 'No, but we've admired each other from afar.' He was a fine Pastor Manders, and Celia and Tom matched him. Celia, the most professional and sensitive of actresses, affected to be an amateur who did it for fun without really being involved – a hangover, I suppose, from the days when acting was regarded as an ungentlemanly and unladylike profession.

When We Dead Awaken was even more of an achievement, for it is a play (Ibsen's last) that is seldom staged, largely because the central character of the deranged Irene and the very brief final act are both difficult to bring off. Wendy Hiller played Irene magnificently, and Michael cut the second interval and, as I have described, effected the change to the top of the mountain by releasing sleeves suspended above the stage which covered the slopes with snow. At the dress-rehearsal, one of these sleeves failed to open until a few minutes into the act, when to our horror we saw it slowly unwind immediately above Brian Cox, as he delivered a passionate declaration of love, and deposit its contents on him, leaving the lady confronted by a snowman. Fortunately this was not repeated at the premiere. Michael summed up this strange and haunting play in his programme notes: 'At times it may seem impossible to rise to the music, but the score itself can only be regarded with wonder.'

Peer Gynt was staged that year in Central Park, New York, with Stacy Keach, whom I had known when he was a student at LAMDA, in the lead. Unbeknown to me, Joe Papp, the redoubtable producer, made a video of it without finding out whether the cinematic rights of my translation were free. I had promised them to Michael Elliott, who had plans to make a film of it in Norway, and so had to say that the video could not be shown. In the hope of persuading me, Papp arranged a showing of the video at a venue in Windmill Street off Piccadilly Circus, a street then occupied largely by pornographic cinemas. I could not find the place, and wandered up and down the pavement peering into every entrance and praying that nobody I knew would see me. The video was dull, it was a hot afternoon and I fell asleep. I am told that Papp has never forgiven me on either count. To make things worse, Michael's film never materialized.

16

An Ingmar Bergman Production

In 1970, Ingmar Bergman came to London to restage for the National Theatre a production of *Hedda Gabler* he had done in Stockholm. Bergman's unwillingness to direct outside Sweden was legendary, but Olivier had somehow persuaded him. Bergman made two stipulations: that he should have a suite at the Connaught Hotel, because they had quiet rooms and understood his dietary problems, and that he should direct only for the first week, since he was also preparing a film. In addition, an assistant was to be present, to note what he said and to rehearse the actors for the rest of the time; possibly he, Bergman, might be able to come back during the final week before the premiere if what he called his 'film manuscript' was sufficiently advanced.

I was used to strange goings-on at the National. In 1965 I had flown back from Sweden the evening before we began rehearsals for Michael Elliott's production of *Miss Julie*. I had not yet heard who was to play the title role, only that, for some reason which I have forgotten (presumably other commitments), it was to be either Maggie Smith or Geraldine McEwan. At my usual Indian restaurant I bumped into Kenneth Tynan, then the National's literary manager, who told me that it was to be Geraldine. After my meal, I phoned Michael Elliott who said he understood it was to be Maggie. When we reached the rehearsal room next morning we found that Albert Finney, who was to play Jean, was equally in the dark. So the director, the leading man and I sat waiting to see which leading lady would come through the door. It turned out to be Maggie. But this was nothing to what happened with *Hedda Gabler*.

One of the National's directors had been deputed to meet Bergman at Heathrow airport. He was late, so that Bergman, after sitting alone with his bag for a while, decided to take the next plane back to Stockholm. He was, he later told me, actually on his way to the SAS booking desk when the director arrived, put Bergman into his small car and drove him to London. Bergman comforted himself with the knowledge that a suite at the Connaught would be awaiting him; but it transpired that the National had instead booked him a small bedroom at the Waldorf, overlooking the traffic of Aldwych. Bergman stared at the room, threw a chair at the director and ordered him to drive him back to Heathrow. The director phoned Olivier, who hurried over, somehow managed to calm Bergman and promised him that if he could endure one night in this room he, Olivier, would put him up for the rest of his stay at his flat. He said he would return and take him to a dinner which he had arranged for Bergman to meet the cast.

I was among those invited to the meal. We had been bidden to meet at eight sharp, since Bergman was insistent on punctuality, at a new restaurant south of the river. I arrived a few minutes early, and was joined by two members of the cast, John Moffatt and Sheila Reid. We were directed upstairs to a private room, pleasantly lit by candles, with a table laid for twelve. As Big Ben struck the quarter, Olivier and Bergman arrived. Bergman was in an open-necked shirt and very cheerful and pleasant; Olivier's famous charm had evidently worked. He chatted agreeably until Big Ben struck half-past eight. Seven of the twelve had not yet come.

Olivier said: 'I don't know where the others can be. I hope you're not too hungry, Ingmar.' Bergman said: 'I have a strict diet. For breakfast a cup of black coffee, for lunch a yoghurt. So . . . But we wait.' Olivier said: 'Great heavens, then we must start. When the others come they'll find us eating and that'll make them ashamed.' The proprietor was summoned and gave us each a menu. The main dishes included boeuf bourgignon and best end of lamb. Olivier, whose ignorance about food equals his charm, gave an incorrect description of these and other dishes, and advised the lamb. Bergman said: 'In Sweden I live on an island called Fårö, sheep island. For two months I have eaten nothing but sheep. Boiled sheep, fried sheep, grilled sheep. I think: when I come to England, I do not have to eat sheep. In England they have beef.' 'Have the boeuf bourgignon, then.' 'I am not allowed to eat sauces.' 'A steak, then. (To the proprietor.) The best steak you have for Mr Bergman.' But unfortunately the restaurant did not have steaks, nor beef in any other form.

Bergman settled for the lamb, and Olivier, by now impatient,

32 With Trevor Howard at a rehearsal of *The Father*, Brighton, 1964

33 Theatre XI vs President's Town XI at Stratford-on-Avon, 1969.
Included are the author, Harold Pinter, Peggy Ashcroft, Ian Carmichael, Julian Bream (in hat), Tom Courteney, Tom Stoppard (Wicket Keeper) and David Warner

34 The Royal Exchange Theatre, Manchester, on its opening night, 15 September 1976

35 Michael Elliott   **36** Espen Skjønberg in *Rosmersholm*, Manchester, 1981

ordered shellfish vol-au-vents for all of us. Predictably, they contained a sauce. Bergman speared a shrimp, fastidiously wiped the sauce off it with a knife, and ate it dubiously. It took some time for him to finish the dish.

Maggie Smith and Robert Stephens now arrived, very merry, and started a conversation with the other actors of such high and private camp that even I could only partly follow it. Bergman was ignored as though he was someone's uncle who had been allowed to join the party. Suddenly he put down his knife and fork and said: 'This sheep is too fat. I can't eat it.' Olivier offered to swap it with his boeuf bourgignon. 'I cannot eat sauce.' Eventually he took the boeuf bourgignon, speared a cube of meat, wiped the sauce off it and ate it as he had eaten the starter. Shortly before nine, Jeremy Brett arrived. He explained to Bergman: 'The car in front of me got involved in an accident. Not my car, the one in front. Although I was not personally involved, we have a law in England that if you witness an accident you have to give evidence. So I had to wait until the police arrived.' This brought our number up to eight. The other four chairs remained unfilled. Whether the absent guests, who included Tynan, simply failed to turn up, or whether the theatre had forgotten to notify them, I never discovered.

Bergman's mood was by now such that I felt sure he would not stay beyond the next morning, and I saw my royalties going down the drain. John Moffatt, perhaps feeling the need to bring Bergman into the conversation, said: 'Now tell us about *Hedda Gabler*.' Bergman said: 'It's a boring play. But one can make something of it.' This momentarily silenced even Maggie Smith. Someone asked: 'Why did you choose to do it in Stockholm, then?' 'I am head of the Royal Dramatic Theatre and I have a powerful actress, Miss Gertrud Fridh. I have to find a part for her. There are not many such. Every time I meet her in the corridor she looks at me. So I go into the library and look at all those plays on the shelves and I say: "There must be some play here for such an actress." Then I take down this old play, *Hedda Gabler*.' (Wrinkles his nose in contempt.) 'By Ibsen.' (Makes a gesture as of emptying a bucket down the lavatory.)

This is the general Swedish attitude towards Ibsen, but it is not the British view of him, and we gaped in horror. Bergman continued: 'I think, can there be anything in this old play for people today? Then I read it, and you know, there is much in it that works. Of course there is much in it that is boring, but that we hop over. [i.e. cut]' In the event, he cut fifteen of the 100 pages of the text.

Something of a gloom settled over the company. Big Ben struck a quarter to ten, and as though on cue Olivier, on my right, began to behave strangely. He glanced at his watch, and ordered coffee for all, not asking if anyone wanted a sweet. (I did and whispered so to the waiter; nobody else got one.) Bergman asked Olivier a question. Olivier looked hard at his watch, asked Bergman to repeat the question, looked at his watch again and answered tersely. Nobody could consult his watch like Laurence Olivier. We all looked at our watches. Surely we could not be overstaying our welcome. It was less than an hour since the last guest had arrived, or anyway the last that we could see. The conversation became desultory. As Big Ben struck the first note of ten, Olivier, again as though on cue, said: 'Ingmar. As I mentioned, although I have this flat in London I live in Brighton. I like to sleep there if possible because although, of course, I have a nanny and Joan and the chauffeur, I do think it very important that one should take one's children to school oneself. You as a father will appreciate this.'

This was not the most fortunate remark, for Bergman is not famous for his closeness to his numerous children by various liaisons. However, he politely replied: 'Of course.' Olivier continued: 'Well, although there is an 11.28 train, I would much rather get the 10.27 so as not to be too late. Will you think me very rude if I run?', and off he went. Considering how badly the evening had begun, and indeed continued, one could not help feeling that for this one morning Joan or the nanny or the chauffeur might have stood in. But in fact, with Olivier's departure the mood lightened. Bergman clearly felt less constrained, gossiped away amusingly and slightly maliciously, and eventually left quite cheerfully for the Waldorf.

Next morning I arrived early at the rehearsal rooms, a depressing huddle of huts left from the war, to find Bergman standing alone in the middle of the floor. 'Had a good night?' I asked. 'A good night! I did not sleep a wink. That traffic. And this cabin! What is this for a rehearsal room? Everywhere there are pillars.' And indeed the room was full of them, holding up the roof.

I have explained that Bergman had stipulated that an assistant director should be provided to note what he did and rehearse the cast in his absence. For some reason Olivier had decided that the best person for this humble job would be himself. He sat watching closely as Bergman, with great precision, blocked the first act, occasionally complaining when a pillar stood where he wanted an actor to be, or when a dog barked outside. Suddenly Olivier said: 'Ingmar.'

Bergman turned. 'Ingmar, this is only a suggestion – you know this play so much better than I do, and you're Swedish like the author [Olivier could never get it into his head that Ibsen was Norwegian] – but would it be an idea, this is only a suggestion of course, would it be an idea if when that chap comes in she doesn't at first see him, and he comes up close behind her, and then she suddenly turns and there he is!'

No one knows the value of silence more than Bergman, and that which followed was considerable. At length he said: 'Perhaps. We see,' and continued directing. That afternoon Olivier made another suggestion. This time Bergman did not turn but stood quite still and silent for a full minute. Then, still with his back to Olivier, he murmured: 'Yes,' and proceeded with his work. The rest of us looked at each other, feeling rather like spectators at a boxing match who had suddenly found ourselves in the ring.

Next morning Olivier was not at rehearsal, and a young man whom none of us knew sat with a notebook writing down every move and direction that Bergman gave. I went to the lavatory and found Olivier standing in the narrow corridor, hands in pockets. He put his hand on my shoulder. 'How's it going?' 'Fine, Larry. Come and see.' 'No, no.' Pause. 'Ingmar's a great director, Michael.' He seemed set for a long dialogue, and I was bursting to get to the loo. 'Everyone's happy with him, aren't they, Michael?' 'Of course.' 'He's a great director.' 'Aren't you coming in?' 'No, no.' At last I managed to get round him and relieve myself. When I got back to the rehearsal room I told the others of this encounter. One of the actors went out and returned slightly pale, to report the same experience. The head of the National Theatre was barring the way to the lavatory like the Ancient Mariner at the wedding.

Olivier had told me to be on hand throughout rehearsals in case Bergman needed an interpreter. Bergman's English was in fact perfectly adequate, though he occasionally turned and barked a single Swedish word for me to translate, a much more difficult task than to render whole sentences. It soon became apparent that he did not regard *Hedda Gabler* as a play that could be allowed to speak for itself, or Ibsen as a dramatist who knew best how to tell his story. Ibsen gradually and subtly reveals that Hedda is pregnant; Bergman had her enter alone before the action begins, stand in front of a mirror and press her hands down against her belly in loathing as though trying to smooth away the, to her, ugly protrusion. He then had her take one of her father's pistols from its case, kick her shoes off, slowly raise the barrel and point it at her temple, all the time watching herself in the mirror, and then put the pistol back in its case. None of us understood why she should kick her shoes off, though we realized that the action must possess some great significance which we were too stupid to perceive. At length someone asked. Bergman said: 'I know a man who is Olympic medallist at the pistol. He tells me that the great pistol-shooters always remove their shoes to get firmer contact with the ground.' Nobody dared ask what that had to do with Hedda Gabler. Sometimes a character, instead of leaving the stage, was made to hang around and observe the others; years later I saw him use this device, equally pointlessly and distractingly as it seemed to me, in a production of *Hamlet*.

Hedda Gabler is one of the most economically written of all great plays, but Bergman cut it as though it was a film. Much of Ibsen's humour went out of the window, as well as all the references to Loevborg's 'vine-leaves in his hair', plus any mention of drawing the curtain and hating the sun, since this clashed with Bergman's set of unbroken red screens. No fewer than six of the eighteen pages of the great final part were regarded as dispensable. At the same time, one could not but frequently admire his skill, precision and imagination. Some of his advice to the actors was very perceptive. To Robert Stephens, playing Hedda's lover Ejlert Loevborg, he said: 'What are you? A poet, yes, a handsome lover. But first and foremost, you are alcoholic. You have given it up, but *you* know, once an alcoholic, always, perhaps, again an alcoholic. And when Hedda offers you the glass of punch, you begin to sweat.' He also, like Olivier, had the ability to make whoever he was talking to feel that he or she was the only person in the world who mattered. Nobody was allowed to smoke in the rehearsal room, as this, like noise and sauces, made him feel sick.

After five days he told us that he would be returning the next day to Sweden to complete his 'film manuscript'. 'Perhaps I come back here for the last week of rehearsal, I cannot tell. As you know, I had intended that an assistant should note what I want and instruct you. But Lord Olivier [he always mockingly underlined the word 'Lord'] has such a powerful personality, I fear he would put himself into my production – as I, if I were his assistant, would do with one of his. This young man has replaced him, but I think, you have all worked together before, you can conduct yourselves like a chamber orchestra, till I return.' And that is what happened.

Back he came for the final week, and all went well until we came to the technical rehearsal. This took place in the Cambridge Theatre, where the production was to run. It was one of those occasions when everything went wrong with the lighting. Bergman lost his temper, a frightening sight. He turned on Olivier and shouted at him: 'You call yourself the National Theatre of England. Any provincial theatre in Sweden could do better than this.' Of course it was not Olivier's fault, but all he needed to do was to apologize and assure Bergman that things would be all right. But Olivier cannot bear to be criticized for a performance in the presence of other actors, and he evidently felt the same about this. He went as white with anger as Bergman. Things were getting very difficult.

The dress rehearsal, without an audience, was slow and pretty lifeless. In the interval I went to a pub by the stage-door and found Olivier barring the entry, as he had barred the way to the lavatory a month earlier. He looked gloomy. 'Ah, Michael. How do you think it's going?' 'Fine, Larry.' 'You don't find it slow?' 'Well, yes, but dress rehearsals always are. And Swedish tempo is slower than ours.' 'I think it's terribly slow.' 'You must tell him, then.' 'No, no. He won't take it from me.' He looked at me, and for a moment I feared he was going to ask me to give Bergman a note. But mercifully he offered me a drink instead.

Bergman had explained that he could not stay for the premiere the next day, and at the end of the dress rehearsal he announced that he would like everyone connected with the production – actors, stage hands, me, even the voice coach – to come to Maggie's dressing-room so that he could thank us all. We wondered why he could not thank us there and then, but soon understood. When Olivier came with the rest of us to the dressing-room, Bergman refused to have him there. Even less generous is what he writes in his memoirs about Olivier's apartment which Olivier put at his disposal after the fiasco at the Waldorf. 'At first sight, the apartment seemed elegant, but it proved to have an ingrained dirtiness. The expensive sofas were stained, the wallpaper torn. There were interesting shapes of damp on the ceilings. Everywhere was dusty, smutty. The breakfast cups were ill-washed, the glasses bore lip-marks, the wall-to-wall carpets were torn.' I visited this apartment several times and never noticed any of these things.★

The premiere the following night was not helped by the presence in a box of Tennessee Williams, who indulged in his customary habit of laughing insanely at the most dramatic lines. However, the production was a great critical and public success. I thought it, if not exactly a *Reader's Digest* Ibsen, at best a clever paraphrase, a 'Hedda Without Tears'. My agent Peggy Ramsay accurately summed up my feelings when she said that for anyone who didn't know or didn't like Ibsen, it made a very striking evening – a fair description of many of Bergman's productions of non-Strindberg classics.

Bergman was nothing but charming, and even flattering, to me throughout this period. I have seldom met a person with greater charm, though Olivier's is certainly equal. But I felt with Bergman something that I have never felt with any other human being. I had no grounds for it, and could not pinpoint any reason for it, nor could I describe it. It was something much more disturbing than malice or malignity. Two actresses who worked with him in Sweden told me they felt the same. When he left London after his final address to the cast, he said to me: 'When you are in Stockholm, get in touch and we will meet.' I never did.

★ In an interview published twelve years later, Bergman claimed that 'Olivier . . . didn't really want me to come. He wanted my idea for the play, and then he wanted to take over and stage it himself, in my choreography . . . Of course it was a silly idea, but he was very charming and he . . . succeeded in convincing me' (Ingmar Bergman, *Four Decades in the Theatre*, by L. L. and F. J. Marker, p. 225. Cambridge University Press, 1982). Bergman also remembered the food at our introductory dinner as being 'Javanese [*sic*] and uneatable.'

17

How Graham Greene Became a Film Actor

In 1965, Graham Greene, together with several other distinguished clients, was hugely swindled by an eminent but corrupt accountant. Hitherto, Graham had resisted the temptation to become a tax-exile, but now he decided to emigrate, first to Paris, then (though he retained the Paris flat on the boulevard Malesherbes) to Antibes. 'Owing to a certain X . . . who managed to rob me of half my savings,' he wrote to me from Paris on 21 January 1966, 'I have had to take up residence abroad from January 1st. I can't help remembering our first voyage together to Paris when you were *en route* to the Far East and how ill the passage made you.' (I see that he inscribed the copy of *The Comedians* which he gave me: 'Christmas 1965, on the point of departure'). Both the Paris and Antibes apartments were, like his bachelor flats in St James's Street and later in Albany, comfortable but curiously impersonal and far from grand, though I remember the fine Jack Yeats oil painting and the army of tiny whisky bottles which airlines give to their first-class passengers and which multiplied over the years like a child's collection of toy soldiers. In both Paris and Antibes, he ate regularly at unpretentious little restaurants round the corner, where he was welcomed as one of the family. Although his French never became really good, Graham settled into his new surroundings with an ease which surprised me. I knew how content he could be in hotel rooms with a few books, but I did not think he would so readily acclimatize himself to lifelong exile. (As a tax-exile he was allowed to spend I think only ninety days a year in England.)

Although he was now into his sixties, he continued to travel as restlessly as ever, preferably to trouble-spots or to places where he sensed that trouble was imminent. It had become a habit, he was to write in *Ways of Escape*, 'to visit troubled places, not to seek material for novels but to regain the sense of insecurity which I had enjoyed

in the three blitzes on London'. His political foresight was so acute
that his appearance in any sensitive area aroused apprehension. Alec
Guinness, a fellow Roman Catholic, once gloomily remarked to me:
'I hear Graham is now in Rome.' On 16 October 1967, Graham wrote
to me: 'Just back from Israel. I managed to bring them their worst
incident in the Canal in two months, but miscalculated and found
myself in the middle of it. Three hours (nearly) stranded on a sand
dune feeling too old for war . . . My 63rd birthday celebrated on
field rations and warm grape juice on the Syrian hills. Could have
been better.' The following year he sent me a gloomy account of
the film of *The Comedians*, which he had scripted ('detestable work').
After congratulating me on my news that I was to become a father
for the first time at the age of forty-seven, he wrote: 'I thought the
Comedians film was pretty dull myself, but it was an impossible film
to do – so much had to be left out for length. Liz [Taylor] was hell.
Anyway I've got this flat [in Antibes] out of it and repaired the losses
caused by the villain – [his accountant].'

In October 1972 I visited him in Antibes. A girl I knew had got a
part in François Truffaut's film *La Nuit Américaine* (known in Britain
and America as *Day for Night*), which he was shooting in Nice and
had invited me to stay with her. Nice is only a few miles from
Antibes, and one result of my visit was that Graham got his first
film part – or at any rate the first in which his face was seen, for
his hand had appeared as *The Stranger's Hand* in the minor film of
that name which he had written long before for Mario Soldati.

Truffaut wrote much of his scripts off the cuff, adding new scenes
as they occurred to him, and one morning as I was sitting in the sun
watching the filming, his assistant, Suzanne Schiffmann, asked me:
'Are you English or American?' When I replied 'English', she asked:
'Have you a dark suit?' In my ignorance of sartorial customs in the
south of France, or anyway in Truffaut's circle, I had in fact brought
a suit with me, and on learning this Suzanne explained: 'Monsieur
Truffaut wants a scene with an English insurance agent. But I must
first control with him that you are the right type.' For a few dizzy
seconds I supposed that I had at last got into films, but when Suzanne
went across to Truffaut and whispered to him, he gave me the briefest
glance and shook his head. She came back to me and said: *'Je regrette,
monsieur, mais Monsieur Truffaut dit que votre visage est trop intellectuel
pour la rôle.'* I said I would be willing to shave off my beard, but no.
I was not the right type.

That evening, I went to dine with Graham and his Yvonne in

Antibes, and when I told him this sad story he said to my astonishment: 'I wonder if I'd be the type.' I said: 'Why on earth would you want to appear in a film?' 'Well, Yvonne's daughter Martine is an announcer on Monte Carlo television and wants to get into films, and I'd like to get her an introduction to Truffaut.' 'Can't you just write to him?' 'No, I'd need to meet him.' I explained that I had been rejected as looking too intellectual, so what chance would he have, and anyway it was well known that he had always refused to appear on television for fear of being recognized and pestered in the street. However, I said that my friend and I had been invited to a party that evening by two of the actresses in the film, Jacqueline Bisset and Nathalie Baye – there was a delightful arrangement in the Truffaut *équipe* by which two different members, sometimes stars, sometimes technicians, gave parties which everyone, including Truffaut, attended – and I could take him along and ask Suzanne if he was the type. He agreed, but made us promise not to tell anyone who he was. 'Say I'm Henry Graham, a retired businessman living in Antibes.' When I protested that someone would be bound to recognize him, he said: 'Nobody knows my face down here.'

So we all went to the party, and as Graham was chatting away to someone in his ragged but serviceable French, I asked Suzanne, not very hopefully: 'Do you think my friend Henry might be a possibility for your insurance agent?' She looked at him for a few moments, and said: 'He is the perfect type. I will control with Monsieur Truffaut.' She did so, returned to me and said: 'Monsieur Truffaut says he will do perfectly.' 'Oh, that's splendid.' 'But there is a problem. We have a very small budget, and for such a role Monsieur Truffaut usually gives no money, only a signed copy of one of his books.' She hesitated. 'But if your friend needs money – ' 'No, that's all right. He has a pension.' So she and Truffaut went over to Graham and the deal was concluded. His scenes would be shot the day after tomorrow; he and I would be collected in a car at Antibes, and he would be given his lines when he arrived.

Next morning Graham telephoned to our hotel and said: 'I can't do it. *Paris-Match* would find out and pester me. It'd come out about me and Yvonne. Can you telephone Suzanne and make some excuse?'

'What shall I say?'

'Tell her I've got stage fright and would make a mess of it.'

I phoned Suzanne, who said: 'This is terrible, terrible. Today is a public holiday and we cannot find anyone else before tomorrow.

Monsieur Henry seemed so excited about it last night. Is it a question of money?'

I decided to come clean.

'My God,' said Suzanne. 'Is that who he is? Well, you must persuade him to come.'

'I don't know if I can do that. He seemed very determined. What can I say to him?'

'Tell him it is not sporting to drop out like this.' I hardly thought this argument would carry much weight with Graham, but I passed on her message and curiously it seemed to move him, for he hesitated. 'It would be letting them down,' I said. 'They'd have to alter the schedule.' Eventually he agreed – less, I suspect, from any residue of the public-school spirit than because he was tickled by the idea of appearing pseudonymously in a film by a distinguished director whom he admired. He insisted, however, that no one but Suzanne and my girlfriend should know his true identity. Suzanne readily agreed to this: 'I would not dare to tell Monsieur Truffaut anyway.' 'Why not?' 'He gets very angry if anyone has tried to deceive him.'

Next morning I met Graham at the railway station in Antibes (he did not want to be collected outside his flat in case the driver should see his name on the entryphone). He was in a grey suit and carrying a rolled umbrella. 'I thought the umbrella would be good,' he said. A lad arrived in an old, battered and filthy *deux-chevaux*. As he drove us to Nice, I kept addressing Graham absent-mindedly as Graham. 'For God's sake call me Henry.' When we arrived, Suzanne handed him a sheet of paper with a few lines typed on it in English. Graham put on his glasses, read it and at once took out his pen. I said: 'Henry, you are a small-part amateur actor. You cannot rewrite the lines.' 'I don't want to say "three-quarters of an hour".' 'What on earth's wrong with that?' 'I can't pronounce my Rs. Do you think they'll let me say "half an hour"?' This was agreed, and in due course he was summoned inside the studio to do his scene.

Suzanne asked if I would mind not coming in as the studio was very small and crowded, so I waited outside in the sun with my friend and Nathalie Baye. Half an hour passed; an hour; an hour and a half. Nathalie knew Graham's identity; I think by this time everyone did except Truffaut. 'How long is this scene?' I asked. 'Only a few lines.' 'How can they be taking such a time?' 'François likes to shoot a scene many times.' 'But an hour and a half?' Two hours passed, two and a half. We began to worry. Remembering what Suzanne had said about Truffaut's anger if he found he had been deceived, I imagined terrible scenes taking place, Monsieur Henry exposed and humiliated, threatened, perhaps even assaulted. What would *Paris-Match* make of this? But at length, after nearly three hours, everyone emerged, Graham and Truffaut with their arms around each other, both in high good humour. What, we wondered, could be the explanation?

It appeared that after a lot of takes, Truffaut had suddenly said: 'Monsieur Henry. You have acted before?' Flattered, Graham said: 'No, not since I was a child', and then, fishing: 'What makes you think so?' But instead of the expected compliment, Truffaut replied: 'When I look at you through the view-finder, I know your face.'

Graham said that at this point he felt exactly as he used to when caught out as a schoolboy. Truffaut said: 'You have been in films?' 'No.' 'Perhaps documentary?' 'No, none at all.' 'In the newspaper?' This was a difficult one. Before Graham could think of a reply, Truffaut continued: 'I know your face. Where have I seen it?' There was a silence. Truffaut looked around and saw that everyone else was staring at the floor. Graham realized now that everyone except Truffaut shared the secret, and Truffaut realized it too and began to get angry. 'What is this? Are you all hiding something from me?' The joke had gone horribly wrong. Suzanne went over to Truffaut and whispered in his ear. Truffaut's eyes bulged and his tiny frame began to swell. For a ghastly moment, Graham thought he was going to attack him. Then he gave a great laugh, cried: 'What a wonderful joke!', rushed at Graham and embraced him. They remained excellent friends until Truffaut's death twelve years later. Graham's scene was duly included in the film, and there he is, listed among the credits at the end: Henry Graham. I was rejected as looking too intellectual, so they gave the part to Graham Greene.

For many years, Graham had sent me a copy of each new work of his shortly before it appeared, with a sentence from it inscribed as a *dédicace*. These usually referred to drink: 'I told him that I don't drink more than anyone else, but he said some livers are weaker than others' (*The Human Factor*); 'We were not satisfied with two bottles, were we?' (*Monsignor Quixote*); 'There was heavy drinking' (*Getting to Know the General*). Sometimes I brought along a book of his which I had acquired earlier for him to sign. In a 1947 paperback of *The Lawless Roads* with a youthful photograph of him on the back, he wrote: 'For young Michael from old Greene. Did I look like that once?', and in *The Lost Childhood*: 'The lost Berkhamsted – the lost Stockholm – the lost Tahiti.' Once I managed to find a second-hand edition of *The Name of Action*, one of his two early novels (*Rumour at Nightfall* was the other) which he so disliked that he refused to allow them to be reprinted. 'God damn you,' he wrote on the flyleaf. 'Burn this juvenilia.' Had I been less foolishly honest, or cowardly, I could also have acquired *Rumour at Nightfall*, for during my stint at Bomber Command I found a copy of it in the public library at High Wycombe. Its loss in wartime would hardly have bothered anyone. I bet someone else has stolen it by now.

I especially longed to obtain a copy of his even more hated (by him) early volume of verse, *Babbling April*, published by Blackwell of Oxford while he was still an undergraduate, but this seemed impossible. Apart from it having been a small edition, he had bought up and destroyed as many copies as he could lay his hands on. However, I found that a friend of mine owned one, borrowed it and had it photocopied (it contains only thirty-two pages). When Graham was next in England, I drove him down to the Hind's Head at Bray, where I had eaten as a schoolboy on my days out at Earleywood and Wellington and, as we sat at a table, said: 'I've an old book of yours. Would you sign it for me?' 'Of course,' he said, and took out his pen. I said: 'Will you sign it whatever it is?' 'It isn't *Babbling April*?' 'Not only is it *Babbling April*. It is a pirated edition.' 'That I can do something about,' he said. 'Do you know who pirated it?' 'I did.' He wrote in it: 'This filthy and clandestine copy of a terrible book', adding a quotation from one of the poems: 'Look at him smiling there'.

The friend who had lent me this copy said that bibliographically it did constitute a separate edition, and advised me to get it bound, suggesting that I approach Sydney Cockerell at Grantchester, perhaps the most distinguished exponent of his craft in Britain; but I would have to write first and ask if he would undertake this, as he did not accept everything that was offered to him. I duly wrote, saying that the book was something that even he had probably never been offered before, a pirated but dedicated copy. Cockerell replied that this was indeed a unique request, and that he would be amused to do it, though he felt bound to warn me that nobody was yet sure how long photocopies would last, and that it was possible that in future years I, or my heirs, would find ourselves in possession of a book of blank pages containing nothing but the handwritten dedication. I suppose that of all the books I own, this must be the most valuable. What will it be worth if the text disappears?

In a letter he wrote to me in 1969, Graham said he thought the three best novels he had written to that date were *Brighton Rock*, *The Power and the Glory* and *Travels with my Aunt*, which appeared that year. He also rated highly his next book, *The Honorary Consul*, which took him three years, not least for the way the characters changed during the course of it, compared (he said in a broadcast) with those in *The Power and the Glory*. There is no trace in it of its difficult gestation, nor does it read like the writing of a man of sixty-eight.

In the spring of 1981, the journalist Chapman Pincher published a book accusing the late Sir Roger Hollis, a former head of British Intelligence, of having been a Russian agent. As an old MI6 man, Graham had strong feelings on the matter. 'I have great doubts about the Roger Hollis story and Mr Chapman Pincher,' he wrote to me on 13 April. 'It looks to me like a classical piece of disinformation and destabilization – perhaps engineered, who knows, by Kim?'

Graham retained his affection for Kim Philby, his wartime colleague in MI6, even after the latter's exposure and defection to Russia. He continued to correspond with him, and visited him several times in Moscow in both 1986 and 1987. I could never agree with him about this, remembering all the deaths of brave and dedicated men that Philby had caused, such as the hundreds of exiled Albanian dissidents who had been parachuted into that country to try to overthrow the draconian Hoxha regime. But Graham set out his views on the subject clearly in his speech of acceptance of the Shakespeare Prize at Hamburg in 1969, which he published under the title *The Virtue of Disloyalty*. 'The writer should always be ready to change sides at the drop of a hat. He stands for the victims and the victims change. Loyalty confines you to accepted opinions; loyalty forbids you to comprehend sympathetically your dissident fellows; but disloyalty encourages you to roam through any human mind; it gives the novelist an extra dimension of understanding . . . The novelist's task is to draw his own likeness to any human being, to the guilty as much as to the innocent.' He concluded: 'That is a genuine duty we owe to society, to be a piece of grit in the State machinery. However acceptable for the moment the Soviet State may find the great classic writers, Dostoevsky, Tolstoy, Turgenev, Gogol, Chekhov, they have surely made the regimentation of the Russian spirit an imperceptible degree more difficult or more incomplete.' Similarly, in his speech of acceptance of the Jerusalem Prize in 1981, *Freedom of Thought*, he praised the dissident Catholic, Father Hans

Kung: 'With all respect, the price of liberty in a Church as much as in a State is eternal vigilance . . . As a Roman Catholic I thank God for the heretics. Heresy is only another word for freedom of thought.' He was deeply disappointed with the general conservatism of Pope John Paul II. And in *Ways of Escape*, he wrote: 'A writer who is a Catholic cannot help having a certain sympathy for any faith which is sincerely held.'

In his eighty-fourth year, as I write these lines, Graham is not very different, in appearance or personality, from the man I first met over forty years ago: the tall figure that still rises quickly from a chair, the nervous schoolboy laugh and sense of mischief and delight in cocking a snook at authority. Twenty years ago I asked Claud Cockburn, who had been a classmate of his at Berkhamsted, how much Graham had changed since he was fourteen, and Cockburn replied: 'Not at all. Classic case of arrested development.' That is one way of describing it; another would be to say that every good writer retains the eye of the child however much he or she may mature intellectually and emotionally. The poet and critic Richard Church astonished me many years ago when I published my first book by advising me: 'Never lose your naivety.' It is a measure of how youthful Graham has remained that it would be difficult if not impossible to tell from internal evidence – apart from an increasing interest in politics and an at first increasing, then decreasing interest in religion – which novels he had written in his twenties and which in his seventies. Who would guess, apart from the historical references, that *Travels with my Aunt* was written nearly half a century after *It's a Battlefield*?

18

A Punch on the Nose

It cannot be often that punching someone on the nose leads to a lucrative contract, but that happened to me in 1972. I was eating a curry in a restaurant next to a very drunk man who began to abuse his female companion loudly in obscene language. After a while, I said: 'Can't you speak more quietly so that the rest of us don't have to hear?' He then abused me similarly, I asked him to stop, and when he didn't I slapped him on the nose with the palm of my hand, the first time I had punched anyone since Oxford, and hopefully the last. It bled, he stopped, and the restaurant owner panicked and telephoned the police. I paid and left, but outside the door met the police coming in. I told them what had happened, they asked me to wait, went in and spoke to the man, came back and said: 'That's all right. Here's his name and address in case you need them.' It turned out to be the playwright David Mercer. I said to the police: 'I admire this man. We have the same agent.' The police looked at me as though I was drunk too. What followed must have nonplussed the other diners, for I re-entered, went up to him, said: 'You're a marvellous writer. I'm a client of Peggy Ramsay too', and told him my name; he said: 'You're a bloody marvellous translator. Have a brandy', and we sat down and became good friends. The lady departed and I gave Mercer a lift back to his flat in Hampstead, dropping him twenty yards from the door because the street was one-way, but something must have happened before he got there, for next day he told Peggy that although he had liked me I had for some reason left him miles from his home in Golders Green so that he had had to get a taxi back. He wrote a short one-act play about the incident called *Blood on the Tablecloth*, but unfortunately it was not one of his best and I don't think it has ever been performed.

A short while later Mercer was contracted to write the script for a film of *A Doll's House*, and insisted that he should base it on my translation, so that my punch earned me a handsome fee. As things turned out, the leading lady insisted on a good deal of rewriting because she felt that Ibsen had not put the feminine point of view adequately (an attitude similarly adopted by a female playwright a few years later, when she adapted the play and completely rewrote the final scene). The result was that instead of being about a self-distrusting girl who leaves a domineering husband, the film became a tale of the bossiest woman one could dread to meet walking out on a downtrodden husband. Each evening Mercer was summoned by the star and told how the next day's scene needed to be reshaped. I had intended to fly to Norway to watch the shooting, but three friends of mine in the cast wrote begging me to stay away; I am notoriously impossible to sit next to in a theatre when displeased, and they reckoned that I would not last half an hour on the set. I am used to having my translations plagiarized without permission or payment; on this occasion I was well paid and got a prominent credit, but scarcely a line of mine was used. At the preview the director told me: 'I'm afraid this is not quite the film I had in mind.' Mercer and I remained excellent friends until his death.

Unlike Shakespeare, Ibsen and Strindberg both work wonderfully well on television because their plays are intensely private. One needs to feel that one is spying and eavesdropping on the characters. Their large-scale works, however, apart from *Peer Gynt* which always draws an audience, are seldom staged because they have such big casts. But they are well suited to sound radio, and Martin Jenkins in particular directed a series of fine productions of plays in this medium, which few theatre-goers can have seen in this country, including three Strindbergs never previously performed here – *Erik the Fourteenth*, *The Virgin Bride* and *Master Olof* – the rarely seen *Dream Play*, a splendid *Brand* with Brian Cox and a *Peer Gynt* with (at my entreaty) an all-Irish cast. I had long wanted to see this, for the rustic background of the opening three acts and the last is difficult to make totally convincing in any English rural accent, but it would be virtually impossible to assemble twenty Irish actors anywhere outside Ireland itself for the duration of rehearsals and a theatre run. But one can do this for the four days that a radio play needs, and the result was remarkable. I suggested Denis Quilley for Peer, assuming that with that surname he must be at least of Irish descent. After the recording, he confessed to me that he had not a drop of Irish blood in his veins, but his accent was so perfect that none of the rest of the cast suspected this.

In 1973, Robin Phillips, who had directed the Royal Shakespeare Company's *Miss Julie* a couple of years earlier, staged a strong *Rosmersholm* at Greenwich with Joan Plowright as Rebecca West (one of her best performances). I watched the dress rehearsal with her husband, Laurence Olivier. At the end, he turned to me, and said: 'Bloody difficult playwright, Ibsen. Much more difficult than Strindberg.' Ibsen is not in fact more difficult than Strindberg, but all his characters demand the kind of close-relationship acting which has always been Olivier's weakest point; he has never been able to portray convincingly a father, a husband or a son, except the kind that cannot relate to those around him, such as Archie Rice in *The Entertainer*, James Tyrone in *Long Day's Journey into Night* or the Captain in Strindberg's *The Dance of Death*. When I congratulated Olivier on his performance in the last-named role, he replied: 'It wasn't difficult. There isn't a line that I haven't said to one of my three wives.'

That year I gave up my flat in Stockholm after seventeen years. The disadvantage of having a second home abroad is that one tends not to go anywhere else abroad. The previous year I had visited Rome and Tokyo, and realized that Stockholm no longer held any surprises for me. I knew what would be around every corner. The theatre was not as good as it had been in the forties and fifties, and the narrowness of Swedish literary society against which Strindberg had inveighed (as Ibsen had against that of Oslo) began to get through to me. A handful of literary and dramatic critics dictated taste, and personal prejudice played a much larger part in their judgements than in more cosmopolitan cities such as London and New York. This did not damage me personally, since I was not writing for the Swedish market, but I felt it none the less. My former girlfriends were married and raising families. Buildings and whole quarters that I loved had been or were being pulled down, and the city seemed to me to be losing much of its individuality and charm. Had I squeezed that orange dry, or was it I that had changed? Anyway, I sold the flat on Döbelnsgatan with its two balconies, and changed my tiny one in Paddington for a larger one in Marylebone, where I had spent my childhood and youth; I no longer needed to run away from those early years of failure and frustration.

At this time I became acquainted with a new generation of directors in Britain. Michael Ockrent imaginatively staged two rare and difficult Strindbergs, *A Dream Play* and *To Damascus*, at the tiny Traverse Theatre in Edinburgh, with the young Simon Callow and Roy Marsden. Both plays have many characters, but Ockrent showed that they can be effectively performed by a small company with everyone except the principal actor playing several roles, something that I have seen accomplished several times since with *Peer Gynt*. Then the young John Caird directed *The Dance of Death* for the RSC, with a magnificent Captain in Emrys James – much closer to Strindberg's conception of the character than Olivier's dynamic but romanticized interpretation. And Martin Esslin, the head of BBC radio drama, asked me to write a play about Strindberg. This, *Lunatic and Lover*, with Alan Badel as Strindberg, was runner-up for best radio documentary drama of the year; then Andy Jordan, who ran his own enterprising fringe company, Bristol Express, got me to rewrite it for the theatre and staged it brilliantly on the Edinburgh Fringe in 1978, when, thanks largely to his contribution, it won a Fringe First and transferred successfully to the Old Red Lion in Islington, one of the best venues on the London Fringe. These pub theatres, holding fifty to a hundred people in an upstairs room, have been a valuable addition to the London scene; I often see more rewarding plays and productions there than in the bigger theatres. The new regime at the National Theatre under Peter Hall never used my work, Hall having a professed policy of never employing any translation that has already been performed elsewhere. This often, except with French plays, seemed to result in his using 'translators' who did not know the language and worked through an intermediary – the method I had found so disastrous with *Little Eyolf* in my salad days. (Michael Frayn tells me that when they asked him to translate Chekhov and suggested various literal translators to help, they were taken aback to learn that he read Russian fluently; he had foolishly supposed that that was why they had asked him.) Hall even made his own version, a particularly clumsy and ineloquent one, of *Borkman*. I cannot say that I was sorry not to be involved, as all the National's Ibsens since Bergman's *Hedda* – *Borkman*, *Brand*, *The Wild Duck* and *Rosmersholm* – have been disappointing, partly, perhaps, because of the dreadfully unintimate Olivier and Lyttleton auditoriums (though *Rosmersholm* in the tiny Cottesloe was no better). *Borkman* was glamorously cast, but I know that few of the actors in it felt that justice had been done to the play, Ralph Richardson being especially unhappy with the result. The Olivier and Lyttleton theatres are suited only to out-front acting, which can work with some large-cast plays, even in a sort of way with Shakespeare, but is death to anything intimate, such as Ibsen.

In 1976 Tony Richardson directed *The Lady from the Sea* in New York, with his former wife, Vanessa Redgrave, as Ellida. The rest of the cast were undistinguished – why can even the best American actors never cope with European classics? – but Richardson staged it skilfully and Vanessa was as good as she could be in a void with no establishable relationships. The production was a hit, and my agent Bob Freedman phoned me in London to say that it was playing to 102% capacity. When I queried this figure, he explained that they had people standing. The company even paid my fare across the Atlantic to see the production. The head of it met me at the airport and, as he drove me into Manhattan, said they were having a 'cullockwy' that evening in which he hoped I would partake. I had no idea what a 'cullockwy' was, thought it might be a barbecue or something of the sort, and readily agreed. It turned out to be a colloquy, or talk-in; after the performance I had to sit on stage with Vanessa and answer questions from the audience. I made a bad start. A ravishing creature in jeans with shoulder-length fair hair asked something. As I began to answer, people at the back asked me to repeat the question which they had not heard. I said: 'The young lady asked – ' The ravishing creature shouted: 'I'm not a lady.' I had to apologize to him. I was addressed throughout as the author. When I tried to explain that I was only the translator, a fierce old man at the back said: 'These were your words we heard? O.K. So you're the author.'

New York is a manic-depressive city. During the *Hedda Gabler* débâcle in 1960 every skyscraper leaned over as I passed and knocked me on the head. Now I was part of a hit; and an important part, for in everyone's eyes I was the author. As I passed those same skyscrapers, I soared to the roof of each, muttering a silent apology to Ibsen's ghost.

That autumn of 1976 Michael Elliott and his co-directors, Casper Wrede, James Maxwell, Richard Negri – all old colleagues from the 59 Theatre Company at Hammersmith – and Braham Murray opened the Royal Exchange Theatre at Manchester. When Michael had first told me of the Arts Council's suggestion that he should run a theatre there, I was very dubious and counselled him against it. I feared that the kind of plays he would want to present would appeal only to a minority in the industrial North. How wrong I was. After some preliminary distrust of this group of southerners who had descended into their midst, Manchester and all the other towns within fifty miles rose in vigorous support. In the eleven years since its foundation, the Royal Exchange Theatre has averaged over 80% capacity nightly, a remarkable figure for a 720-seat theatre presenting, on the whole, demanding plays. The city became a second home to me, as to Michael; I came to love its people, their warmth and enthusiasm, even its buildings. I am of the generation that was brought up to regard all Victorian architecture as hideous. When I took my daughter, then nine, there for the first time, she stared round St Ann's Square in which the theatre stands and said: 'I think Manchester's beautiful.' I looked, and she was right.

When Richard Negri's design for the theatre was shown to the architects, they raised one objection. When full, it would crash through the floor into the Danish Food Centre beneath. Their solution was to link it by steel girders to the great pillars supporting the Exchange roof and so spread the weight. I was as pessimistic about this as I had originally been about the whole project. It seemed impossible to me that this plan could work. Everyone on the opening night would be killed, like the Philistines at Gaza. But again I was proved wrong. The theatre has survived (though not the Danish Food Centre). Since 1976, three-quarters of the most memorable productions that I have seen have been at the Royal Exchange: Michael's *Philoctetes*, *Crime and Punishment*, *The Lady from the Sea* and *Moby Dick*; Casper Wrede's *The Three Sisters*, *Hope Against Hope* (about the Russian dissident poet Osip Mandelstam) and *Oedipus*; Braham Murray's *The Dybbuk* and *Macbeth*; Adrian Noble's *The Duchess of Malfi*; Nick Hytner's *Don Carlos*.

The Royal Exchange also introduced a major European actor to British audiences. I had seen Espen Skjønberg give several remarkable performances in his native Norway, first thirty years before as Oswald in *Ghosts*, and more recently as the Captain in Strindberg's *The Father* and Judge Brack in *Hedda Gabler*. Casper persuaded him over to Manchester to play the crazed old schoolmaster Ulrik Brendel in *Rosmersholm*, a notoriously difficult part to bring off, and subsequently Old Ekdal in *The Wild Duck*, Ulysses in *Philoctetes*, the drunken doctor in *The Three Sisters*, and Shylock. The critics and audiences at once perceived that here was an actor unlike any we had in Britain, of a ferocious power combined with a superb technique, like Wilfrid Lawson at his best, before that great actor had begun to forget his lines – in fact, like a sober Lawson, if anyone who knew Wilfrid can imagine that. Skjønberg's Brendel and Old Ekdal are for me definitive, in the sense that I cannot imagine either part being played otherwise or better. In 1985 *Drama Magazine* named him Best Supporting Actor of the Year for his performance in *The Three Sisters*, one of the few times this coveted award has been given either to a foreign actor or for a performance outside London. His Shylock was finer than any performance of that role that I have seen by a British actor, worthy to stand beside Frederick Valk's unforgettable interpretation for the Old Vic in the forties.

Almost everything that I had written since the ill-fated *May Game* in 1954 had been suggested to me by someone else: the Ibsen and Strindberg translations, the Ibsen biography, both versions of *Lunatic and Lover*, and a radio play about Herman Melville, *Call Me Ishmael*. (I think the only exception, apart from editing a cricket anthology, *Summer Days*, and writing a short history of my cricket club, the Jesters, was a television play I wrote in 1964 about Ibsen's relationship with the young Emilie Bardach when he was sixty-three and she eighteen, *The Summer in Gossensass*, which Casper directed brilliantly with that other great Norwegian actor, Claes Gill, as Ibsen, and I am not even sure that that was originally my idea.) Ever since the publication of my Ibsen biography various publishers had suggested that I should write one about Strindberg, but I shrank from it for the reasons I have stated. In 1978 my agent David Higham took me out to lunch to put the question again, but again I refused. When he left for the office, I stayed drinking coffee with his wife Nell, and somehow, I cannot think how or why, by the time we finished I had agreed to write, not a full biography but a shortish book to be called *Strindberg the Dramatist* which would deal only with his plays, not, except in passing, with his life or his numerous non-dramatic works. But before I began it, a Scandinavian friend sent me an advance copy of a Swedish biography of Strindberg which was in the press, and I was so incensed by its, as it seemed to me, uncritical approach to Strindberg both as a writer and as a human being that I decided to attempt a full biography as I had with Ibsen. I have already described the problems I encountered; it was a fascinating exercise to write about a man whom I immensely admired but whom in many ways I found antagonizing.

What I had not anticipated, though with hindsight I should have, was the hostility which my approach would arouse among Strindberg disciples, many of whom identify with him very personally. There are two facts about Strindberg which I should have thought no balanced observer could deny, and which in my experience most

Swedes accept: that, like so many great writers – Wordsworth, Shelley, D. H. Lawrence, O'Neill, Brecht – he was extremely uneven, and that he was frequently an impossible human being. But Strindberg's disciples will have none of this. One Swedish critic was so angry with my book that he wrote three hostile reviews of it, in a daily and an evening paper and a book of essays, in the last of which he concluded that I must be a covert homosexual with no appetite for ordinary pleasures. The literary editor of *Svenska Dagbladet* was so annoyed by a favourable review in his own pages that he topped it with a headnote: 'Englishman . . . spends much labour in proving that Strindberg is no longer worth bothering about', which was the opposite of what his reviewer had said. Neither *Dagens Nyheter* nor *Svenska Dagbladet* allowed me the right of reply, which surprised me. Two American-Scandinavian scholars thought I had indulged in a muck-raking exercise, looking only for what was sensationalistic and discreditable.

I was associated with several notable productions in the eighties, including five exciting ones on television. Philip Saville directed *The Ghost Sonata*, with a scarifying performance by Donald Pleasance as the Old Man, and Kenneth Ives *The Father*, with Colin Blakely, Dorothy Tutin (even better than she had been in the 1968 production), Irene Handl and Edward Fox. Michael Darlow directed my two favourite Ibsens, *Little Eyolf*, with a very strong cast headed by Diana Rigg, Anthony Hopkins, Peggy Ashcroft and Charles Dance, and *The Master Builder*, with Leo McKern and Miranda Richardson, whose father Alan had been a friend of Sidney Keyes and me at Oxford. I have never seen the great dialogues between Solness and Hilde more powerfully or subtly done. These productions were matched by Elijah Moshinsky's *Ghosts*, with Judi Dench, Michael Gambon, Kenneth Branagh, Freddie Jones and Natasha Richardson (Vanessa Redgrave's daughter). In the theatre, Adrian Noble directed for the Royal Shakespeare Company a splendid *Doll's House*, with Cheryl Campbell a brilliant Nora, and Clare Davidson staged a *Miss Julie*, with Cheryl Campbell and Stephen Rea, which transferred from the rebuilt Lyric, Hammersmith, to the Duke of York's. And Suzanne Bertish, Ian McDiarmid and Jonathan Kent, all former RSC actors, directed themselves in *Creditors* at the Almeida in Islington, an experiment that came off wonderfully well. There were also some fine productions in the provinces, notably Greg Herzov's *Doll's House* at the Royal Exchange in Manchester, with a Nora by Brenda Blethyn which equalled Cheryl Campbell's,

Michael Meacham's *Little Eyolf* at Leicester, with Heather Sears as a remarkable Rita, and, also at Leicester, Michael Boyd's *Hedda Gabler* with Sian Thomas, the best overall production of that play of the forty-odd that I have seen.

I am sometimes asked which are the best ten Ibsen and Strindberg performances that I have seen. That is a hard one. Certainly Frederick Valk's Solness, and Leo McKern's; McKern's and Brian Cox's Peer Gynt; Patrick McGoohan's Brand; Judi Dench's Mrs Alving; Tom Courtenay's Oswald, and Kenneth Branagh's; Espen Skjønberg's Ulrik Brendel and Old Ekdal; Mai Zetterling's Hedvig (I missed Dorothy Tutin's, which was rated its equal); Vanessa Redgrave's Ellida in *The Lady from the Sea*; Pamela Brown's Hedda, with Joan Greenwood's not far behind; Mary Miller's and Miranda Richardson's Hilde Wangel in *The Master Builder*; Cheryl Campbell's Nora, and Brenda Blethyn's; and Wendy Hiller's Irene in *When We Dead Awaken*. That's nineteen, but I cannot cut it down further. And in Sweden, Ulf Palme's Hjalmar Ekdal and Eva Dahlbäck's Gina in *The Wild Duck*, Tora Teje's Mrs Alving, Åke Claesson's Pastor Manders and Max von Sydow's Gregers Werle. In Strindberg: Wilfrid Lawson's incomparable Captain in *The Father*, and in the same role Espen Skjønberg and, on a good night, Trevor Howard; Mai Zetterling's Tekla in *Creditors*; Helen Mirren's Miss Julie and Albert Finney's Jean; Dorothy Tutin's Laura in *The Father* (and Beatrix Lehmann's, opposite Lawson); Emrys Jones's Captain in *The Dance of Death* and Donald Pleasance's Hummel in *The Ghost Sonata*. In Sweden, Ulf Palme's Jean in *Miss Julie*, both his King and (in the film) his Göran Persson in *Erik the Fourteenth*, and his Captain in *The Dance of Death*; Per Oscarsson's Master Olof; Tora Teje as the Judge's Wife in *Advent*; Anders Henrikson's Gert in *Master Olof* and his Hummel in *The Ghost Sonata*; and Marie Göranzon and Peter Stormare in Ingmar Bergman's 1987 production of *Miss Julie*.

But when I am asked who is the greatest actor I have ever seen, I do not have to hesitate.

19

My Greatest Actor

The name of Frederick Valk must be unknown to most people under fifty, for he died in 1956 and in films he played only supporting roles, mostly camp commandants and the like. But when I am asked who is the greatest actor I have seen, I have no doubt; it was Valk. Likewise, if asked to name my ten greatest individual performances in *all* plays, I start with Valk's Othello, Shylock, Solness in *The Master Builder* and Old Karamazov in *The Brothers Karamazov*, and then think about Olivier, Edith Evans, Richardson, Lawson, Gielgud, Donat and the rest. My admiration of Valk is not a private eccentricity. It was shared by the two shrewdest dramatic critics of this century, James Agate and Kenneth Tynan. In addition to what G. H. Lewes, writing of Edmund Kean, called 'animal power', he had pathos, sensitivity, intelligence and humility. All he lacked was a perfect command of English, which is not surprising, since he did not begin to act in that language until he was forty-four.

Reference books sometimes describe him as Czech, and he was a Czech national when he came to England in February 1939. But he was born Frits Valk, a German Jew, in Wuppertal in the Ruhr, in 1895. He had a fine singing voice and it was touch and go whether he should take up a career in acting or music, but the theatre prevailed, and by the time Hitler came to power in 1933 he was well established. That year, sensing what was to come, he moved to Prague, where he worked for six years as leader of the German theatre there (half a million of the eleven and a half million inhabitants of Czechoslovakia were German-speaking). An active anti-Nazi, he escaped to England sixteen days before Hitler occupied the country. A list of the roles he played in Germany and Czechoslovakia makes remarkable reading. In Shakespeare, Richard III, Lear, Shylock (both when he was twenty-eight), Othello, Macbeth, Petruchio, Angelo,

236

Hotspur, Pistol, Henry IV, Caesar, Oberon, Quince, Theseus, the Ghost and First Player in *Hamlet*, Aufidius in *Coriolanus*, and Tybalt; Mephistopheles in both Goethe's and Marlowe's *Faust*; Sophocles's Oedipus; Ibsen's Brand, Solness in *The Master Builder*, John Gabriel Borkman, Brack in *Hedda Gabler*, the Button Moulder in *Peer Gynt* and Bernick in *The Pillars of Society*; Büchner's Woyzeck and Danton; Stanhope in *Journey's End*; Flecker's Hassan; Higgins in *Pygmalion*; Schiller's Wallenstein, and Franz Moor in *The Robbers*; Goethe's Prometheus; Cecil Graham in *Lady Windermere's Fan*; and four Strindberg leads, Charles XII, Gustav in *Creditors*, the Captain in *The Dance of Death* and the Advocate in *A Dream Play*. The list underlines the breadth of German repertory between the wars; no leading British actor of his generation would have covered anything like this range in a lifetime, much less by the age of forty-four.

His English was good enough for him to find work quickly in London, and by July he was at Wyndham's Theatre as a German doctor in *Alien Corn*, by the American dramatist Sidney Howard. He still called himself Frits Valk, but as war became imminent he changed his first name to Frederick. In 1940 he played the lead in another Sidney Howard play, *They Knew What They Wanted* (a role Charles Laughton had taken in the film), and Dr Kurtz in Robert Ardrey's *Thunder Rock*; then in 1941 he was Nick the barman in an Old Vic tour of William Saroyan's *The Time of Your Life* (he was as gifted in comedy as in tragedy), alternating it with Shylock.

In late 1941 or early 1942 I saw his Shylock, and although I had seen and admired him in *Thunder Rock* I was quite unprepared for what hit me now. It was a workmanlike production by Esmé Church, and of the several actresses who played Portia opposite him I was fortunate in seeing surely the best: Jean Forbes-Robertson. Valk could have been forgiven if he had, at this stage of the war, sentimentalized the Jew, but nothing could have been further from the case. His Shylock was mean, but he was so because of the attitude of everyone around him. It was an age of fine acting in Britain: Olivier, Richardson, Gielgud, Donat and Redgrave were all at, or approaching, their peak. But now I found myself confronted with a power and – what can I call it? – savagery unlike anything I had experienced. It was the kind of ferocity that one usually sees only from actors who are alcoholics. Wilfrid Lawson had it; so had Robert Newton. But Valk was not an alcoholic; he was in perfect control of his powers. Yet unlike some great technicians, his technique never showed. The word 'acting' never crossed my mind as I watched him. Some of my acquaintances shrank from his performance; it was not the kind of acting they were used to; what they were seeing was not nice; it was profoundly upsetting. I could not argue with them. As G. H. Lewes wrote of Edmund Kean, 'it was as vain to protest against his defects as it was for French critics to insist upon Shakespeare's want of *bienséance* and *bon goût*'. I simply knew that I had been moved and shaken as never before in a theatre, or anywhere else. For the first time, as it seemed to me, I fully understood the meaning of grief, rage and despair. As C. E. Montague wrote of *Ghosts*, I felt that previously these things, which I thought I knew as well as the next man, 'can only have been known as one knows a beast safely caged in a zoo, since now they are going about glaring at you with fanged mouths open; they have turned terrifyingly real'.

A few months later I saw Valk play Othello in London. This, again, was an Old Vic tour; the director was Julius Gellner, the Iago Bernard Miles (and very good he was). Othello is a greater challenge than Shylock, for Shylock appears in only five scenes. I have seen several actors succeed as Shylock, no one else as Othello; even more perhaps than Lear, it is the most demanding of Shakespeare's roles, perhaps of all roles. Orson Welles lacked something; Olivier's performance I did not admire; I am sure I would have thought more kindly of them if I had not seen Valk. I felt as Kenneth Tynan did when reviewing another actor's attempt: 'I have seen Mr Valk in the part, and there, in the simple equation Valk = Othello, is an end of it.' Other critics agreed. *The Times* praised his 'superbly masculine rendering . . . which does not fail, when the time comes, of that ground swell of passion which shakes the heart'. James Agate in the *Sunday Times* hailed it as 'the best Othello since Salvini', who had retired from the stage in 1890.

Five years later Valk played the role again, this time with Donald Wolfit as Iago (one of Wolfit's finest performances), and Kenneth Tynan, then an undergraduate of twenty, wrote a memorable account of the occasion for an Oxford magazine which subsequently appeared in his first book, *He That Plays the King*, and which is about to be reprinted for the first time for over thirty years in a volume of his collected criticism. It is easy to say why one dislikes a performance; the most difficult task for a dramatic critic is to convey why he or she found an evening in the theatre magic and exciting, and no British critic, not Hazlitt nor Shaw nor Agate, possessed this gift to the same degree as Tynan, even at that early age. 'I have lived for three hours on the red brink of a volcano,' he began,

and the crust of lava still crumbles from my feet . . .
He broke every law of our stage-craft, this berserk Colossus.
Following the imperious rules of his agony, his voice would
crack and pause, minute-long in mid-line; and there would be
speechless signallings the while, and rushes as of a wild bull.
Then the voice would rise and swoop again into unknown
pastures of word-meaning, scooping up huge, vasty syllables
of grief as though carving an ancient bed of clay. He seemed,
at times, almost to sing, so unlike our custom was his
elocution; a bully's song, a bludgeoner's song, yet its strains
moved to pity, as great verse should . . . You could almost
hear thin skins splitting and half-shut minds banging and
locking themselves around you; the theatre was perturbed,
but pin-still.

To the complaint of some critics that Valk's accent destroyed the
poetry, Tynan replied:

This was no time for R.A.D.A. modulations and exquisite-
ness; a man was hacking a horrid path for himself, and it was
not pretty, or fanciful . . . The play, the words, all plays,
all words, were too small for this passion. It transcended the
prescribed limits of acted drama, and strode boldly through
Hell-lake and bade the white-clad recording imps take notice
of foul disorders and evil conceits; of the climax of a great
anguish; of the dilapidation of a sturdy tower; of the molten
intoxication of a warrior and demi-god.

James Agate, repeating his earlier praise, declared Valk to be 'an
actor whose passion and power have not their like in this country',
and concluded: 'If Valk is not a great Othello, and if the duel with
Wolfit is not magnificent throughout, then let me retire'.

Valk did not appear on the London stage again during the war,
except when he took over from Anton Walbrook in Lillian Hellman's
Watch on the Rhine, though he led several Old Vic tours in the provinces, as Kutuzov in an adaptation of *War and Peace*, Ibsen's John
Gabriel Borkman, the Egyptian Doctor in Shaw's *The Millionairess*
and Stefan in Coward's *Point Valaine*, a performance which Coward
saw and admired. I next saw him in 1946 in two plays at the Lyric,
Hammersmith, as Nick the barman in Saroyan's *The Time of Your
Life*, in which he surprised those who, like myself, knew him only as

a tragedian by his splendid gift for comedy, and as Old Karamazov in an adaptation by Alec Guinness (who himself played Mitya) of *The Brothers Karamazov* directed by the twenty-one-year-old Peter Brook. This performance evoked another eloquent appraisal from Tynan:

> . . . Valk, as the lousy, boorish old patriarch, was shattering. His bull neck, thrust out defiantly as he drove home some crapulous jest; his colossus stride of feet; his laborious guttural voice; his thunder-darting eyes – Valk is pre-eminently an actor in whom physical attributes obtrude to the extinction of all other values. Yet he is subtle; the timing of his interminable pauses, which defy interruption, is uncanny. He is the most insidious of battering-rams, the most persuasive of earthquakes; he burns like a hard, gem-like holocaust. He acts with his sweat and stamina; rock-like and immobile, he exudes power, and in action he is a fighting *toro*, too wily for the slimmest, most cajoling matador to cite and kill.

James Agate, in the *Sunday Times*, wrote: 'This week's performance has put an end to any shilly-shallying I may have entertained on the subject of Mr Valk, and I announce my intention – in case it should interest anybody – of henceforth alluding to the player who filled the role of Old Karamazov as "that great actor, Frederick Valk". I, who saw Irving, say that Valk is a great actor.'

These reviews might possibly suggest that Valk was an actor of great power but limited discipline. Nothing could have been further from the truth. He was, as I have said, the most disciplined of performers, with a technique which kept his great gifts under masterful control. To take one example: he had an exceptional voice, capable of tremendous volume. Normally he spoke quietly, yet in tones audible throughout the largest theatre; but he could do something I have never seen any other actor do, explode suddenly into full volume as when one's elbow brushes against the volume knob of a record-player so that the sound terrifyingly fills the room. I remember him doing this at the moment when Othello seizes Iago by the throat and says: 'Villain, be sure thou prove my love a whore!' He had all the power of his great contemporaries in Germany, Emil Jannings and Werner Kraus (the latter of whom he especially admired), but he had what they lacked: an immense warmth and humanity.

In his introduction to *Shylock for a Summer*, Diana Valk's moving account of her husband's visit to Canada in 1955 to play Shylock at Stratford, Ontario, Tyrone Guthrie, who directed that production, described Valk's appearance:

He was of somewhat more than middle height, but the
head and chest were those of a giant; and the limbs seemed
by comparison rather short and thick; the whole effect was
immensely powerful but squat. A great head on a great barrel, round, incredibly thick, but not fat; hard, not soft. The
face, like the whole figure, was broad in comparison with its
length; wide-set eyes, a short thick nose, a wide mouth and
very square jaw. The neck was short and immensely thick.
But any impression of coarseness was immediately obliterated
by the eyes, the directness of their glance, the candour
and intelligence of their expression, their extraordinary and
benevolent magnetism. His colouring was extremely swarthy;
dark, but not black hair; a darkly sallow complexion quite
unlike the ruddy colouring of a robust Briton; the eyes
were a warm bright brown and, for all their brilliance, the
'white' of the eyes was not white at all, but like dark
ivory.
   It is often the case that extremely powerful men have
silly squeaky little voices. Valk's voice matched his physique;
a warm and velvety baritone with an upper register of
extraordinary brilliance and power. Probably it was due
to the gigantic muscular development of the diaphragm, but I
do not think I have ever heard a man's voice which had
the same ringing, uninhibited power at the top . . .
   In spite of heroic efforts he never entirely mastered the
illogical intricacies of English pronunciation. Inevitably,
therefore, his English-speaking career was restricted to roles
in which 'an accent' was permissible. Unfortunately, this
restricted the great classical parts for which he was otherwise
so suitable, and which he so dearly longed to play. But,
as always, nature takes away with one hand and with the
other offers compensation. I think the great set-back to his
career, the painful adjustment to being a refugee, made
him the man he was, more thoughtful, gentle, humble and
wise than the great star he might, in other circumstances,
have been.
   Apart from the language, he had to adapt himself to the

241

style of the English-speaking stage. In Central Europe acting is larger, louder, more uninhibited; more emphasis is placed upon the virtuosity of the soloist and less upon the values of teamwork. Frederick Valk made this adaptation well. He was a fine member of a team, and always placed the meaning of the play before any opportunity which might permit him to score individually. His chief fault as an actor, in my opinion, was a tendency to rush at an emotional scene like a bull at a gate. It was hard for him to control the powerful torrent of his own feeling, the trombone tones of that great voice, and to build up a climax by slow degrees, step by disciplined step. On the other hand he preserved from his old training a splendid technical breadth and freedom in the use of both the voice and the whole body . . .

One of the features of his character was his love and reverence for all young growing things – be they people or animals or plants, or a young country like Canada or a young institution like the Canadian Shakespeare Festival. We mourn the fact that this genial, gentle giant is no longer physically in our midst.

Alec Guinness, in his memoirs *Blessings in Disguise*, similarly recalls Valk as 'a bull of a man, simple and endearing', and these last two qualities, not the most common in great actors but so essential to Othello, were important factors in his success in that role. Tynan, reviewing Richard Burton's Othello a decade later, remembered Valk's as 'a great stunned animal, strapped to the rack'. But the most memorable features of his Othello, Shylock and Old Karamazov, had been the explosive power. No one, I think, was quite prepared for the equal mastery which he then showed in three Ibsen roles: Solness in *The Master Builder*, Pastor Manders in *Ghosts*, and John Gabriel Borkman. All three are deeply inhibited men whose passion can find no satisfactory outlet, and Solness and Borkman in particular are among the most difficult of all roles to bring off. No British actor in my lifetime has quite succeeded in either on the stage, though Leo McKern, who is Australian, was a magnificent Solness on both radio and television. They demand a completely different approach from that required for Othello and Shylock (as, in general, Ibsen does from Shakespeare), and I can only suppose that Guthrie had not seen these performances when he wrote that Valk's one fault was that he was inclined to 'rush at an emotional scene like a bull at a gate'. This may have been his instinct with Othello and Shylock (and I am not sure that he was wrong; is not that how those two characters would have behaved?), but it was certainly not true of his Solness, nor, from all reports, of his Borkman or Manders, both of which, alas, I missed through being abroad. What I remember most from his Solness is its stillness, the sense of tremendous power chained. 'His Solness,' wrote *The Times*, 'is a man in whose genius and reckless charm we can believe; the remnants of those qualities are there along with the remorse bred of age and introspection and the fantastic fear of youth, and the still more fantastic craving for it.' Kenneth Tynan went even further.

This performance is the most towering thing to be seen in the West End for many months. It is also the strongest, and I am not excepting public buildings, works of sculpture, or even the pavements we tread on . . . Mr Valk's Othello was like a great dam bursting; his playing in *The Brothers Karamazov* was a triumph of coarse *gouaillerie*; and now his Solness has made his star blaze red across all this continent, and other lights are tapers. You felt at once that this man had built monuments, stone upon stone, and was capable of sheer, muscle-tight toil; you could not consent to it as mere stage pretence . . . He seemed an Alp, and when he fell from his crazy tower, the very fall of the House of Usher seemed like crackling matchwood. Mr Valk rules our stages.

That was in January 1947; and it was in December of that year that I first met Valk. I was editing a selection of Sidney Keyes's plays, stories and letters. They included a play about Minos of Crete, and I sent this to Valk in case it should interest him. He replied courteously that he found it promising but immature, and invited me to visit him and his wife when I came home from Uppsala for Christmas.

They lived in a small early-Victorian house in Notting Hill Gate. I say 'small', but when I revisited it recently it did not seem as it had when I met Freddie in it. As Guthrie says, he was not a tall man, about five feet ten, but of tremendous breadth and bulk; how he seemed to fill those rooms! Having seen him only in the roles I have named, I expected someone formidable and alarming. I was twenty-six and had never met a great actor. Instead, I found a man of extraordinary gentleness, warmth and understanding, as was his wife Diana, the daughter of a Winchester housemaster who later became a canon of

Salisbury Cathedral – an incongruous father-in-law, one might have supposed, for Valk, but he loved Valk and Valk him. I must have overstayed my welcome, for it was not until Diana had gone to bed and Freddie began to empty the stove that I could tear myself away.

Over the next nine years until his death we met often. He had a passion for football, which I shared. He claimed to have been a useful left back in his youth, which I can well believe; once, he told me, an opposing outside right whom he had flattened looked up at him from the ground and asked: 'What do you weigh?' We went to many matches together when he was not working. We usually stood, partly for economy but also because the average football seat simply did not hold him. Once, for an international at Wembley, I booked seats, and it proved decidedly uncomfortable for me and, I am sure, whoever was on his other side. He knew every football ground in London, at any rate in the first two divisions, and how to get to the best standing room. At Tottenham we had to make for a squalid little alley incongruously called Park Lane; and for Arsenal, he had found that it was best to take the Tube to the station beyond and walk the short distance back. He was very knowledgeable about all the teams and would engage in technical discussions with the spectators around him. We were often taken for father and son since, although fair-skinned and red-haired, I was similarly built on a smaller scale and bore a certain facial resemblance to him.

Despite the acclaim which his performances received, Valk made little money from them, for they were almost always on Old Vic tours, which paid poorly, or in small theatres such as the Arts, where for his Master Builder and Borkman I believe he got £10 a week. He did a certain amount of film work, but always in small parts. One December I said to him: 'What a year you've had!' He said: 'How much would you think I earned this year?' 'I've no idea.' 'I just made a thousand pounds' – a tiny amount, even in those days. He longed for the time when he could 'really make something for Diana and the boys'. When I referred to his having won the Ellen Terry Award for his Old Karamazov – not for the best supporting performance but for the best performance of the year – he said: 'It was the worst thing that could have happened to me.' 'Why?' 'Who is going to want an actor in a supporting role who in another supporting role has won the award for Best Actor?' And indeed, he seldom got offered a supporting role in a play thereafter. In a piece about the Prince Regent called *The Gay Pavilion*, by Walter Lipscomb, which was seen in London shortly

37 Frederick Valk as
John Gabriel Borkman, 1950

38 Sir Ralph Richardson

39 Wendy Hiller in *When We Dead Awaken*,
Edinburgh Festival, 1968

40 Brian Cox

41 With Nora, 1972

after the war, he had a single short scene as the mad King George III and ran away with all the notices. 'Five minutes of magnificent acting by Frederick Valk as George III,' wrote W. A. Darlington in the *Daily Telegraph*, 'and if all the evening had been as good . . . I should now be hunting the dictionary for superlatives.'

I seldom heard him criticize another actor. I asked how it had been to play opposite Wolfit, who, apart from being a notorious upstager, had directed that second *Othello*. 'Oh, Donald's a nice fellow.' Pause. 'Mind you – ' Another pause. 'Yes?' 'Sometimes he gave me rather difficult positions.' 'What kind of positions?' 'Well, in the scene where I have to say: "Never, Iago! Like to the Pontic Sea . . .", he made me sit in a basket chair, which creaked. I said: "Donald, could I not deliver this speech standing up?" He put his hand on my shoulder, and said: "Freddie. I have played Othello myself, and I know all the best positions".' Pause. 'He did. And he was making sure that I didn't have any of them.'

When he first came to England, Freddie had been struck by the different attitude adopted by the stars. The first thing that surprised him had been when at the lunch-break on the opening day of rehearsal, the stars had eaten not only in the same pub as the rest of the cast but at the same bar. When he was a young actor in Berlin and Hamburg, the stars would be driven by their chauffeurs to an expensive restaurant or hotel, whence they would return late for rehearsal, to show that they were stars. For the same reason there would inevitably come a show-down between them and the director. In London, day after day passed with no such confrontation. 'I thought, in England they are clever, they leave it until the last week.' Still no confrontation. 'They do it at the dress-rehearsal.' When that too passed without incident, Freddie became really worried. 'They do it an hour before the opening.' But there was no confrontation. Such a thing, he said, would have been inconceivable in continental theatres in the thirties.

In a film called *Saraband for Dead Lovers*, Freddie played the Elector of Hanover, father to the future George I of England (Peter Bull), and had to arrive in one scene on horseback. He explained that he had never ridden a horse, so lessons were arranged for him at a fashionable riding-school. He was smartly kitted out in full rig, including a brown bowler hat, at the company's expense, and spent several happy mornings riding in Rotten Row in Hyde Park. I said: 'I don't remember you on a horse in that film.' He replied, 'When it came to the shooting, they wanted me to arrive at a gallop. I said I

had never been taught to gallop. So in the end I came in a coach.'
But he had enjoyed his stint in Hyde Park.

Although I missed Valk's Manders and his Borkman, I was
fortunate in being in England in 1950 when he played Matthias
in *The Bells*, Leopold Lewis's old melodrama which had provided
Henry Irving with his most famous role. Kenneth Tynan, for whom
Freddie had played Chris Christopherson in O'Neill's *Anna Christie*
when Tynan was directing at Lichfield after leaving Oxford, staged
The Bells at the Bedford Theatre in Camden Town. Like all of
Tynan's productions, it was eccentric but imaginative, and Freddie
gave a tremendous performance as the murderer who, on the night
before his daughter's wedding, dreams that he is on trial and that
a mesmerist is summoned to compel him to confess the truth and
re-enact the murder. I remember his roar: 'Into the fire, Jew!' as
he forced the corpse of his victim into the oven (horrible words
to hear so soon after the revelations of Auschwitz), and his final
line when the wedding guests come to wake him and, appearing
through the curtains round his bed with his hands to his throat,
he cries: 'Take the rope from my neck!', and falls dead. He made
it seem a powerful old play, though I don't know who else could
have brought it off. The following year he was splendid in a
terrible production by Basil Dean of *Hassan*, not in the title role,
which he had played in Germany, but as the Caliph. During the
interval on the first night I committed a gaffe worthy of Sir John
Gielgud himself, the acknowledged Grand Master of the Clanger.
Standing in the loo next to an elderly man in a dinner-jacket,
I observed: 'Isn't it a splendid play?' 'It's an interesting play.' I
said: 'But what a ragged production.' To this he made no answer,
and I saw that he was staring hard at his organ. I reflected that
old men sometimes have problems urinating and said no more.
As we prepared to leave, the critic Ivor Brown entered. The old
man said: 'Hullo, Ivor', to which Brown replied: 'Hullo, Basil.'
But Dean was a famous monster, and I have never regretted my
remark.

In 1955 Freddie enjoyed his triumph in Canada, first with Shylock
at Stratford, Ontario, and then with *Othello* and *They Knew What
They Wanted* in Toronto. In May 1956 he opened in the West End
as the Russian Ambassador in Peter Ustinov's comedy *Romanoff and
Juliet*, and on 4 June wrote to me in Sweden the last letter that I was
to receive from him. He was delighted to be doing comedy again,
and pleased with the play's success.

Ustinov has definitely ended his period of Promise. His play
has a touch of genius, his wit is prodigious and his humanity is heartwarming. It makes everybody happy, audiences as
well as actors, and it is fascinating to see London playgoers'
faces change from that cool mask of 'All right – go ahead
and try to amuse me if you can' to a complexion of wild
delight . . . There seems to be quite a lot going on in the
London theatre. Devine has set up management at the Royal
Court Theatre, encouraging young playwrights. There is a
man (aged 24) who has written a remarkable play called *Look
Back in Anger* . . . Come to London, Michael, and let's talk.

At the end of June I saw him in the play and we had a long chat in
his dressing-room. The future seemed to be opening for him; he was
to go with the Ustinov play to Broadway at the end of its London
run, and had received several other Broadway offers as the result
of his performances in Canada, which had been admired by critics
and producers from New York. 'At last I'm going to make a little
money for Diana and the boys.' A month later he had a stroke while
visiting a Czech friend in London and died almost immediately. He
was sixty-one.

Twenty years later, as we were lunching at the Savile, Ralph
Richardson asked me: 'Whom do you think the greatest actor you
have seen?' I hesitated out of politeness to him. He said: 'Valk?' I
nodded, and so did he.

20

Memories of Ralph Richardson

Not many people can claim to have heard Ralph Richardson sing, for although he had wide interests, music was not one of them; Sir John Gielgud tells that when he first got to know him, Ralph owned a gramophone but only one record, a popular song of the period called 'Tea for Two'. Nor, until Gielgud pointed it out to him, had he realized that there was anything on the other side. But the first time I saw him, when I was nine, he had a singing part in a musical, *Silver Wings*, which opened the new Dominion Theatre in Tottenham Court Road in 1930. Harry Welchman and Lupino Lane were the stars, and I still remember the ending of Act One, when an aeroplane crashed through the roof on to the stage and Lupino Lane crawled out of the wreckage. Ralph played the pilot; but I cannot remember anything of his performance, sung or spoken – I think he can only have sung when everyone else did – and was surprised when fifty years later he told me he had been in it. I saw him often in the thirties and forties, at first in modern plays such as Priestley's *Cornelius* and Barry Lyndon's *The Amazing Dr Clitterhouse*, and then in the great Old Vic seasons of 1944–47 at the New Theatre when his roles included Peer Gynt, Falstaff, Cyrano, Bluntschli in *Arms and the Man*, Tiresias to Olivier's Oedipus, and Lord Burleigh in *The Critic*, surely the most memorable performance there can ever have been of a completely silent role, unless by some actress as the daughter in *Mother Courage*.

My first meeting with him in 1950 was an uncomfortable experience. I had just joined the Savile, where one ate at communal tables. I came in to lunch early and took a place at an otherwise empty table, hoping that nobody grand would sit next to me. To my horror Ralph, then newly knighted, took the place on my left. What could I possibly find to say to so great a man? The wine waiter asked:

'Wine or beer, Sir Ralph?' Ralph fixed the man with enormous eyes. 'Shall it be wine? Or shall it be beer?' Assuming this question to be rhetorical, the wine waiter remained silent. Ralph continued: 'It shall be neither. It shall be milk. A pint of milk.' Taking this to be one of Ralph's obscurer jokes, the waiter laughed sycophantically, then, seeing Ralph's glare, fled in terror and returned with a pint of milk. Ralph raised the glass, quaffed half of it, and then what I had been praying would not happen happened: he turned those great eyes on me. Useless to attempt to evade them; mesmerized, as a rabbit is said to be by a snake, my eyes met his. The first word to be uttered to me as a member of the Savile was about to be spoken. With a large white ring round his mouth and his wildest expression, Ralph cried: 'Nectar!' What could one reply? What, if anything, I did say, I have no idea. I thought I would never dare to enter the place again, and although I saw him frequently there over the next nine years, I avoided him fearfully until we became properly acquainted at Liverpool in the circumstances I have earlier described.

Parenthetically, Victor Pritchett told me later of a similar experience which he had had at the Savile in 1938. Like me, he took a chair at an empty table. Almost immediately the place on his right was taken by W. B. Yeats and, a minute later, that on his left by H. G. Wells, who began to eat greedily with his mouth open. Yeats, who had only a few months to live, apparently hated any talk of death. Pritchett says that the following dialogue then took place across him between the two great men:

WELLS: Isn't it Yeats?

YEATS: Ah. Good morning, Wells.

WELLS: You're looking very old, Yeats.

YEATS (*goes slightly grey*): None of us gets younger, Wells.

WELLS: Ah, the days we had when we were young. Do you remember how we used to walk on Hampstead Heath with X and Y?

YEATS: Yes. I wonder what they're doing nowadays?

WELLS (*eating noisily*): Dead.

YEATS (*greys further*): Both of them?

WELLS: Yes. And when we went together to the Bedford to see Dan Leno with young Z.

YEATS: How is Z now?

WELLS: Dead. (*Pause.*) And Yeats, do you remember the
time we went boating at Richmond and took those girls with
us? One of them wore a pink dress and had beautiful long
gold hair.
YEATS (*moved, puts down his knife and fork*): Yes, I remember
her. She was very beautiful. What's happened to – surely she
can't be dead? She was much younger than us.
WELLS: No, she isn't dead.
YEATS: Thank heavens for that.
WELLS (*illustrating, graphically*): Paralysed, all down one side.
(*To waiter.*) I'll have the steak.*

Ralph had left school at an early age and was largely self-educated.
He had very wide interests. Anything scientific or, especially,
mechanical, fascinated him. Whomever he sat next to at the Club,
or met, he would question minutely about their work, however
unglamorous it might appear. When he died, the dressing-room
attendant at Lord's, where he played tennis weekly in the court
behind the pavilion, told me that Ralph always managed to find
new things to ask him about his job. On two famous occasions on
television Ralph was supposed to be the interviewee but ended up
questioning the interviewer (in one instance Michael Parkinson, in
the other Bernard Levin), and when he appeared together with the
then world motor-cycle champion Barry Sheene the programme
became an interview by Ralph of Sheene, and a very expert one.
He had joined the Savile as a young actor in 1933 rather than the
actors' usual club, the Garrick, so that he could avoid theatrical
conversation, though if one did ask him about acting, direction or
plays he was as shrewd as one might expect. Like so many of his
generation, he was suspicious of directors. They were welcome to
stage the play as they wished, but he reckoned he knew better
than they how to approach a role ('I just want them to give me
a decent place to stand with a bit of light'), and better than at any
rate some dramatists when a play needed cutting. In his seventies

---

*Fifty years later, Pritchett recalled 'the contrast of the two voices – Wells high-
pitched and Cockney and Yeats's exalted utterance about the beautiful woman.
Wells was very sly and cocky, Yeats was all Irish lamentation . . . one cheeky
and jeering, the other almost operatic with melancholy' (letter to the author, 26
September 1988).

he appeared in a new play by John Osborne called *West of Suez*, and I asked him what he thought of Osborne. 'Charming fellow.' I said I had heard that Osborne never allowed a line to be cut. 'I've cut a lot.' 'How did you manage that?' 'I just leave things out, and when he comes round afterwards, before he can open his mouth I say: "Old chap, you've got to forgive me, my memory's going".'

We never worked together, except once on radio in Ibsen's last play, *When We Dead Awaken*, when he was not at his best. For some reason, he appeared in few Ibsen roles – the only others, I think, were Peer Gynt, Brand on radio, Judge Brack in *Hedda Gabler* on TV, and, in his last years, John Gabriel Borkman and Old Ekdal in *The Wild Duck*. He would have been ideal for so many – Dr Stockmann in *An Enemy of the People*, Hjalmar Ekdal in *The Wild Duck*, Torvald Helmer in *A Doll's House*, Tesman in *Hedda Gabler*, Manders in *Ghosts*, Dr Wangel in *The Lady from the Sea*, Solness in *The Master Builder* – but although I tried to persuade him to play several of these, Borkman was the only one that interested him. For years we discussed this. I told him that he should do it with Celia Johnson as Ella, the woman Borkman should have married but rejected to advance his own ambitions, and either Peggy Ashcroft or Wendy Hiller as her twin sister with whom Borkman entered into a loveless marriage. Once he told me that David Merrick had invited him to do it on Broadway with Maureen Stapleton and Mildred Natwick as the sisters and then, with the same cast, in London. I said I thought that whatever might be right for Broadway he should not do it with American actresses, however good, in London, and I am afraid I must have convinced him. I say afraid, because when at last he did act it in London it was in an unconvincing production with Peggy Ashcroft wrongly cast as Ella and Ralph much below his best, as he was well aware. When, before seeing it, I congratulated him on his notices, he shook his head and said: 'I haven't brought it off.' More than any actor I can think of, he knew when he had failed.

His wife Mu once remarked to me: 'Ralph's a very sexy man but he never comes over sexy on the stage', and the same was true of Peggy Ashcroft. Although both sexy and maternal in private life, sex and maternity were two things she never seemed able to portray on the stage, even when young. Ibsen once observed: 'My central characters are, almost without exception, passionate people and they need to be acted with passion', but Peggy, whom I admire and greatly like, tended to act Ibsen's women as though they were Shaw's, from above the neck instead of below it. Hedda she encompassed but not, to my mind, Rebecca West or Mrs Alving or Ella Rentheim. One must feel that had Borkman and Ella married they would have been great lovers, and Ralph and Peggy never suggested this.

Ralph was, I think, unique among great British tragic actors in that he achieved this reputation, and rightly, without succeeding in any of the big Shakespearean tragic roles. Tynan put his finger on the problem when he observed: 'Richardson's round, sober cheese-face can so easily, in moments of high passion, suggest Bottom bewitched', and again, in another context, when he said that Ralph had a failing of sometimes seeming 'much too amiable'. His Macbeth and Othello were both calamitous, as was his Prospero, which, like his Macbeth, he played during the 1952 Stratford season when he was personally unhappy. Wisely, he did not attempt Hamlet or Romeo; nor did he play Lear, in which he would surely have been magnificent. Olivier has told how during their great season at the New Theatre in 1946 both he and Ralph wanted to play Cyrano and Lear, and that Ralph yielded the latter to play the former, in which he gave one of his finest performances. In the last twenty years of his life I often asked: 'Why don't you do Lear?', but he always silently shook his head.

Ralph's Falstaff and Vanya were, like his Cyrano, incomparable. Tynan summed up his Falstaff in one of his finest critical passages:

> Richardson's Falstaff was not a *comic* performance . . . Here
> was a Falstaff whose principal attribute was not his fatness
> but his knighthood. He was Sir John first and Falstaff second,
> and let every cock-a-hoop young dog beware. The spirit
> behind all the rotund nobility was spry and elastic . . . there
> was also, working with great slyness but great energy,
> a sharp business sense; and, when the situation called for it,
> great wisdom and melancholy.

Ralph owned a series of unusual pets, mostly ferocious and inclined to attack his visitors. Luckily I never encountered any of his succession of ferrets, but I knew, and feared, a malignant brute named José. Some of us were chatting after lunch at the Savile one day when Ralph wandered over and, in accordance with his custom of not wasting words by leading into a conversation, asked: 'Do any of you chaps know the best place to buy a parrot?' Like so many of Ralph's opening sentences, this stopped the conversation stone dead.

Then Dallas Bower, the film director, said: 'Have you tried Winsor &
Newton?' We all looked bewildered, none more so than Ralph, and
who could look more bewildered than he? He said: 'I thought they
only sold painting tackle.' 'Didn't you say you wanted a palette?'
'Ah, no, no, no. Parrot.' And he cocked his head to one side and
emitted a series of squawks. Someone suggested Harrod's. Ralph
then went to Spain to film *Dr Zhivago*. Some months later I was
reading a paper at the club when I felt a hand on my shoulder and
Ralph, whom I had not seen in the interim, said:

'I was walking through the market place in Madrid, and what do
you think I saw?'

'I can't imagine.'

'The most beautiful parrot you ever clapped eyes on in your life.'

I remembered our previous conversation.

'Did you buy it?'

'I did.'

'Didn't you have trouble bringing it into England?'

'Her Majesty the Queen issued a special passport. With his name
on it. José. Valid for one entry into the United Kingdom only.'

'How splendid. Does it talk?'

'Only Spanish.'

'Oh dear.'

'But I'm having lessons, so I shall be able to converse with him.'

Remembering Ralph's inability to pronounce the simplest foreign
word correctly, it occurred to me that it might be quicker to send
the parrot to the Berlitz School to learn English, but I thought I had
better not venture this suggestion.

José terrified everyone except Ralph. Once I noticed some deep
and recent scars across his fingers and asked if he had an accident.
'It's only José. He does it in fun.' José was not kept in a cage but sat
on an open perch, spreading his wings like an eagle and screeching
at anyone who entered. On one visit I thought he looked somehow
different and more than usually baleful.

'José looks a bit different today, Ralph,' I said, quietly in case the
brute understood.

'Ah, poor chap. He doesn't get on with Lucky.'

'Who is Lucky?'

'My chauffeur. José goes for him occasionally, only in fun. Lucky
said either he or José would have to go. I managed to work out a
compromise. I clipped José's wings, so he can't fly.'

'What a good idea.'

'It means the poor chap can't get any exercise. I have to take him for a spin on my bike each morning.'

'On your bike?'

'On my shoulder. He loves it.'

I thought this could only be one of Ralph's flights of fancy. But the actress Rosalie Crutchley who lived down the road told me that a regular sight each morning now was Ralph chugging round the Outer Circle of Regent's Park at a gentler pace than usual with José on his shoulder.

Ralph was a strange mixture of literacy and linguistic naivety. When we did *When We Dead Awaken* he had extraordinary problems with the pronunciation of Taunitzer See, which one might think would scarcely tax an intelligent child. His spelling too was very erratic. At the Savile we wrote our lunch orders on a form, and it was a daily pastime to see how Ralph spelt the various dishes. This he did according to the often idiosyncratic way in which he pronounced them: for example, 'spinich' and 'luttace'. 'Cheesebord' was another which appeared regularly. But he was very widely read, and deeply, not a skimmer or a dipper. Once, looking at his large library, I said, as I sometimes do when visiting friends: 'Let me guess which of these you haven't read.' He replied: 'I've read every one of them', and I am sure he had, even the difficult late novels of Henry James, of whose work he was especially fond.

Ralph went to the theatre more often than some actors. Once he told me that he had been so bored by a play that he had left in the interval. I said: 'Isn't it difficult for you to do that? Surely people recognize you and notice you haven't come back?' 'If I think it might bore me, I sit in the gallery,' he replied. 'Nobody recognizes me there, so I can leave when I want.'

Once he took me to a movie.

'I'm going to the cinema this afternoon. Care to come?'

'What's the film?'

'*In Cold Blood.*'

This was the Truman Capote movie about a real murder case. I said I would. It was at the Curzon, perhaps four minutes' walk from the Savile, but his Rolls arrived with uniformed chauffeur (Lucky, I suppose), and took us there in style. As we entered, Ralph spotted a confectionery stall in the foyer. His eyes gleamed.

'You must have some sweets.'

I was about fifty at the time.

'No, really.'

'Ah, you must have something. Have some chocolate peppermint creams.'

It occurred to me that perhaps he wanted some for himself, so I said: 'Well, thank you, that would be nice.'

He put his arm round my shoulders, led me to the stall and cried: 'A box of chocolate peppermint creams for my young boy friend here.' Every head turned wonderingly towards us. It must have been the only time in his life that Ralph can have been suspected of homosexuality, which he regarded as a baffling aberration. It is told how when he was playing Othello to Olivier's Iago in 1938, Olivier conceived the idea of Iago having a secret passion for Othello, and decided that on the first night, not earlier in case Ralph objected, he would, when Othello falls in a fit, plant a kiss on Ralph's lips. This happened. Ralph said nothing about it to Olivier but took the director, Tyrone Guthrie, aside after the final curtain and said: 'Tony, have you noticed anything odd about Laurence recently?'

He enjoyed a game of snooker after lunch. 'Care for a spot of blowball?' he would ask. None of us knew why he called it that. He was not very good, except when it came to the two final colours, which he would pot from sometimes quite difficult angles. When I mentioned this, he explained: 'I like last acts.' Sometimes he wore a heavy gold watchchain in his waistcoat, and once he brushed the cue ball with this as he lined up his shot. To touch any ball with one's clothing constitutes a foul, but under Savile rules a dangling tie did not count. Could a watchchain be categorized as a tie? No other snooker player in memory had worn one, so the problem had not arisen. A longish debate ensued, during which Ralph stood to attention doing his prisoner-in-the-dock act. Eventually it was decided that for this once the offending object was a tie, but that he must not do it again.

On one occasion, some of us were discussing capital punishment, in the days when it still existed in Britain. Suddenly Ralph said: 'My brother murdered a chap once.' There was an awkward silence. No one liked to ask the question which immediately occurred to us all.

Ralph continued: 'During the First War. Went into a pub, didn't like something this fellow said, took out his gun and shot him dead.'

Someone ventured to ask: 'What happened to him?'

'He was arrested. Hadn't any defence. The whole pub saw it.'

'Was he . . . imprisoned?'

'By good fortune, we were about to raid some place in Belgium or Holland. Some port or other.'

Someone suggested Zeebrugge; Ralph nodded. 'My brother was a great expert at blowing things up. The fellows at the Admiralty said: "Send for Richardson". "He's in prison." "Get him out." They did, and he blew the place up. Got a medal.'

'What about the murder?'

'They forgot about that. Bad luck on the other chap, of course.'

He told me how, as a child at Brighton, he had become friendly with the great wrestler George Hackenschmidt, who would take him shrimping and then do a fry-up for them both at his house. 'Tremendous big fellow,' Ralph said, and was incredulous when I told him that Hackenschmidt stood only five feet eight and was the shortest of all the great champions. I happened to read that Hackenschmidt was still alive in his eighties somewhere in London, and Ralph said: 'I must visit him. Let's go together.' But only a few weeks later I read in the paper of Hackenschmidt's death. What a dialogue that would have been.

Ralph could sometimes be awkward to act with, the result not of selfishness but of eccentricity. An actress who played opposite him once told me that on her first night, as she embarked on a longish speech, Ralph began murmuring his next cue, the closing words of her speech, and continued to do so until she reached those words, whereupon he made his reply. Ralph's diction was so perfect that the audience heard him all the time. When she politely asked him not to do this in future, he expressed incredulity that he had done it at all. The unhappier he was in a role, the more eccentric he became. Many stories are told about his Macbeth in the 1952 Stratford season, which Tynan summed up as 'a sad facsimile of the cowardly lion in *The Wizard of Oz* . . . He moved dully, as if by numbers, and such charm as he possessed was merely a sort of unfocused bluffness, like a teddy-bear snapped in bad light by a child holding its first camera.' Leaving the stage in the midst of one particularly unfortunate performance, he grasped a young actor standing in the wings and said: 'If you ever come across a little bit of talent with the name Richardson on it, let me know. I'd like to have it back.' To another actor he confided as he walked off: 'If I was a member of the audience, I'd ask for my money back.' He had difficulty in establishing a routine for the final duel with Macduff, and developed a mnemonic which he would cry during rehearsal; it began 'One, two, clash your swords, three, four, round we go.' I am assured that on the first night he murmured this so audibly as to be heard above the sound of the swordplay by all but the very deafest of the audience. Seldom can any tyrant's end have been greeted with such hilarity.

His devotion to his motor cycle sometimes caused his friends embarrassment. He would offer other members of the Savile lifts home, and they, thinking he meant his Rolls-Royce, would accept, only to be led round the corner and find Ralph's finger pointing at the pillion. The eminent American historian Milton Waldman told me that, when aged around eighty, he mentioned to Ralph at lunch that he was going for a heart check-up, was offered a lift and a few minutes later found himself in the predicament described. Waldman protested that he could not possibly ride pillion in his condition, but somehow he found himself on it with his arms round Ralph's waist and his face pressed into Ralph's tweedy back. 'I think we can just make it,' said Ralph, and weaved through the Oxford Street traffic to deposit Waldman on his specialist's doorstep. But Waldman's embarrassment had only just begun. The specialist greeted him, looked at him thoughtfully, took his pulse and asked: 'Did you walk here?' 'No.' 'Taxi?' 'No.' 'How did you come?' 'By motor cycle.' 'You drove here on a motor cycle? At eighty, with a heart condition?' Feeling, he told me, more foolish than he had done for sixty years, Waldman had to reply: 'Actually, I rode pillion.' The specialist said it was no use examining him in his present condition and told him to return in a week, by taxi.

Like most actors of his generation, Ralph could not sustain any accent but his own for more than a few sentences except as a caricature. Apart from its disadvantages on stage, this also meant that when he told stories, which he did very well, all the characters spoke like Ralph, sometimes with ludicrous effect. Once as I was about to pay my lunch bill at the Savile, I saw Ralph standing by the cashier's desk with a pained expression. Before I could ask if anything was wrong, he turned his great eyes on me and, with his customary lack of prelude, said: 'There isn't anything particularly odd about a jam omelette, is there?' He continued: 'I had a fine steak, and thought: "I'll end with a jam omelette". I told the waitress: "Bring me a jam omelette, my dear". She came back and said [Irish waitress speaking like Ralph]: "Sorry, sir, we have ham, cheese and herb, but no jam". I said: "Would you ask if they could make a jam one for me?" She came back and said: "They want to know who it's for." I gave her my name and she came back the third time and said: "Sorry, sir, no jam omelette." What I want to know is, who would I have had to be to get a jam omelette?'

Of the actors of his youth, he especially admired (as did Gielgud) Charles Hawtrey, for his complete naturalism, 'as though he wasn't acting at all'; and of actresses, Mrs Patrick Campbell. As a young man, he told me, he had gone on his motor cycle one Monday evening to see her play Hedda Gabler in I think Portsmouth, and was so excited by her performance that he drove over again on the four following nights. 'On the Friday she was so perfect that I didn't go on the Saturday in case she might be a little less good.' He said he thought the best actress he had ever played with was Madge Titheradge, whom I saw a couple of times in the late thirties and who was indeed a marvellous artiste.

Ralph had a pithy way of summing up people and things in very few words, often in rather out-of-date slang. Sitting with Michael Elliott and me at lunch once, he asked Michael what he was doing, to which Michael replied that he was directing *Ghosts*. '*Ghosts*?' said Ralph. 'I get these plays confused. Isn't that the one about the boy who gets the clap?' Michael, after a pause, could only answer: 'Yes.' From that time, whenever Michael and I were working on a play, we always tried to imagine how Ralph would have summarized the plot.

He had in general an excellent memory, though when it failed him it sometimes did so in spectacular fashion. I spotted him on one occasion at the Savile when he had just returned from six weeks' filming in Yugoslavia, and asked how he was, to which he replied: 'My memory's going.' He elaborated. 'A chap whose face I knew came up to me in the bar just now. Knew him well. Awfully nice fellow. American. We had a long chat. Couldn't place him. I was on the point of saying: "Old chap, remind me of your name" when by good fortune he said something which enabled me to identify him as the chap who'd been directing this film in Yugoslavia.' On another occasion he told me he had just recorded *Borkman* on radio (before he did it on stage), and when I asked who had played Ella he replied: 'Very good actress named Wordsworth.' None of us could think of any actress of that name. It turned out to be Sylvia Coleridge.

He did not often dry on stage, but when he did he did so in the grand manner. The director Michael MacOwan told me how he was present on the opening night of *The Alchemist* in 1947, when Ralph played the housekeeper Face. The play opens with him saying: 'Believe it, I will', to which his master Subtle retorts: 'Thy worst, I fart at thee.' The director, John Burrell, raised the curtain on the empty alchemist's shop with the noise of an angry crowd approaching outside. Ralph and George Relph as Subtle then rushed in upstage with their pursuers visible behind them, shut the door just in time to keep them out; then Ralph turned to deliver his opening line, and forgot it. Ralph was famous among other things for his skilful exploitation of silence on stage, which made the prompter more than usually unwilling to intervene. At length, after a very extended pause indeed, there was no alternative. MacOwan said he thought this must have been the only occasion in theatrical history when the run of a play had opened with the prompter's voice.

Later that year Ralph somehow contrived to forget one of the most famous lines in all drama. He was playing John of Gaunt in *Richard II*, with Alec Guinness as the King. It was the schools' set book of the year, and the matinée audience consisted largely of children, many of whom had had to learn the main speeches by heart. As is sometimes the case when a great actor's role ends halfway through the play, Ralph got slower and slower and his pauses longer and longer. At last John of Gaunt's big moment arrived, his deathbed adjuration to the King. 'This blessed throne of kings . . . (Long pause.) This . . . sceptred . . . isle. (Longer pause.) This . . . earth of . . . majesty . . . (Huge pause.) This . . .' Ralph's eyes moved from side to side. What prompter in his right mind would have dared to open his mouth? Still the line would not come. At length 800 treble voices from the audience piped: 'Seat of Mars!'

About a year before he died Ralph appeared in a new play about an old man and three elderly sisters, one of whom was played by Celia Johnson (who, tragically, died shortly before the opening night in the West End). The sisters had somewhat unusual names, which Ralph had difficulty in remembering. This led to some strange exchanges on tour. Ralph: 'Hullo, my dear. How is your sister . . . Antigone?' Celia: 'Andromache, you mean? Oh, she's much better.' Ralph: 'And Felicity?' Celia: 'Yes, Francesca's fine.' During the opening week at Richmond, Ralph forgot a line and failed to hear the prompter who was on the far side of the stage. He crossed and cocked an ear. The prompter repeated the line. Ralph then spoke it, which was the third time the audience had heard it, sensed a slight tension in the house, nodded towards the wings and said: 'Jolly useful chap, that.'

He was the most generous of hosts. If a guest had no car, and the evening ended too late for Ralph to summon his own chauffeur, he would ring for a taxi, give the driver a £10 note and say: 'Take this lady anywhere she wants to go.' The first time I visited his house, wearing my best suit, I was admitted by the butler who opened the living-room door to reveal Ralph in a dinner-jacket. I was about to apologize when I saw behind him Ivor Brown, the drama critic, in an ancient grey suit and John Gielgud in green corduroy. As I tried to work this out, Ralph said: 'I was changing for dinner when I thought: "I haven't told young Meyer what to wear. I'll put on a dinner-jacket. Then if he comes in a suit, I'll be the one who's wrongly dressed."' And that is how the evening continued, Ralph remaining in full fig.

After dinner Mu and Ivor Brown's wife Irene Hentschel retired, and we four men, after a glass of port, went up to Ralph's study. Finding that the cigars were elsewhere, he left and returned with a large box and José on his shoulder. As he leaned over Gielgud to offer the cigars and brandy, José spread his wings and uttered a ghastly screech. 'Oh, Ralph, do take that dreadful bird away.' 'He's only playing.' The conversation for some reason then turned to pornographic literature. Ivor Brown said he thought no book of any quality had been written in that genre. 'What about *Fanny Hill*?' said Ralph. Ivor said he had never read it. Ralph's eyes gleamed. 'I've a spare copy which I shall be delighted to give you.' He burrowed into a cupboard and emerged with the volume in a lurid dust-jacket. 'No, really,' said Ivor, in some embarrassment. Ralph put on his conspiratorial look. 'You don't want Irene to see it. I'll wrap it up in brown paper.' And he took brown paper and string from his desk and made an elaborate parcel, with many a loop. Ivor did not look happy as he sat clutching it. How could his wife not ask what it was? On reflection I think that Irene would in no way have been shocked and that Ivor simply did not want to read it.

Around eleven o'clock the Browns left, and for the next two hours Ralph and Gielgud exchanged reminiscences of forty years in the theatre. How I wished I had a concealed tape recorder! No two men could have been more unalike; perhaps that is partly why they so loved and respected each other. I must have drunk a good deal, for next morning I could not recall too much of what had been said. Now, twenty years later, I remember only that Olivier was mentioned, and I said: 'Ralph, what is Larry really like? I've worked and socialized with him and he's always been charming, but I never feel I know what the real man is. Like the Marcel Marceau sketch when he takes off a series of invisible masks and replaces them with others. What's he really like?' Ralph pulled at his pipe and pondered. Clouds of smoke filled the room. At length: 'I've known Laurence [unlike the rest of us, Gielgud included, Ralph always called him Laurence] as long as I've known you, Johnny. Marvellous actor.

Love the fellow. But I've no idea what the real man's like. Johnny, what do you think?' Pause, then: 'Well Ralph it's extraordinary now I think of it I've known him all these years and I admire him as much as you do he's always been most generous to me we share a dressing-room now at the Vic and he insisted that they put my nameplate above his on the door who else would have done that you would of course but who else and he's such wonderful company such a marvellous mimic and raconteur I always adore seeing him. But I've no idea what he's really like.'

Something embarrassing once happened to someone close to Ralph, which everyone seemed to know about except Ralph himself. It was felt that he should be informed and that Gielgud, as his oldest and closest friend, was the man to tell him. Gielgud protested that, being notorious for his lack of tact, he was the person least suited for the task, but he was overruled and invited Ralph to dinner at the Caprice. Nervous at the ordeal ahead, he talked even faster than usual throughout the meal until they reached the coffee and the moment could no longer be postponed. At length: 'Ralph you know I always adore meeting you you understand so many things unlike me I don't understand anything outside the theatre not always that whereas your range is so amazingly wide BUT Ralph there is something very particular I wanted to discuss with you it's very personal you may even find it embarrassing how shall I begin? Ralph when one gets to a certain age not necessarily quite our age how shall I put it a way of life that has seemed satisfactory somehow doesn't seem quite so totally satisfying . . . one feels a need for change . . . to do something that may even seem slightly desperate . . .' Ralph's eyes widened with understanding. He took Gielgud's hand in his and said: 'Johnny! You're thinking of getting married at last!'

Children, as one might expect, seldom failed to bring out the magic in him. He treated them, as they love to be treated, as adults. When I brought my small daughter to his dressing-room after a performance one evening, he delighted her by offering her 'Orange? Or whisky? Or gin?' Soon after she was born he and Mu visited us for dinner. We lived in an unfashionable part of Hampstead next to a housing estate which contained a villainous group of children not unlike the Dead End Kids in the old film of that name. Many and varied were the objects they threw over the wall into our tiny garden. It was a hot July evening and, knowing that the other guests would wish to dress informally, I asked Ralph to do the same, lest he should arrive in a suit or even that dinner-jacket. He came with Mu in the Rolls. Before they could disembark the car was surrounded by a horde of children of every colour. Such a car had never been seen in our street before. Mu made for the house, but Ralph remained to answer every question the children put to him, opening the bonnet to explain some of the more complicated mysteries. Never can even he have held an audience more spellbound. It must have been a full five minutes before they would let him go. An equal tribute to his magic is that the Rolls was undamaged when he and Mu left at midnight; the previous week a Mercedes had had its windscreen smashed. I had assumed that Lucky would deliver and collect him, and spent much of the evening glancing nervously out of the window and keeping an ear cocked.

Although Ralph was not generally interested in games, he had been a good squash player in his youth, several times representing the Royal Automobile Club in the Lansdowne Cup (as R. D. Richardson). He must have been a psychologically formidable opponent in the claustrophobic confines of a squash court. Around the age of fifty, needing some less strenuous activity, he took up real tennis, or 'court tennis' as it is known in the United States, and thenceforward, when-ever possible, he would play once a week at Lord's cricket ground. For the last ten years of his life he played every Friday afternoon at three, and as I had the two o'clock court we always met then if not elsewhere. Even after his eightieth birthday he would arrive on his motor cycle in a shining white helmet to play for an hour against the great professional Henry Johns, who was only eight years Ralph's junior but still moved as lightly as a ballet dancer.

These occasions were well worth watching. Ralph naturally could not run much in his last years, so that Henry had to put the ball within his reach without making it seem too obvious. Real tennis is played across a net like lawn tennis, but with back walls and a side wall roofed by sloping penthouses, and we marvelled at the variety of angles which Henry managed off wall or penthouse to leave the ball ending up at the same distance on either side of Ralph. Henry, being the professional he was, issued advice across the net as sternly as though he was coaching a young beginner, and as no theatre director had dared to address Ralph for forty years. Ralph would mutter little mnemonics to himself, as audibly as everything else he said, and in his own strange wording. Once after Henry had admonished him: 'Hold your racket still, don't wave it around', he heard Ralph murmuring, as they changed ends: 'I mustn't wave at the Indians. They'll run away.' On another occasion, when Henry for once lobbed a ball gently into an empty corner and Ralph just failed to reach it in time, he cried: 'Sorry, Henry. When I got there, the bus had gone.' The Lord's court has notable acoustics like the old Greek theatres, and as Ralph stood at the receiving end, far from us spectators seated behind the server, we could clearly hear his murmurings as he awaited service. When he made a poor shot, he would utter an epic cry of anguish, varied, when Henry indulged himself with the occasional winner, by an equally epic cry of admiration.

After this exercise, Ralph and Henry would sit to cool off before showering, and the conversations between these two, each supreme at his craft, were rewarding, for Henry was as penetrating a questioner as Ralph, so that both would be drawn out on the subtleties of their art and the great practitioners they had admired in their youth. Ralph once remarked that some of the tennis players of the twenties and thirties must have been odd chaps, which caused Henry to remark: 'There don't seem to be any great eccentrics nowadays like there were then. Is that true in the theatre too?' 'I can't think of one,' said Ralph.

Ralph was always immaculately and expensively dressed, and once he said to me that he was ashamed of his white flannels, which were beginning to show signs of age. 'I wanted to buy some new ones, but Mu says it's ridiculous to spend eighty quid on sports trousers at my age.' I was about to say that they wouldn't cost a quarter of that sum when I realized that he did not think of any article of clothing except in terms of Savile Row. I mentioned this to Henry, who told Ralph that he could get him a pair of the kind that Test cricketers wear for I think seventeen pounds. Ralph looked incredulous, but Henry measured him and the following Friday had three pairs for Ralph to try, one of which fitted him perfectly. Ralph was as amazed that this could be achieved off the peg as he was at the price, and talked about it for weeks.

The last time I saw him was at Lord's in September 1983. He looked less than his usual robust self, and two things struck us all as strange. He had come by car instead of on his motor cycle, and Mu was with him. I had never seen her at the court before. When he went into the court he could not get even the edge of his racket to the ball. Henry took him to the far end away from the spectators and lobbed a few balls on to the penthouse to give him an easy stroke, but Ralph still could not manage a touch and after a few minutes he gave up and returned to the dressing-room. I left for a couple of weeks in Sweden and soon after my return heard on the radio the news of his death. Mu told me that the day before I had last seen him the two small fingers of his right hand had gone numb. This did not much bother him at the time, but it turned out to have been a slight stroke, the first of several of increasing severity. He subsequently went into hospital, where he deteriorated so rapidly that he refused to allow even his closest friends to see him. After four days he said to the doctor: 'I want a straight answer to two questions. Shall I live? And if I do, what will I be like?' The doctor replied: 'You will live, but you will be in a wheelchair for the rest of your life.' 'Thank you,' said Ralph, and from that moment he refused all food and medicines and died in three days. It was a Roman way to go, and very Ralph. No one who knew him could imagine him lingering on as a helpless invalid.

He was given a splendid memorial service in Westminster Abbey. The application for tickets was so great that they could have filled the building several times over. Someone described him as the most loved person in Britain after the Queen Mother. Alan Howard and Albert Finney read the lessons, Laurence Olivier gave the address, and John Gielgud spoke the passage from *The Pilgrim's Progress* which ends: 'All the trumpets sounded for him on the other side.' I imagined Ralph holding up the queue at the pearly gates as he questioned St Peter: 'What kind of oil do you find best for these hinges . . .?'

Epilogue

From 1958, when I underwent my painful apprenticeship with *The Lady from the Sea* and *John Gabriel Borkman* (I don't count my crib version of *Little Eyolf* in 1955), until 1984, when I finished my Strindberg biography, I spent twenty-six years on Ibsen and Strindberg. I do not regret that my career took this course. Had Peter Hall staged *The May Game* in 1955 as he intended, and had it been a success, I would not have been willing to turn my back on creative writing, nor to regard myself as a window-pane. But not being creatively fertile, how would I have filled the gaps between one work and the next? Moreover, it is a curious fact, though I have not seen it stated anywhere, that with very few exceptions a dramatist's effective creative career lasts for at most fifteen years. They go on writing, but their later plays interest few people. This is true even of dramatists whom one thinks of as having had lengthy careers, such as Coward and Priestley. No one nowadays bothers or is likely to bother about any of the plays which Coward wrote before *The Vortex* in 1924 and after *Present Laughter* in 1942 (eighteen years), or anything by Priestley before *Dangerous Corner* in 1932 and after *An Inspector Calls* in 1946, or any of Tennessee Williams except those from *The Glass Menagerie* in 1944 to *Sweet Bird of Youth* in 1958, or any by John Osborne except those from *Look Back in Anger* in 1956 to *A Patriot for Me* in 1965, though all of them continued to write for another quarter of a century. Pirandello wrote all his plays between 1922 and 1932, and Brecht all his best plays (except *The Threepenny Opera*) between 1933 and 1945. The average dramatist's career is as short as a boxer's or a footballer's, and I have always thought it must be terrible to find oneself at fifty still full of plays but with nobody interested in the new ones. Why this should be true of dramatists but not of novelists I do not know. Nor are those

265

who have tasted success in the theatre normally willing to turn to the less glamorous business of writing novels, though occasionally a novelist who has subsequently succeeded as a dramatist, such as Graham Greene, returns to his first love. I greatly doubt whether my career as a dramatist, had I had one, would have lasted for anything like fifteen years, and what would I have done for the remaining twenty or thirty? I am sure I was not a novelist, otherwise I would have tried harder to follow up the reasonable success of my first effort in that field.

I am fortunate that my translations are still performed, more frequently indeed than when they first appeared a quarter of a century ago, so that nowadays on an average I have one staged or broadcast somewhere in the world every four or five days. I find it ceaselessly stimulating to discuss them with directors and actors, some of whom were not born when I wrote them. I love driving to remote provincial towns and fringe theatres to see new productions, and discovering exciting young talents in bud as well as mature ones that for some reason have never achieved fame. This more than anything differentiates the British theatre from its counterparts abroad. Every country has its stars, but none other shares this depth of quality, so that even someone who has worked in the theatre as long as I have is repeatedly astonished by seeing some splendid performer of whom he or she has never even heard. And because I was lucky enough to work on two great masters, I am continually finding new subtleties in their plays; they are inexhaustible.

As one who has spent over half my adult life annihilating myself, as a translator and biographer should, I find it difficult to turn the spotlight on to that self. Like Eliot's Mr Prufrock, I am not Prince Hamlet, nor was meant to be. I am one of those described by Thomas De Quincey in his autobiography, who 'though liberated from all reasonable motives of self-restraint, *cannot* be confidential – have not it in their power to lay aside reserve', though I can be cheerfully gregarious on the surface. I do not regard myself as an intellectual but as an intuitive person, whose reactions come from below rather than from above the neck. Until I was nearly forty I was quick-tempered and, as I have said, a dilettante. I do not much like that early self, not that I am much enamoured of my present self; I dislike my egocentricity, idleness and unwillingness to become emotionally involved with anyone. I know that, despite the way things have turned out, I should have stretched myself creatively. Never having had to earn a living was partly responsible, though a sense of guilt about that at least ensured that I did what work I have done, so that eventually the income from my translations and biographies came to exceed my expenditure. Even when on holiday I have a compulsion to spend the morning alone, if possible at a desk; I used to feel equally compelled to spend the evening with someone, though now in my late sixties I rather prefer to spend them alone.

For some reason I have always, for as long as I can remember, been plagued by nervous habits in private conversation, coughs and sniffs and the like, which abandon me as soon as I have to speak in public, as when lecturing, which I usually do without notes, or broadcasting. My chief pleasures have been sex, food, cricket and real tennis, and watching almost any kind of sport except horse- and motor-racing. I am priggish about drunkenness and gambling, even small bets on such things as snooker, and penny-paring about small things, so that I am sometimes to be seen standing at a bus stop in the rain while empty taxis pass. Thanks largely to Sweden, I sorted myself out sexually comparatively early, and have been lucky in these relationships. Most of them lasted several years, and I was always the one who was left, which suited me; in the end my lack of emotional commitment, which I suppose held a certain attraction, meant that my partners moved on, or back, to marriage. Sharing a home with anyone for more than a month makes me restless; I like closing my own front door behind me. Yet nearly all the relationships which I have had have ended without recrimination, and in most cases we have remained affectionately in touch.

In the summer of 1961 I surprised myself and all who knew me by falling in love. I call it that because I do not know the difference between it and what people call infatuation. She was Swedish, of high intelligence and classical beauty, tall, fair and seemingly extrovert; how could I, or anyone else, tell that beneath all this lay a destructive and, ultimately, self-destructive manic depression? She had, she told me when it was too late, a compulsion to break off every relationship when it was at its peak, partly because she could not bear that it should fade, and partly because she could not bear to be the one who was abandoned. She left a trail of destruction and hatred behind her. Once she said to me: 'I have no friends. All women hate me, because when I enter a room every man's eyes turn towards me, and all men hate me because I have either said no to them or broken with them.' In a letter from the ship back to Sweden at the end of that summer, she wrote to me: 'I realize again that I have no line, no thread, to keep to in life. Once one part is over, it seems to be gone for ever, and I start a new one. At least I am afraid it will be so. Life consists of doors, which one opens and closes, and never opens again. One just finds a new door, hoping to find some happiness behind, and if so even more hoping not to have to close it again too soon.' She was two different personalities, and at any moment one was liable to be confronted by the half determined to destroy what pleased the other half. That summer left me resolved never again to commit myself like that, nor have I. More than ever, I distrusted love. Some years afterwards, we met again in Stockholm and became lovers once more. She seemed much calmer and we had a happy few days. Six weeks later she gassed herself.

I am well aware what I have missed through this inability to love. Does it make me part of a minority? George Gissing believed that 'Love is the personal experience of the very few. You can no more choose to be a lover than to be a poet.' If this is so, how lucky are the few. One of the great poets of this century, Rainer Maria Rilke, wrote in *The Notebook of Malte Laurids Brigge*: 'To be loved is to be consumed. To love means to radiate with inexhaustible light. To be loved is to pass away, to love is to endure.'

When I was forty-six, a much younger girl with whom I was involved suggested that we should have a child. I said I didn't want to marry, to which she replied that neither did she. I reflected that this might be the last time that this opportunity might arise, and ten months later, in September 1968, our daughter was born. I was present at her birth, which was difficult; her heart stopped while she was in the womb, and when she was delivered by forceps both the oxygen cylinders in the operating theatre were found to be empty. While the anaesthetist and the midwife argued about the responsibility for this, an elderly nun hurried out and returned with a full cylinder. After a horrid delay, the infant began to bawl, and I have loved her ever since. I found myself able and willing to accept the emotional commitment from which I had always shrunk in personal relationships; it made me, not a complete person, but a less incomplete person than I had been. Her mother and I parted a year later, but we remain close, and our daughter has always been loved by, and loves, us both. We named her Nora, after not the character in *A Doll's House* but my mother. I have always been determined that she should have the parental love that I never had after my mother's death, and for me it was a revelation to have someone whom I could love without the fear of rejection. The great discoveries of life are always platitudes.

Appendix

Barnhill
Isle of Jura
Argyllshire
23. 5. 46

Dear Michael,

Thanks so much for your efforts. No, I haven't a licence (there's no policeman on this island!) so don't worry about the black powder. I made some which is not as good as commercial stuff but will do. If you could get the percussion caps I'd be much obliged. Tell them the largest size they have, ie. something about this size ⊓.

I'm just settling in here — up to my eyes getting the house straight, but it's a lovely house. Richard isn't coming till the

Letter from George Orwell (p 72)

end of June, because Susan has to have a minor operation & I couldn't cope with him singlehanded, so I've had to board him out. However the reports are that he is getting on well. Our difficulties at present are (a) that I can't yet get a jeep (hope to get one at the end of the month) & am having to make do with a motor bike which is hell on these roads, & (b) owing to the drought there's no water for baths, though enough to drink. However one doesn't get very dirty here. Come & stay some time — It's not such an impossible journey (about 48 hours from Delhi) & there's plenty of room in this house, though of course conditions are rough.

All the best —

George

6.8.46.

Dear Meyer.

Yes, I can put you up on Saturday, 10th,
Your best way of getting here is from 10.50 from
Waterloo to Salisbury by a train arriving
12.35. The village taxi will meet you at
Salisbury — a genial red faced clean-shaven
man whom you can identify. Bring your
bat, as you will have to play for Heytesbury
v Devizes, at 2.30! Our ground is in good
condition, but every ball arrives at a
different height — usually either a shooter
or at nose level, owing to the winds which
have accumulated. If only the weather is
decent, you will enjoy the game greatly,
& this place is now looking its best. .
             yours sincerely,
                          S

Letter from Siegfried Sassoon (p 78)

271

247219 Lt. Sidney Keyes,
1st Bn, Queen's Own R.W.K. Regt,
British North African Force
26.iii.43

My Dear Michael,

As you probably know already, I have now gone into semi-permanent & not very honourable exile among the Berbers: but have left behind a sort of posthumous child in the form of a new collection of verse called The Cruel Solstice (Routledge 6/- in autumn). John will show you the MS – though you've read them all before. They are fairly good.

The sea voyage was surprisingly luxurious, & I was sorry to see the end of it. Meals used to consist of 2 meat courses, sweet, soup, cheese & coffee, perfectly served by Javanese waiters. The first one shook me rather, but I soon settled down to about 10 days of solid eating. No drinking, though, the boat was dry. The enemy took very little action indeed about us; & I slept through the single rather desultory attack we had. Gilkes, by the way, was on the same boat & is about here somewhere. At the moment, I have a small office suspended between floor & roof of a disused brickworks near a town I cannot name. Everything – including me – is quite incredibly filthy; the rain comes through the roof, & when I wash, my canvas bucket leaks on to the soldiers 20ft below. One night I shall fall out of bed & give them a shock! It is rather like being a Bat. Just outside, we have a miniature three-fenced-in-fields cornland, with sexy frogs which keep up what can only be described as a ROAR & croaking all night & most of the day; & probably with malaria, I shall eventually find out about the latter, I suppose. Yesterday I went into the town, but saw neither Boyer nor Lamarr, nor even Joseph Cotten. There isn't much food, but plenty of (bad) drink. And widely night I saw a new Sacha Guitry film, made last year, called La Destinée fabuleuse de Désirée Clary. It was not very fabulous, but surprisingly good considering the circumstances. It cannot have cost more than about 2½d to make. The flicks here are a bright spot, as they are beginning to revive some of the good French films of 1937-39 — (e.g. Renoir's Underworld & Three Waters).

Night is falling, or it may be just the light in here. Anyway, I must stop for tea. God knows when this will reach you; but please write. Best wishes to your father & brothers, and love to all the literary boys. I consider myself Oxford Poets' first line!

Yours ever,
Sidney.

P.S. You should read a book called A Narrow Street — it's a good one about Paris, though by an American newspaperman.

Dear Sir:

If you remember the summing up by the judge in the recent Sitwell case, you will be advised to p. it in following apology, which will end the incident. If you do not, I shall have to write through a solicitor: but I don't want to do so.

We regret that our reviewer (Mr Sidney Keyes) in our Feb 5th issue referred to Mr Robert Graves as 'a flashy author' and as 'a partner in the Graves-Riding mutual admiration society.' We apologise to Mr Graves for the above statements which are untrue in substance and implication.

P.T.O

Letter from Robert Graves (p 116)

The reference to the 'mutual-admiration
society' is of course the one which I regard as
the most damaging. I do not disguise my
admiration of Miss Riding's work, but
your reviewer if he wished to justify factually
this most improper remark would have to
prove that Miss Riding had publicly expressed
                        was that we engaged in 'log-rolling':
her admiration of me or my works: or this
he could not do. 'Flashy' has not been used
in a good sense since 1780, or I resent
the depreciatory sense as applied to me x
~~personally,~~
~~as~~ though I could not object to the
adjective as applied to my work — it would
then be 'fair comment' however inaccurate.
Miss Riding & I have collaborated in several
works, and once for some years in business
partnership: this aggravates the offensiveness of
your reviewer's remarks. Yours faithfully
                                    Robert Graves

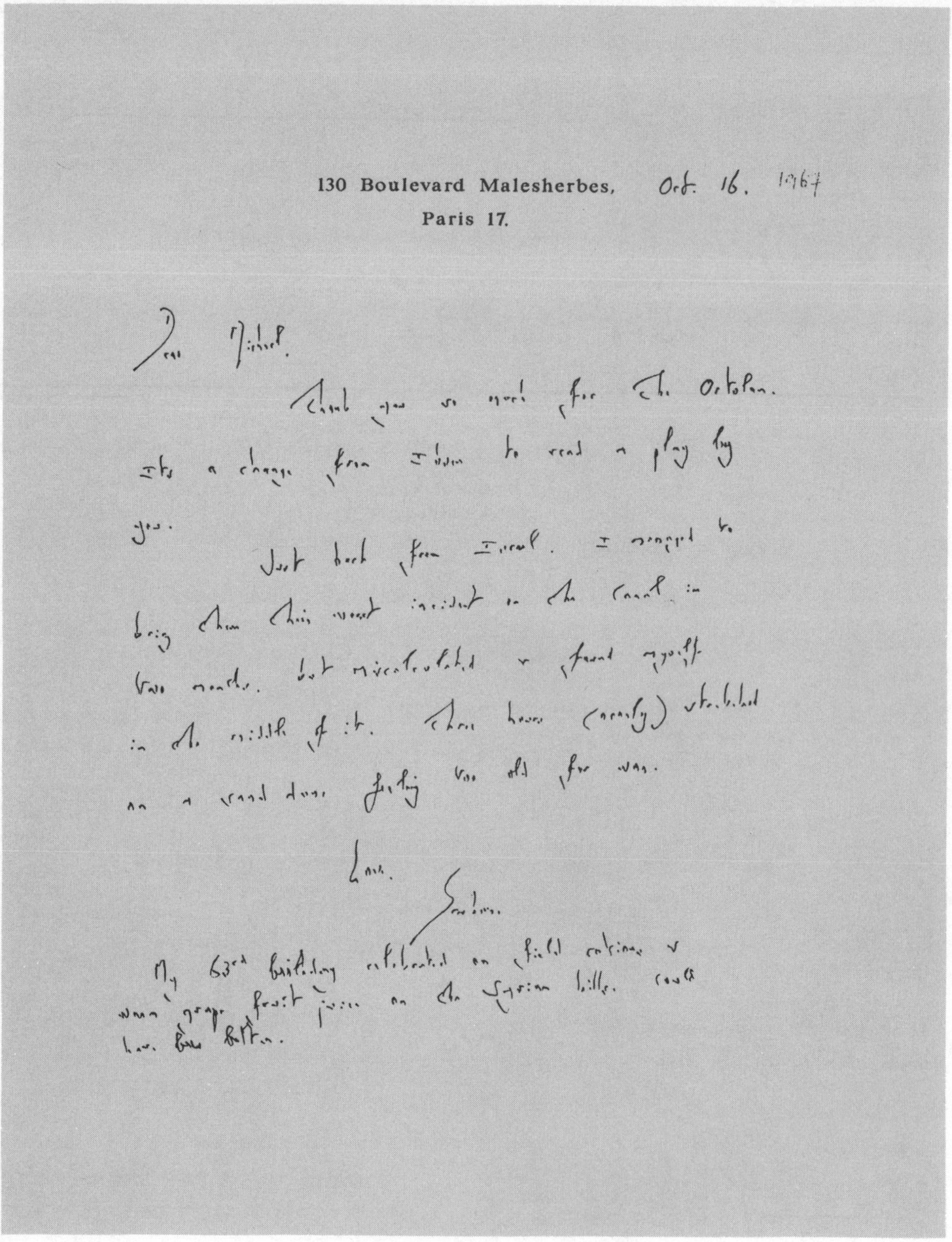
130 Boulevard Malesherbes, Oct. 16. 1967
Paris 17.

Dear Michael,

Thank you so much for The Ortolan. It's a change from Ibsen to read a play by you.

Just back from Israel. I managed to miss this recent incident in the Canal by two weeks, but miscalculated & found myself in the middle of it. Three hours (nearly) stretched on a sand dune feeling too old for war.

Love,

Graham.

My 63rd birthday celebrated on field rations & warm grape fruit juice on the Syrian hills. Could have been better.

Letter from Graham Greene (p 220)

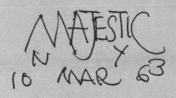

MAJESTIC
N Y
10 MAR 63

My dear Michael,

Thanks very much for
your letter and the copy
of "When We Dead Awaken"
with your excellent preface.

I wish the play was
all that the preface leads
one to hope for — although
it is extremely well translated.

The first act is fine,
although a little more
humour in the sculptor
make-up might lead one
to expect more of his
master-piece.

The second act is
good — reflective, poetic,
but one waits for the the
trail at least for
dynamite to explode.

The third act opens
with a scene which is rather
silly in my opinion, but,
when the sculptor comes on
and one thinks "at last
we are going to have a
scene —— nothing
whatever new happens!

Letter from Sir Ralph Richardson in New York (not in text)

There is a re-statement of situation — no development in the sculptor's character but a devil of a lot of stage difficulties, is a situation which poor old Richardson could not untangle.

I am very grateful for you for thinking of me and I wish to God I could find a part to play — but I could not play this.

Ninety per cent of what this play has to say has been already said with magic charm which and humour and mystery in 'Peer Gynt' don't you agree? No — you don't — I am very stupid I am afraid!

EVER

Ralph.

The Cherwell

Cherwell, 1941 (starting on p 31)

EIGHT OXFORD POETS

Selected by MICHAEL MEYER & SIDNEY KEYES

Keith Douglas

Gordon Swaine

John Heath-Stubbs

Michael Meyer

Roy Porter

Drummond Allison

J. A. Shaw

Sidney Keyes

GEORGE ROUTLEDGE & SONS

BROADWAY HOUSE, 68-74, CARTER LANE, E.C.

Eight Oxford Poets, 1941 (pp 42–4)

Index

Index

Index

Chekhov, Anton, 41, 83, 91, 128, 188, 189, 199, 225, 230, 232, 252
Chengtu, 151
Cherry Orchard, The, 199
Cherwell, 29–39, 42, 64, 81, 96, 116
Cherwell, Lord, 30
Chicago, 195
Chichester, 193–4, 206–7
China, 137, 150–1, 157–8
Christ Church, *see* Oxford
Christ's Hospital, 29
Christie, Dame Agatha, 96
Church, Esmé, 237
Church, Richard, 226
Churchill, Randolph, 125
Churchill, Sir Winston, 30, 98
Claesson, Åke, 235
Clare, John, 37
Claude de Lorraine, 170
Cleese, John, 192
Clench, Greta, 50
Clench, Stanley, 49–51
Cleverdon, Douglas, 84
Clifford, Hubert, 106–7
Clodd, Mr (shepherd), 80
Clutton-Brock, Alan, 54
Cockburn, Claud, 226
Cockerell, Sydney, 224
Cocteau, Jean, 112
Codron, Michael, 128, 131
Coghill, Nevill, 28, 39
Cohen, Louis, 6
Cohen, Samuel, 5
Cohn, Leonie, 57
Coleridge, 258
Collection, The, 191
Collie, C. H., 44
Collins, William, Ltd, 62, 68, 96, 131
Collins, Sir William, 68, 96–7, 102–3, 131
Comedians, The, 219–20
Complaisant Lover, The, 174–7, 183, 187–8
Comrades, 91
Compton, Fay, 40
Conan Doyle, Sir Arthur, 59
Confidential Agent, The, 182
Connaught, H.R.H. Duke of, 25
Connolly, Cyril, 21, 123–4
Conrad, Joseph, 123, 188
Constantine, Learie, 104
Consumers' Association, 120
Cooper, William, 43
Corbishley, Father, 98
Coriolanus, 237
Cornelius, 248
Corot, J. B. C., 170
Cosmann, Milein, 46
Courtenay, Tom, 195, 207, 209, 235
Coward, Sir Noël, 15, 40, 239, 265
Cowie, Laura, 16
Cox, Brian, 167, 207–8, 210, 228, 235
Crabbe, George, 45
Crankshaw, Edward, 107

Cranmer, Philip, 20
Crazy Horse strip club, 137–8
Creditors, 162–4, 166, 170, 234, 235, 237
Crick, Bernard, 66, 68, 74
cricket, 1, 8, 12, 14, 17–18, 25, 31, 35, 40, 47, 62, 78, 79, 80–1, 84, 86, 96–7, 99, 104, 118, 121, 123, 128, 129, 152, 167, 168, 178, 199, 233, 262–3, 267
Cricket Match, The, 128
Crime and Punishment, 125, 195, 232
Critic, The, 248
croquet, 122
Crosland, Tony, 122
Cruel Solstice, The, 32, 55–6
Cruchley, Rosalie, 254
Cuba, 173
Cul-de-sac, 131
Curman, Sigurd, 203–4
Cusack, Cyril, 41–2, 201
Cyrano de Bergerac, 248, 252

Dagens Nyheter, 234
Dagerman, Stig, 133–5, 188
Dahlbäck, Eva, 235
Dance, Charles, 234
Dance of Death, The, 90, 170, 229, 230, 235, 237
Dangerous Corner, 265
Danielsson, Bengt, 180–5
Danielsson, Bror, 94
Danielsson, Marie-Thérèse, 180–5
Danton's Death, 163, 166, 237
Darkness at Noon, 51, 122
Darlington, W. A., 245
Darlow, Michael, 234
Davenport, John, 104–6
Davidson, Clare, 234
Daviot, Gordon, 16
Day, Derek, 104
Day for Night, 220–3
Day Lewis, Cecil, 29, 32, 60–2, 104
Dean, Basil, 246
'Death and the Maiden', 37–8, 101
Delafield, E. M., 32
De la Mare, Walter, 49
Dench, Dame Judi, 234, 235
Desire Under the Elms, 40
Devine, George, 102, 126, 194, 247
Dews, Peter, 207
Dickens, Charles, 70, 183
Dickson, Dorothy, 2
Disraeli, Benjamin, 39, 54
Dix, Tim, 152–7
Dr Zhivago, 253
Doll's House, A, 91, 151, 208, 227, 234, 235, 251, 268
Don Carlos, 232
Donat, Robert, 113–14, 207, 236, 237
Donner, Henry W., 94
Dostoevsky, Fyodor, 125, 170, 195, 225, 232, 236, 240
Doubleday, 167–8, 185, 200
Douglas, Keith, 29–33, 42, 45, 56
Douglas-Home, Sir Alec, 21

283

Index

Hitler, Adolf, 26–7, 236
Hobart, 5
Hobbs, Sir Jack, 17
Hobson, Sir Harold, 127
hockey, 31, 39, 74, 77, 98, 104, 121, 127
Hodgson, A. C. W., 10
Hoff, Harry, 42
Hoffnung, Gerard, 35
Holden, Inez, 66–7
Hölderlin, Friedrich, 37
Hollis, Sir Roger, 225
Holloway, Baliol, 15, 16
Holloway prison, 10
Hollywood, 133, 135, 175, 187, 201
Holmes, Sherlock, 59
Homage to Catalonia, 68
Homer, 21
Honorary Consul, The, 225
Hong Kong, 136, 150
Hood, Thomas, 78
Hooper, Mr, 150–1
Hope Against Hope, 232
Hopkins, Anthony, 192, 207, 234
Hopkins, Gerard Manley, 98, 100
Hordern, John, 127
Hordern, Sir Michael, 191
Horizon, 66
Hornibrook, P. M., 17
Housman, A. E., 116
Howard, Alan, 264
Howard, Brian, 54–5
Howard, Sir Michael, 20
Howard, Sidney (playwright), 237
Howard, Sydney (actor), 15
Howard, Trevor, 199–200, 206, 235
Howe, George, 16
Howes, Bobby, 15
Hoxha, Enver, 225
Hughes, David, 168
Hulton, Sir Edward, 117
Human Factor, The, 223
Hurwood, Alan, 17
Huxley, Aldous, 25–6
Hylton, Jack, 128
Hytner, Nicholas, 232

Ibsen, Henrik, 36, 41, 47, 60, 61, 64, 72, 82, 83, 89,
    90, 91, 93, 94, 113, 128, 130–1, 151, 159–71, 182,
    185, 188–200, 202, 204–5, 207–18, 227–39, 242–
    244, 246, 248, 251–2, 254, 258, 260–1, 264–6, 268
Immigrants, The, 111
Importance of Being Earnest, The, 4, 16, 40
In Cold Blood, 254
In Parentheses, 99
In Retreat, 57
Innes, Michael, 28
Inspector Calls, An, 265
International During the War, The, 119
Invitation to the Waltz, 61
Ireland, Patrick, 20
Iron Laurel, The, 32, 45–6
Irving, Sir Henry, 63, 82, 246

Isherwood, Christopher, 34, 124
Isis, 29
Israel, 220, 225
It's a Battlefield, 59, 226
Ives, Kenneth, 234

Jackson, Sir Barry, 47, 51
Jackson, Guy, 84
Jakarta, 137, 139, 144, 178, 183
Jamaica Inn, 167
James, Emrys, 230, 235
James, Henry, 104, 108–9, 112, 125, 188, 254
Jannings, Emil, 240
Jeal, Alfred, 18
Jenkins, Martin, 228
Jepson, Selwyn, 115–16
Jerrold, Douglas, 70, 76
Jesters Cricket Club, 104, 233
Joad, C. E. M., 32
John Gabriel Borkman, 64, 160–1, 167, 169, 170,
    191, 208, 230, 237, 239, 242–4, 246, 251, 252,
    258, 265
John Gordon Society, 124–5
John Paul II, Pope, 226
Johns, Henry, 262–3
Johnson, Celia, 209, 251, 259
Johnson, Dr Samuel, 103
Jones, David, 98–9
Jones, Freddie, 234
Jordan, Andy, 230
José (parrot), 252–4, 260
Josephson, Ragnar, 203
Journey from Obscurity, 97
Journey's End, 237
Joyce, James, 70, 188, 201
Judgement Day, 40
Julius Caesar, 237
Juno and the Paycock, 40

Kaufman, George, C., 16
Kavanagh, P. J., 126, 164
Keach, Stacy, 192, 210
Kean, Edmund, 236, 238
Keeley, T. C., 43, 48–9
Kenderdine, Captain R. J., 120
Kent, Jonathan, 234
Kerr, Deborah, 41
Keyes, Sidney, 32–8, 42, 44–6, 49, 55–6, 58, 60,
    63–4, 77, 101, 116, 121, 234, 243
King, Francis, 32–3, 42, 159
King Lear, 40, 59, 76, 155, 236, 252
Kingsley, Ben, 192
Kingsmill, Hugh, 58–60, 76–7
Kipling, Rudyard, 54, 104, 115
Kippax, Alan, 17
Koestler, Arthur, 51, 75, 121–3, 137
Koestler, Cynthia, 122–3
Kon-tiki, 180
Kotzebue, August von, 36
Kraus, Werner, 240
Kulle, Jarl, 88
Kung, Hans, 225–6

Index

Index

Index